Transforming Public and Nonprofit Organizations

STEWARDSHIP FOR LEADING CHANGE

Transforming Public and Nonprofit Organizations

STEWARDSHIP FOR LEADING CHANGE

JAMES EDWIN KEE

KATHRYN E. NEWCOMER

MANAGEMENTCONCEPTS

MANAGEMENTCONCEPTS

8230 Leesburg Pike, Suite 800
Vienna, VA 22182
(703) 790-9595
Fax: (703) 790-1371
www.managementconcepts.com

Printed in the United States of America
10 9 8 7 6 5 4 3 2 1

Library of Congress Cataloging-in-Publication Data
Kee, James Edwin.
   Transforming public and nonprofit organizations : stewardship for leading change / James Edwin Kee, Kathryn E. Newcomer.
      p. cm.
   ISBN 978-1-56726-227-8
   1. Administrative agencies--United States--Management. 2. Nonprofit organizations--United States--Management. 3. Servant leadership. I. Newcomer, Kathryn E., 1949- I. Title.
JK421K44 2008
658.4'092--dc22
                                                                2008001654

ABOUT THE AUTHORS

James Edwin (Jed) Kee is a professor of public policy and public administration in the Trachtenberg School of Public Policy and Public Administration at the George Washington University (GW) and Co-Director of the Midge Smith Center for Evaluation Effectiveness. At GW, he has also served as chair of the Department of Public Administration; Senior Associate Dean responsible for long-range planning and budgeting, faculty development, and curriculum planning; Interim Dean of the School of Business and Public Management; and Giant Inc. Professor of Public/Private Management.

Professor Kee joined GW in 1985 after a 17-year career in government in the states of New York and Utah, where he held a number of legislative and cabinet-level positions. He is past president of the National Association of State Budget Officers and was Utah Governor Scott M. Matheson's representative to the National Governors Association.

Professor Kee's teaching and research interests are in the areas of leadership, public-private partnerships, and public financial management. He has written extensively for such journals as *Public Administration Review, Public Budgeting & Finance, International Journal of Public Administration,* and *The Harvard Law Review.* He co-authored *Out of Balance* (1986) with Governor Matheson. He provides training in leadership and financial analysis throughout the United States, Canada, Africa, the Middle East, and China.

Professor Kee received his BA from the University of Notre Dame and his MPA and JD from New York University.

Kathryn E. Newcomer is a professor at the Trachtenberg School of Public Policy and Public Administration at GW, where she is also Co-Director of the Midge Smith Center for Evaluation Effectiveness, Director of the PhD in Public Policy and Administration program, and Associate Director of the school. She chaired the Department of Public Administration at GW for 20 years before becoming founding director of the Trachtenberg School. She teaches public and nonprofit program evaluation, research design, and applied statistics. She routinely conducts research and training for federal and local government agencies and nonprofit organizations on performance measurement and program evaluation, and has designed and conducted evaluations for several U.S. federal agencies and dozens of nonprofit organizations.

Dr. Newcomer has published four books: *Improving Government Performance* (1989), *The Handbook of Practical Program Evaluation* (1994, 2nd edition 2004), *Meeting the Challenges of Performance-Oriented Government* (2002), and *Getting Results: A Guide for Federal Leaders and Managers* (2005). She has also edited a volume of New Directions for Public Program Evaluation, *Using Performance Measurement to Improve Public and Nonprofit Programs* (1997), and numerous journal articles. She is a Fellow of the National Academy of Public Administration and currently serves on the Comptroller General's Educators' Advisory Panel. She has also served as President of the National Association of Schools of Public Affairs and Administration (NASPAA). Dr. Newcomer has received two Fulbright awards and has lectured throughout the world on performance measurement and public program evaluation.

Dr. Newcomer earned a BS in education and an MA in political science from the University of Kansas, and her PhD in political science from the University of Iowa.

*To present and future public servants as they transform
their organizations in the public interest.*

Contents

Figures

Tables

Foreword

In the late evening of 6 September 2005, I was winding my way toward a bed and a hot shower on board the USS *Iwo Jima,* which was docked at the cruise ship pier in New Orleans' Riverwalk. As we say in the Coast Guard when a ship has lost power, electricity, and the ability to sustain its crew, the city was "down hard, dark, and dirty." I encountered a civilian who looked as "down hard, dark, and dirty" as I felt. I asked him who he was and he told me he was a senior official from the City of New Orleans. I had just flown down from Baton Rouge after being tasked by Secretary Chertoff and the President to assume the role of Deputy Principal Federal Official for the response efforts in and around New Orleans. I asked, "What can I do for you and the city?" He replied, "We need hope."

Many times the problem is clear, the need even clearer. It was in this case. The adequate response was less clear. What is hope? How is it transformed into action, transformed into effect? What is most important, what can wait? These questions converged on me and I searched for answers. That conversation with the city official was the "tipping point," the galvanizing event in my personal search for "what to do?"

The answer, in the short term, was not profound, it was not elegant, and it wasn't even understandable in normal bureaucratic terms. The most immediate need was to muster, consolidate, support, and sustain the emergency services the city so desperately needed. The city official said to me, "I need somewhere to house my police and fire fighters and their families." I replied, "You got it."

Most of us will never encounter a situation like I did on 6 September 2005. We will, however, experience the challenge and opportunity to decide what an organization will do with its future or what we will do with the organizational space we live in.

Transforming Public and Nonprofit Organizations: Stewardship for Leading Change raises the questions in a larger context: What is the central problem in repositioning government to meet the challenges of the 21st century? What is the cause for action? What is the effect we collectively seek to achieve? These questions are not easily answered.

Professors Jed Kee and Kathy Newcomer have chosen to ask the hard questions. The response to Hurricane Katrina, while focused on the penultimate natural disaster of our era, is indicative of the challenges facing public administrators today. Those challenges come together in the need to create organizations that are "change-centric."

Leaders can create change-centric organizations only through transformational stewardship. It is a higher calling that transcends what we would call "standing the watch." It requires leaders to project their organizations and their personal leadership skills against a future set of challenges. Through research and thoughtful reflection the authors have provided us valuable insights.

Here are some thoughts and take-aways that I had in reviewing this text.

1. Leadership has always been important, but never more important than it is now. True leaders transform their organizations incrementally, or in "step functions," in ways that anticipate the future.

2. You can never communicate and collaborate enough. Transparency of information breeds self-correcting behavior.

3. We need to make our systems work for us and our organizations. We should measure what is important, not just what is mandated if it doesn't inform us or make us wiser.

4. A very wise person once told me, "Thinking that the government will do something just because it is right is like believing you can stop a bullet because you are a vegetarian. You don't make policy until you spend money.

5. We all manage risk; some do it better than others. Our ability to articulate how we do this is the ultimate value proposition to the American people and Congress.

I thank the authors for this effort. They have made a valuable contribution to the current thinking on how public and nonprofit leaders can transform their organizations in these challenging times.

Thad W. Allen
Admiral
United States Coast Guard

Preface

Leaders of 21st century organizations face an imperative to change or transform their organizations in response to ever-growing demands for greater productivity and effectiveness in an increasingly interconnected world. Leaders of private sector organizations must continually reinvent their organizations in the face of changing consumer demands and world competition. Public and nonprofit leaders have only recently faced this pressure to transform business processes and delivery systems. However, events such as the terrorist attacks on the United States on September 11, 2001, the widespread organizational failures to deal effectively with the Hurricane Katrina disaster in 2005, and the challenge of dealing with worldwide hunger and pandemics such as bird flu have highlighted the need for public and nonprofit organizations to become more nimble, connected, and performance-oriented.

We invite public and nonprofit leaders to become more comfortable with the demands of change and transformation, to build organizations that are "change-centric," to carefully weigh and prepare for the risks of change, and to develop a change-oriented leadership style that we call *transformational stewardship*. Transformational stewards continually balance the need for organizational change with the need to protect important organizational values and norms, always keeping the concept of the public interest at the center of their deliberations.

Although public and nonprofit sector change is inevitable and is occurring at an increasing rate, many managers and leaders of public and nonprofit sector organizations are not provided the training and tools they need to become successful change agents. Most books dealing with organizational change focus on the private sector, and they often make the implicit assumption that all change is the same.

We believe that public and nonprofit leaders face unique challenges and responsibilities. Foremost among those is the mandate to protect the public interest. We wrote this book to offer public and nonprofit leaders both theoretical knowledge and practical tools that can help them accomplish their change goals while protecting their organizations as well as the broader public interest.

Our analysis suggests that successful change is possible if the leaders initiating change efforts carefully weigh several important aspects affecting the contemplated change: its complexity, the needs and views of stakeholders, the external sociopolitical environment, and the organization's change capacity. Moreover, leaders who understand and assess the risks of change are better prepared to follow strategies that either overcome or mitigate those risks, and are able to build organizations that welcome and are adaptable to change initiatives.

This book grew out of our lifelong interest in leadership and organizational performance, which culminated in a research project we recently conducted for the George Washington University Center for Innovation in Public Service (CIPS)[1] to study the challenge of change and transformation in the public sector (Kee and Newcomer 2007). In this book we expand our research to include the nonprofit sector and offer a tailored approach to assist leaders of change in both sectors. We also suggest a general approach to leading change, which we refer to as transformational stewardship—a balanced method that recognizes the need to transform organizations while protecting organizational values and stakeholders. Informing our recommendations is our belief

---

[1] The Center for Innovation in Public Service is a collaborative research organization at the George Washington University, located within the Trachtenberg School of Public Policy and Public Administration. Its mission is to provide a forum for dialogue among government, private sector, nonprofit, and academic practitioners and experts interested in improving the leadership and management of public organizations.

that public and nonprofit leaders must keep the concept of the public interest at the center of their change and transformation initiatives.

ORGANIZATION OF THE BOOK

The chapters that follow provide evidence of the need to change, discuss the findings from our research, introduce the concept of transformational stewardship, and focus on several key elements involved in successfully stewarding public and nonprofit organizations through major changes or transformation. The key elements we believe require attention in any change effort include:

- *Transforming leadership*—strong, widespread leadership throughout the organization that provides a foundation for change.
- *Stakeholder communication and collaboration*—understanding the perceptions of key stakeholder groups and designing appropriate communication and collaboration strategies to involve stakeholders in the change effort.
- *Change-centric organizational culture*—organizational cultures, structures, policies, and procedures that support change initiatives.
- *Change implementation mechanisms*—the development of specific change structures that take responsibility for leading the change effort.
- *Performance measurement systems*—systems in place to track performance and the capability to develop metrics to measure the success of change.
- *Sociopolitical environment*—understanding and taking advantage of favorable environmental factors while mitigating adverse factors.
- *Analysis of the risk of failure*—effective analysis of the risk factors in a change effort and the development of mitigation strategies to address those risks.

We explore these concepts in the three parts of this book. Part I, "The Challenges for Leaders," comprises four chapters. Chapter 1 provides an overview of the forces for change in public and nonprofit organizations, highlighting the need to protect the public interest. Chapter 2 outlines our concept of transformational stewardship and explains why that concept is relevant to keeping a high level of public interest and accountability in change initiatives. Chapter 3 provides leaders with a diagnostic approach, or model, for dealing with the change landscape. Chapter 4 discusses six case studies of public and nonprofit organizations, drawing important lessons.

Part II contains five chapters dealing with "Key Leadership Processes." Chapter 5 begins with the important responsibility leaders have to communicate and collaborate with the organization's stakeholders. Chapter 6 discusses the importance of organizational culture and how leaders must foster change-centric cultures to create organizations that are comfortable with continuous improvement and change. Chapter 7 offers approaches to building mechanisms for implementing change, including strategic management and change frameworks that foster a learning organization. Chapter 8 addresses the need to measure change performance, highlighting why performance measurement systems are such an important part of the change process. Chapter 9, contributed by Ron Carlee, examines the change leadership of emergency management functions in a networked environment.

Part III provides our "Vision for the Future." Chapter 10 discusses how public and nonprofit organizations can develop transformational stewards throughout their organizations. Chapter 11 offers our "Invitation to Change in the Public Interest" for leaders of public and nonprofit organizations. The appendices provide two tools for leaders of change: a diagnostic tool for analyzing change risk and an individual 360-degree transformational stewardship survey.

We have written this book for all those who lead change efforts—not only leaders with positional authority within their public or nonprofit organization, but also all those who assume situational leadership roles in a change effort. Depending on the nature of the change, different types of managers may assume a leadership role; for example, the chief technology officer in an e-government initiative or the chief human capital officer in a pay-for-performance proposal may lead change efforts. Middle managers also play an important leadership role in communicating and translating change initiatives to their supervisees and colleagues across their organizations. We view all these individuals in a variety of organizational roles as potential change leaders, and we have written this book and tailored our guidance to them.

Depending on the current state of the organization and the need for change, outside leadership sometimes is brought in to transform the organization. In other cases, the organization may contract with a private firm to coordinate and synchronize skills and resources to implement the change initiative. In most cases, however, the individuals in an organization likely will assume the key change leadership roles. This book is designed to provide all those leading change efforts with the knowledge, methods, and assessment instruments they need to accomplish change goals.

The good news is that successful large-scale public and nonprofit sector change is possible. The case studies presented in this book clearly show that leading major public and nonprofit change efforts is complicated, unpredictable, and risky. But, with the right analysis and preparation, leadership can bring about successful change. We hope this book will provide change leaders with the tools and knowledge they need to evaluate their organizations and make informed choices on how to increase the effectiveness of their change efforts in the public interest.

James Edwin Kee
jedkee@gwu.edu

Kathryn E. Newcomer
newcomer@gwu.edu

Washington, D.C.
May 2008

Acknowledgments

This book could not have been written without the assistance and suggestions of many individuals, starting with many change leaders who have influenced and shaped our perspectives: Senator Robert Kennedy, Governor Scott M. Matheson, Coast Guard Commandant Thad W. Allen, GW President Stephen Joel Trachtenberg, GW Dean David Fowler, Coast Guard Rear Admiral Patrick Stillman, Comptroller General David Walker, Nancy Tate, and Joseph Wholey.

The book grew out of a project on "Leading Change in the Public Sector," undertaken with funding from BearingPoint in George Washington University's Center for Innovation in Pubic Service. S. Mike Davis, now at the Government Accountability Office, was an early project co-director and provided a number of important ideas concerning the concepts of change risk and transformational stewardship. Center research assistants who worked on the project and the case studies of public sector change included Dan Proudfoot, Whitney Setzer Owen, Deborah Trent, Sasha Rosen, and Valerie Oster. Owen was a co-author of a working paper that served as an early draft of Chapter 3. We also thank all those individuals from the agencies involved in the case studies for their kindness and willingness to provide candid assessments of their organizations' change strategies and implementation.

Three other graduate students in GW's Trachtenberg School of Public Policy and Public Administration made important contributions to the book: MPA student Jennifer Griffin was the primary author of the case study on N Street Village and the summary of the Hillel transformation contained in Chapter 4; MPA student Audra Clark tried out an early version of the 360-degree assessment and made several useful suggestions; and PhD candidate Heather Allen provided excellent editorial suggestions throughout the book and finalized the book's references.

We thank Ron Carlee, Arlington County Manager, for his willingness to provide Chapter 9 on emergency network management. A number of the Trachtenberg School's faculty, including Mike Worth and Mike Harmon, contributed their thoughts. Former Associate Business School Dean Lois Graff provided her insights (included in Chapter 7) on transforming GW's undergraduate business program.

Coast Guard Commandant Thad Allen graciously agreed to write the foreword to the book. We are proud to recognize him as a graduate of our MPA program; he has become an outstanding national leader—someone all public servants can emulate.

Finally, we appreciate the good work of the executives and staff of Management Concepts, especially Myra Strauss for her encouragement and assistance throughout the whole process.

While we acknowledge and appreciate all these individuals, the final product is our own. We ask our readers for their indulgence of any mistakes or limitations they may find in our analysis and welcome any suggestions for future editions.

PART I

The Challenges for Leaders

CHAPTER ONE

The Change Imperative

Public and nonprofit sector leadership in the 21st century is challenging and risky. Rapidly evolving global conditions and shifting political and economic influences are changing our ideas not only about "what" the government, nonprofit, and private sectors should do, but about how they should work together. Advances in information technologies and methodologies, as well as rising expectations of leadership, are driving and supporting changes in how public and nonprofit agencies accomplish their missions.

Unfortunately, the tragedy of the September 11 terrorist attacks, the multiple National Aeronautics and Space Administration (NASA) disasters, the failed Federal Emergency Management Agency (FEMA) response to Hurricane Katrina, and the various scandals involving misuse of funds by the leadership of well-known public and nonprofit organizations (most recently the Smithsonian Institution) highlight the need for public and nonprofit leaders to anticipate and respond to many kinds of risk. Public and nonprofit leaders face new and still-emerging circumstances that require them to design and implement more effective ways of doing business, and to improve organizational performance in support of the public interest.

Public and nonprofit sector leaders need to be comfortable with change, while recognizing that change is risky business. Organizational change is inherently unsettling, requiring the modification of traditional structures and sometimes new ways of doing business altogether. Pay-for-performance, competitive sourcing, public-private partnerships, performance-based budgeting, an increased consumer orientation, and other initiatives often create a shifting environment in which public and nonprofit leaders must satisfy a variety of external constituencies while maintaining supportive internal organizational norms and values.

To meet the challenge of change in the public interest, we believe that public and nonprofit leaders in the 21st century must become *transformational stewards*. Transformation and stewardship are reciprocal and mutually reinforcing aspects of public service, and both are vital responsibilities of tomorrow's public and nonprofit leaders. Transformational stewards are leaders who pursue organizational transformation effectively, while serving as stewards of their employees and protecting core public and nonprofit values. We contend that public and nonprofit leaders of the future require heightened creativity and initiative in anticipating and planning for risk, in addition to the skills and commitment to focus consistently on the public interest while implementing change.

The need for transformational leadership in the public and nonprofit sectors is most evident when we examine the pressures for change felt by today's public and nonprofit managers. These pressures emanate from many sources: an aging and increasingly multisector workforce; resource constraints; new horizontal relationships among public, nonprofit, and private sector organizations; globalization; technology breakthroughs; and increasingly complex public problems. In many cases, demands for change conflict with one another, competing for the leader's time and resources.

In this chapter, we begin by defining change in the public interest. We then identify some major changes underway that are affecting public and nonprofit organizations, particularly in terms of how public services are delivered in the United States.

▪▪ WHAT IS "CHANGE IN THE PUBLIC INTEREST"?

The concept of "the public interest" (or whether it can even be defined) is frequently debated in the literature (see, e.g., Sorauf 1957; Schubert 1960; Downs 1962; Goodsell

1990). In practice, the term is often synonymous with the notion of "general welfare," the "common good," or actions benefiting the "general public." While difficult to define precisely, the public interest "has a day-to-day commonsensical, practical salience for the behavior of hundreds of thousands of Public Administrators" (Catron, cited in Wamsley et al. 1990). The concept is somewhat analogous to the legal term "due process," which, while vague, becomes clearer in the discussion of particular cases and provides a unifying symbol of correct action (Sorauf 1957).

Former Irish Information Commissioner, Kevin Murphy, defined the public interest in the following way:

> *In very general terms, I take it that the public interest is that which supports and promotes the good of society as a whole (as opposed to what serves the interests of individual members of society or of sectional interest groups). In this sense I take it that the term "public interest" broadly equates with the term "the common good."*
> (Freedom of Information [Scotland] Act 2002)

The public interest is often contrasted with the concept of "private interest," recognizing that what is good for general society may not be beneficial to particular individuals and vice versa. The "Tragedy of the Commons" is a classic representation of this concept: While individuals may gain from grazing their cattle on the commons, at some point (absent regulation in the public interest) overgrazing is detrimental to the entire society, destroying the pasture and the livelihood of all (Hardin 1968). Current examples of this conflict include overfishing in the oceans and global warming. Individuals may gain from inexpensive fish or cheap power, but the long-term cost to society in general may be significant and contrary to the broader public interest.

Sometimes it is easier to determine what the public interest is not. For example, it is not corruption or injustice, racism, authoritarianism, arbitrary actions, unethical decision-making, or antisocial behavior.

Faculty members at Virginia Tech University, in their "Blacksburg Manifesto," noted that while it may be impossible to define the public interest in a given policy situation, the concept is still useful as an "ideal" and a "process." The manifesto states:

In this vein, the "public interest" refers to a combination of several habits of mind in making decisions and making polity: attempting to deal with the multiple *ramifications of an issue rather than a select few; seeking to incorporate the* long-range *view into deliberations, to balance a natural tendency toward excessive concern with short-term results; considering competing demands and requirements of affected individuals and groups, not one position; proceeding equipped with* more *knowledge and information rather than less; and recognizing that to say that the "public interest" is problematic is not to say it is meaningless.*
(Wamsley et al. 1990)

Simone argues that the term "public interest" encompasses "processes, principles and policies" (2006). In applying the concept of the public interest to media policy, Simone recommends "a participatory process as the preferred method for identifying and applying public interest principles. The ultimate goal of the examination is to discover ways to increase public participation in the ongoing dialogue" regarding the public interest. As an illustration of Simone's approach, ensuring equal access to certain government services might involve all three facets: the policy to make the services available, the principle of equality, and the processes by which that access is ensured. An agency responsible for a particular government service will have to consider all three as it undergoes any change or transformation.

Accepting the notion of the public interest as a useful perspective to guide actions may further suggest an approach to the change process. Wamsley et al. (1990) suggests the following approach:

1. Tentative steps and experimental action, rather than a final "solution"
2. Curiosity and dialogue about ends as well as means
3. Individuals and institutions that "learn" as well as respond
4. Humility and skepticism about "grand designs"
5. Greater awareness of the potential of each individual to contribute to the dialogue about the public interest
6. Greater attentiveness to the words of public discourse.

Goodsell illustrates this approach to the public interest in discussing a National Park Service decision to limit visitors in certain national parks (1990). In its announcement the Park Service emphasized that the park ecosystem must be preserved over the "long run" and that visitors must be given a "quality experience." Further, the Park Service noted that closing the parks when full respects their "carrying capacity" and indicated that indirect controls tried in the past had failed. Finally, the Park Service said that in an experimental park closing it had received only one complaint. This example demonstrates the importance of the *process* of determining the public interest.

The point of discussing these approaches and illustrations is not to argue for a specific set of public interest imperatives; rather, it is to suggest that the concept of the "public interest" is a multifaceted concern that leaders of public and nonprofit organizations must keep in mind as they work to change or transform their organizations. This concern for the public interest must capture existing policy and "official" expressions of the public interest; any fundamental principles at stake; the processes by which citizens and stakeholders are able to engage in dialogue about maintaining the public interest during the transformation; and the special trusteeship responsibilities that leaders have for their organizations and the public (both current and future generations).

While nonprofit leaders may not have exactly the same trusteeship responsibilities as public leaders, nonprofit organizations enjoy a special status in most countries: They are created for certain public purposes, generally have public purposes as part of their charter, and often are based on certain shared values or principles—all of which have to be considered in any change or transformation.

The concept of "change in the public interest" argues that the notion of acting for the good of the general members of society must be at the center of all public and nonprofit change and transformation initiatives. Thus, as public and nonprofit leaders contemplate and initiate change and transformation, their diagnosis of the problem, their strategizing about solutions, and their implementation and reinforcement of the resulting changes must all occur within the context of the public interest.

EVOLVING MODES OF SERVICE DELIVERY

In the United States, public services are increasingly delivered through networks of public, nonprofit, and private agencies. Approximately 88,000 government units (U.S. Census

Bureau 2002) and 1.4 million nonprofit organizations (Urban Institute 2006) are currently operating in the United States. Federal, state, and local governments account for about
30 percent of the nation's economy, and nonprofits account for about 8 percent. Nonprofit
organizations are not only growing in size as a percentage of the economy, but they are also
increasingly working with government agencies to deliver a variety of public services.

The nonprofit sector encompasses a diverse set of organizations, from small neigh-
borhood associations and local arts organizations to multibillion-dollar hospitals and universities. Of the 1.4 million nonprofits, about 300,000 are registered with the Internal
Revenue Service as 501(c)(3) "public charities," a category that includes most arts, education, health care, and human services organizations; many of these are actively involved
in providing public goods and services. The major charities reported raising about $1 tril-
lion in 2004, about 25 percent from charitable contributions. More than 65 million individuals volunteered for nonprofit organizations in 2004 (Urban Institute 2006).

Apart from religious institutions, the largest number of nonprofit organizations
provide human services (including relief organizations like the Red Cross and human-
itarian organizations like Habitat for Humanity). Many nonprofits produce complex
goods or services—health care, education, performing arts—that are difficult to judge
in terms of quality. Further, many of the goods and services provided by nonprofits are
paid for by persons other than the recipients. A donor to "Save the Children" might be
an affluent North American, for example, while the recipient might be a child from a
less developed nation. Because there is no profit motivation, nonprofits are not governed by the same contractual discipline of the private market and are valued most for
their trust and reputation rather than for price or profit.

Nonprofit production of goods and services often serves as a "complement" to
public production, supplementing or replacing government efforts to redistribute goods
and services. Nonprofits also have lower labor costs (because they rely on lower paid personnel and volunteers) than government agencies and thus, arguably, might be more efficient in providing certain goods and services than government. They may have more
flexibility and be able to make use of service charges and fees to partially cover costs—
something government may not politically be able to do. For these reasons, government
agencies are increasingly relying on nonprofits to share public duties and responsibilities.

Public-Private Partnerships

Public services in the United States are increasingly delivered through multiagent and multisectoral networks, via the creation of public-private partnerships (PPPs) that require new types of governance structures and new methods to ensure transparency and accountability. E. S. Savas defines a public-private partnership as "any arrangement between government and the private sector in which partially or traditionally public activities are performed by the private sector" (Savas 2000, 4). This is a broad definition that could accommodate a variety of arrangements, from contracting-out to the use of vouchers. The types of relationships that pose the greatest challenge are public-private partnerships that are ongoing relationships between the government and the private sector in which the private organization produces a public good or performs a public service that has traditionally been provided by the public sector organization.

Public-private partnerships have existed in the United States since its founding. During the revolutionary war, the Continental Congress authorized the use of privateers to harass the British Navy. Later, much of the West was developed through a variety of PPPs, including the transcontinental railway and homesteading. The production of transportation infrastructure has often been undertaken with PPPs, from the development of private toll roads and canals during the nation's early history up to the present Dulles Greenway—a privately financed, built, and operated toll road from Dulles Airport to Leesburg, Virginia.

After World War II, PPPs were often used in urban infrastructure projects. For example, in urban renewal projects, local governments provided tax concessions and improved infrastructure for private development in central cities. The federal government supported these projects through a variety of grant programs and tax credits.

PPPs also have been used to provide a variety of public services and have served as critical mechanisms in such important policy areas as implementing welfare reform and providing health care to the poor and elderly. At the federal level, service contracting grew by 33 percent in domestic agencies during the 1990s (Eggers and Goldsmith 2004) and has played a key (and somewhat controversial) role in the war in Iraq, with the private sector feeding, housing, transporting, and even protecting armed services personnel.

Heterarchy Replacing Hierarchy

Administrative structures in government are moving away from hierarchy and "silo" delivery of programs toward a "heterarchy" of systems (resembling a network or fishnet) that interact to meet the needs of citizens. While the exact shape of this heterarchy is currently under discussion and is far from clearly defined, it is evident that public and nonprofit organizations are moving toward a networked approach to service delivery based on coordination and cooperation among multiple organizations from all sectors. In a heterarchy or network, authority is determined by knowledge and function—through horizontal linkages rather than the traditional hierarchical form of vertical authority.

The most recent examples of leadership successes and failures during the Hurricane Katrina relief effort clearly illustrate this trend. Organizations that emphasize leadership in a networked environment performed well. For example, during the first week of the relief effort, Coast Guard crews rescued an estimated 22,000 people in Louisiana, Mississippi, and Alabama. Coast Guard Lt. Cmdr. Jim Elliot, who helped oversee rescues from Mobile, attributes the success of the effort to a unified command with states and local industries before the hurricane roared ashore. "We know how to join with other organizations to get the job done," he said (Barr 2005). Among other factors Elliot identified as important to the coordinated response were the cross-training of employees and cross-functional teaming.

CHALLENGES TO ENSURING PUBLIC ACCOUNTABILITY

Government service (planning, funding, and providing services directly to citizens) is thus evolving into public facilitation and governance—the provision of public services through a network of public, private, and nonprofit actors. This change in the manner that government delivers services is partly the result of an aging workforce (half of all top U.S. civil service executives are over 50), but mostly the result of deliberate policy at the national level to reduce the number of federal employees despite expanding public responsibilities. Public governance requires a new type of public leadership—leadership that engages the "para-public sector" (nonprofit and for-profit organizations that operate primarily on government contracts) while maintaining public accountability (Kee, Forrer, and Gabriel 2007).

We now speak less about government and more about governance. The trend in public sector employment has been to hire fewer full-time employees, especially at the federal level, and instead to contract out government jobs to the private sector. As Paul Light has alerted us, "the shadow government" continues to grow because our governments hire more and more contractors (Light 2006). As of 2002, Light estimated the number of contractors to be double that of full-time federal employees. "Doing more with less" frequently means doing more with contract employees or through a variety of contractual relationships with private and nonprofit organizations.

One of the most significant challenges in the leadership of complex networks is the issue of public accountability. Public accountability is the process by which public servants balance the interests of participating private market and nongovernmental organizations and government agencies in the provision of public services while maintaining a sense of accountability to the public being served. Under this concept, the public or nonprofit manager serves as facilitator between the public and the private/nonprofit sector. The manager is tasked with upholding the public interest while accruing the benefits of service provision via the para-public network of for-profit, nonprofit, and faith-based providers. These complicated delivery systems make ensuring accountability for both process and performance especially challenging.

In the nonprofit sector, new legal requirements also have led to increased oversight by boards of trustees and oversight and audit committees. The Sarbanes-Oxley Act, for example, was enacted in 2002 in response to private sector corporate and accounting scandals such as Enron and Tyco. Although only a couple of its provisions specifically apply to nonprofit organizations, the act serves as "a wake-up call to the entire nonprofit community. Indeed, several state legislatures have already passed or are considering legislation containing elements of the Sarbanes-Oxley Act to be applied to nonprofit organizations" (Board Source and Independent Sector 2006). In response to the act, many nonprofit organizations are proactively taking steps to change their financial practices and enhance the transparency and accountability of their financial results.

OTHER PRESSURES FOR CHANGE IN PUBLIC AND NONPROFIT ORGANIZATIONS

Issues of structure and accountability are clearly among the important drivers of public and nonprofit change; nonetheless, other, equally important forces also influence how public and nonprofit organizations carry out their responsibilities. Among those forces are the increasingly competitive nature of delivery of goods and services, globalization, and the demand to be more performance-oriented—to prove to consumers, voters, and funders alike that public and nonprofit organizations are using their resources wisely and efficiently.

Competition

Nonprofit and public sector organizations and their employees are facing pressures to become more competitive and entrepreneurial, and they often find themselves competing with the private sector (e.g., competitive sourcing, bidding for contracts) to fulfill their organizational mission. In addition, the growth in the number of nonprofits creates a competitive environment for donor funds, and nonprofits may have to position themselves differently to obtain needed funding.

The "conservative revolution" that began with Reagan in the 1980s and continued through the Clinton and Bush presidencies favored nonprofit enterprises, manifested in a huge expansion in the contracting out of government programs. The number of full-time employees in public agencies has been reduced, but the number of private and nonprofit sector workers involved in public service has increased. This shift also intensified competition by making for-profit businesses eligible for grants and contracts that previously had been restricted to nonprofits (Hall 2005). Some nonprofit leaders have voiced concern that in a competitive fundraising environment the distinction between what is charitable and what is commercial gets blurred: "too many nonprofits are chasing the money and not their mission" (Eggers 2002, xvii).

Public sector employees increasingly find themselves competing with the private sector to "prove" that they can deliver goods and services as efficiently and effectively as their private counterparts. While "competitive sourcing" has existed in government for some time, the Clinton and Bush administrations (see, e.g., the President's Management Agenda, U.S. Office of Management and Budget 2007) have placed new emphasis on this approach. Competitive sourcing requires public employees to depart from the safety of their program hierarchy and create "most efficient organizations" that compete directly with their private (and sometimes nonprofit) counterparts. While the results of such competition are heartening for public employees (U.S. OMB 2007), they nonetheless necessitate major changes in the manner that public organizations operate.

Globalization

The world is becoming flatter; Friedman, for example, notes that the U.S. role in the world's economy has changed dramatically as a result of open-sourcing, outsourcing, insourcing, offshoring, and supply-chaining (2006). One consequence of growing interdependence is that the problems of the world can no longer be treated as distant concerns. Instant communication of problems, such as pandemics or agricultural failures, forces us to become more responsive; the changing nature of who produces the nation's goods and services raises the problem of lack of oversight of health and safety issues in other countries (such as China).

O'Toole and Hanf highlight the growing influence of globalization on all levels of governance, asserting that "the globalized future of public administration is already emerging" (2002). The authors examine how increased interconnection of multinational authorities (e.g., United Nations, World Trade Organization, European Union) and the influence of international nongovernmental organizations are shaping policies at every level of domestic government.

Public and nonprofit managers increasingly are seeing the impact of global actions on their service delivery. For example, international agreements can force modification of local law, and local governments are entering into international agreements with the power to impact national policy. One illustration of the latter is the use by state and local governments of tax breaks to encourage the location of global companies in their jurisdiction. O'Toole and Hanf conclude that: "internationalization shapes the perspectives of U.S. administrators…[the] professional orientations of those involved are molded by their interactions, especially collegial ties with others working on similar challenges…as a result, administrators are likely to develop a more transnational perspective" (2002). Globalization creates the situation in which a public manager's closest working partner may be located across international and intersector borders rather than in the office across the hall.

The nonprofit sector also is becoming more international (Anheier and Themudo 2005). Oxfam, Save the Children, Amnesty International, the Red Cross, and Greenpeace have become "brand names" among international nonprofit or nongovernmental organizations (NGOs). The free flow of funds across borders means that a donor can fund nonprofits in any continent; indeed, the activities of major nonprofits often span the globe. While globalization has enabled nonprofits to operate across national borders, it also has further eroded traditional boundaries between the public and private domain and what is considered "commercial" versus "charitable" (Hall 2005).

The Performance Imperative

Leaders of public and nonprofit organizations are being pressured by their funders (legislatures and donors) to become more performance-oriented. Beginning in the 1980s, the for-profit sector began to be influenced by the works of Peters and Waterman (1982), Senge (1990), and others to create more competitive, performance-oriented, creative learning organizations. The global "new public management" movement of the 1990s (Kettl 1998) produced success stories, especially in the "Westminster" nations (Australia, New Zealand, and the U.K.), that inspired more dialogue on the need to reinvent government.

In the U.S. federal government, the National Performance Review of the Clinton administration, the Government Performance and Results Act (GPRA), and the President's Management Agenda under George W. Bush instituted policies that required managers to document and report data on performance. At the turn of the century, nonprofits began to ask the same types of questions: How can we better focus on our mission, reduce bureaucratic structures, and become more performance-oriented and accountable to our clients and donors?

Just as government is being asked to become more "business-like" and "accountable for results," nonprofit organizations are feeling the pressure to mimic their private and governmental counterparts (Oster 1995). Some of this pressure is coming from donors and other stakeholders, but some is internally generated by nonprofit leadership that is trying to better fulfill the mission of the organization. Both public and nonprofit organizations also are experiencing increased expectations from their constituents, boards of trustees, and legislatures for service delivery to be more consumer-friendly and results-oriented.

THE CHALLENGE FOR LEADERS

The one common element in all these forces for change is the need for public and nonprofit leaders to adapt and transform the way people and processes perform. But change is not easy. While potential rewards may be great, change carries risks for the organization, leaders and managers, and other stakeholders. This is true in the private sector as well as the public and nonprofit sectors, but there is reason to believe that change in the public and nonprofit sectors is more "risky" than change in the private sector.

A private-sector CEO has to satisfy his or her board of directors, and ultimately the stockholders, but can often proceed in relative secrecy, without a great deal of collaboration. In contrast, public and nonprofit sector leaders have significantly more stakeholders. They include those internal to the organization, such as unions, senior political appointees, and nonprofit boards of directors, and those external to the organization, such as political leadership (both elected and appointed), donors, suppliers, and citizens/consumers. Generally speaking, organizational change in the public and nonprofit sectors must be transparent, requires extensive consultation, and is usually conducted in a highly visible arena. Additionally, the nature of political (and nonprofit board) leadership creates a short-term horizon for many of the stakeholders, making long-term change initiatives more problematic.

While change in the ways of conducting business is usually called *organizational change,* the reality is that change is not organizational unless it is first *individual change,* and then *team change.* At these levels, a number of stakeholders with interest in the change efforts emerge. Each of these stakeholders has distinct and often very different perceptions, expectations, and "stakes" in whatever change is being proposed. In addition, the perceptions, expectations, and stakes of the leader influence the course of change. While local stakeholders are more prominent in the leader's daily environment, the increasing complexity and scope of the managerial role in government and the nonprofit sector—with its increased emphasis on public-private partnerships and intergovernmental arrangements—means that all stakeholders must be on the leader's radar to some degree.

Collectively, these relationships and their influences on the change process constitute the "change landscape." Becoming aware of and thinking critically about this landscape are critical first steps toward deliberately negotiating it with proficiency and skill.

Leadership expert William Bridges once noted that change is inevitable, but transformation is optional (1991). However, when we examine the nature of problems that government and the nonprofit sector must address—terrorism, global warming, bird flu and other potential pandemics—the failure of public and nonprofit organizations to learn and evolve is unacceptable. So while transformation may be optional in some theoretical sense, if public and nonprofit leaders and managers are to uphold their responsibility to act in the public interest, they are compelled to learn how to transform their organizations to succeed in the face of new challenges. Change and transformation are difficult, however, requiring sound methodology and change-centric leaders who can balance the need for transformation and the need to be good stewards of their organization and their employees.

THE RESPONSIBILITIES OF TRANSFORMATIONAL STEWARDS

Transforming operations and ways of doing business is challenging and often difficult to accomplish successfully; a large number of change efforts fail. By identifying and understanding the major challenges they face prior to implementing changes, leaders will have the opportunity to strategize and adjust their plans and processes accordingly, and to develop the skills needed in their organization to navigate the perilous change course.

In an effort to capture a variety of change practices and to illustrate the concepts that we have identified as the most significant to change leaders, we examined six case studies, all involving large-scale change efforts in the public and nonprofit sectors. These cases all involved complex changes that were undertaken to transform the current state of the organization and to change the ways the organization provides goods and services. We examined the change initiatives involved in the following cases drawn from federal, state, local, charitable, and religious organizations:

- The delivery of human services in Fairfax County, Virginia
- The U.S. Coast Guard's strategy to recapitalize and integrate its "Deepwater" assets
- The transformation of the Veterans Health Administration
- The initial stages of a significant unfunded federal mandate, REAL ID, that requires a fundamental restructuring of the states' driver's license systems
- The change in leadership of N Street Village in Washington, D.C., under conditions of fiscal crisis
- The restructuring of Hillel, the Jewish nonprofit that serves college students throughout the United States.

We also drew from our own experiences of changes that occurred in state government and at George Washington University. Collectively, these experiences and cases provided rich material for our analysis.

To engineer successful public and nonprofit sector change, leaders must carefully anticipate and analyze change complexity, their stakeholders, their external sociopolitical environment, and their organization's change capacity—initiating change while managing the risks of change. Leaders must adapt and help others adapt to changing mission requirements, new requirements, or environmental forces; stay competitive with the latest innovations and technology; and continue to provide quality services to citizens.

If change is such a risky business, why engage in it? The answer, of course, is that it is often more risky not to change. In our two nonprofit cases, not changing might have led to the demise of the organizations, as they were facing significant fiscal crises brought about by poor leadership as well as internal and external forces. In the Veterans Health Administration case, the very existence of a public veterans' health care system was in question, with political pressure to privatize it. The system was a "burning platform" that could not survive in its current configuration. With the increased pressure and new responsibilities expanding the Coast Guard's mission of protecting our harbors and ports, not changing could have led to mission failure. Fairfax County human service systems might have been able to "muddle along" without changing, but at a high cost to servicing the county's expanding population. Finally, REAL ID presents a change mandated by Congress, and while negotiations continue regarding its implementation, the inevitable outcome of production of national identification cards will occur, one way or another.

In Chapter 2 we develop further our notion of transformational stewardship. Then in Chapter 3 we provide a more complete discussion of our model for leading change in the public interest. Chapter 4 describes the six cases of public and nonprofit changes we researched to both inform and test our model. Each of the case studies is used throughout the remainder of the book to illustrate the model and expand our vision about the role of public and nonprofit leaders as transformational stewards.

PRACTICAL TIPS FOR THE CHANGE LEADER

- Examine your organization's change landscape and the various forces for change, including globalization, competition, and the need to become more performance-oriented.

- Develop a strategy to deal with those change forces.

- Analyze the risks to the organization associated with the change imperative and the risks of not changing.

- Examine how the evolving nature of public service delivery will affect your organization's structure and potential collaborators.

- Develop a list of potential partners in achieving your organization's mission and a strategy to involve them in that goal.

- Determine whether the proposed changes will heighten demands for public accountability.

- Consider how moving from a structure of "government" to "governance" will affect how your organization will be held accountable for its results.

SUGGESTED READINGS ON THE CHANGE IMPERATIVE

Donald F. Kettl, *The Next Government of the United States: Challenges for Performance in the 21st Century.* Washington, DC: Transformation of Organizations Series, IBM Center for the Business of Government, 2005.

Kettl provides clear guidance on how leaders should both predict and prepare for change in order to succeed. Discussing how management challenges have changed in government, he highlights why recent events—such as 9/11 and Katrina—demonstrate that the government needs to change its approach to be able to respond to serious problems effectively.

Thomas L. Friedman, *The World is Flat: A Brief History of the Twenty-first Century.* New York: Picador, 2006 (updated edition), 2007 (paperback edition).

This acclaimed book is useful for academics and practitioners alike. Friedman highlights how the world has become interconnected and explains why these changes cannot be ignored. Globalization is a concept that transformational stewards cannot ignore if they are to lead in the public interest; this book is an excellent starting point.

Gareth Morgan, *Riding the Waves of Change: Developing Managerial Competencies in a Turbulent World.* San Francisco: Jossey-Bass Publishers, 1988.

Morgan provides a farsighted view of a manager's/leader's changing responsibilities at the close of the 20th century and into the 21st century. He prepares leaders for dealing effectively with waves of change, including new technologies, management styles, and employee values; market fluctuations; and globalization. He discusses how to "read the environment" for emerging change issues and to manage proactively, including promoting creativity, learning, and innovation throughout the organization.

Margaret J. Wheatley, *Leadership and the New Science: Learning about Organizations from an Orderly Process.* Birmingham, AL: University of Alabama Press, 1984.

Wheatley provides a clear way of thinking about organizations for a chaotic future. Using examples from many areas (particularly physics), she argues that relationships are the fundamental key to an organization's success. Leaders of nonprofit, public, and private organizations will all find guidance on participation and cooperation in this book.

CHAPTER TWO

Transformational Stewardship in the Public Interest

Our case studies reinforce a premise, widely supported in the literature, that leadership is a critical element in the change and transformation process; effective "change leadership" requires special skills, which we believe are encapsulated in the concept of "transformational stewardship." In this chapter, we first review leadership theories in general, and then more specifically change leadership theories. Second, we describe the concept of transformational stewardship and provide a list of attributes of successful change leaders. Third, we provide some illustrations from our case studies that reinforce our transformational stewardship concepts and approach.

▄▄TAXONOMIES AND THEORIES OF CHANGE LEADERSHIP

Most people feel they know what leadership is, or at least, somewhat akin to pornography, "we know it when we see it." That has not stopped academics and practitioners from developing general theories about the "best" ways to categorize approaches to leadership. We group these taxonomies into the following six categories:

- *Trait* theories of leadership attempt to develop a list of defined characteristics of leadership, such as intelligence, self-confidence, decisiveness, courage, empathy, and integrity. Proponents include Stogdill (1948, 1974); Mann (1959); Lord, DeVader, and Allinger (1986); Kirkpatrick and Locke (1991); and more recently the "emotional IQ" or maturity approach of Goleman (1998) and Goleman, McKee, and Boyatzis (2002).

- The *style* approach emphasizes the behavior of leaders, ranking individual relationships with followers in terms of the leaders' "concern for people" and "concern for production or results." The Blake and Mouton Managerial Grid is one of the best known approaches of this type (1964, 1985).

- The *situational* approach characterizes the leader's role along a "supportive" and "directive" matrix, based on the development level of the followers (Hersey and Blanchard 1993).

- *Contingency* theory—a "leader-match" approach—suggests that the type of leadership style needed depends on three factors: leader-member relations (good or poor), task structure (high or low), and positional power of the leader vis-à-vis the follower (strong or weak) (Fiedler 1967; Fiedler and Chemers 1974).

- The *transactional versus transformational* leadership approach is associated with James MacGregor Burns' influential book *Leadership* (1978) and the work of Bennis and Nanus (1985). Transactional leadership refers to leadership approaches that focus on the exchanges (i.e., promises of rewards or threats of punishment) between leaders and followers. In contrast, transformational leadership refers to a process in which the leader and follower engage each other in creating a shared vision that raises the level of motivation for both. Bass and Avolio (1994) state that this level of motivation encompasses the following: "idealized influence"—charisma or ethical role model of the leader; "inspirational motivation"—communicating the shared vision and values; "intellectual stimulation"—for greater creativity and innovation; and "individualized consideration"—listening carefully to the needs of the followers.

- *Servant* leadership focuses on the follower: The leader is required to take care of and nurture the follower, while shifting power to the follower

(Greenleaf 1970; Autry 2001). Other "holistic" approaches that are generally linked with a strong ethical dimension include "spiritual" leadership (Fairholm 1997; Vaill 1989b) and "stewardship" (Kass 1990; Kee 2003).

While their proponents suggest that the various leadership theories apply to organizations that are fairly static as well as to those that are undergoing change, leadership theories do not always explicitly take "change" into account. Some might argue that leadership is inherently change-oriented—that the function of management is to protect and nurture the status quo, while the function of leadership is to continually examine better ways of doing things (see, e.g., Zeleznik 1977). Clearly, some of the leadership theories, such as transformational leadership, are more change-oriented.

Nonetheless, issues of change leadership have spawned a whole new set of authors, many of whom have written primarily with the practitioner in mind. For the sake of discussion, we have created a taxonomy that divides the works of these authors into three models of change leadership: leader-centered, follower-centered, and change-centric leadership.

In any change effort, a public sector leader or manager must make careful use of his or her power and influence to effect the necessary change. However, the nature of the use of power and influence may be different depending on whether the change leader is leader-centered, follower-centered, or change-centric.

A leader-centered change leader is likely to focus on those aspects of power and influence that revolve around the leader's own power sources (legitimate authority, expertise, charisma). In follower-centered change, a leader is more likely to rely on his or her indirect sources of power and influence (common vision, relationships, organizational norms and culture, empowerment). A change-centric leader is likely to rely primarily on mutual trust and community, drawing on both the leader's and the followers' power to achieve the needed change.

Table 2.1 provides a summary of the three approaches to change and their various strengths and weaknesses.

TABLE 2.1:   Comparison of Change Leadership Models

	Leader-Centered Change Leadership	Follower-Centered Change Leadership	Change-Centric Change Leadership
Role of the Leader	• Directing/shaping change vision • Communicating change to employees • Mitigating resistance to change	• Stepping back so group members have equal leadership • Achieving consensus in decision-making	• Facilitating change from top and bottom • Bringing attention of upper leadership to change initiatives from frontline workers
Approach to Power and Influence	Reliance on positional authority and personal power sources such as charisma and expertise	Reliance on personal power that emphasizes relationships, common visions, organizational norms and culture, and empowerment of followers	Reliance on mutual trust and community, taking advantage of the personal power of both the leader and followers
Potential Strengths	• Efficiency in decision-making • Holistic view of organization's needs • Access to resources	• Promotes participation and equality • Lessens resistance to change	• Strategic capability along with detailed implementation • Facilitates interaction among stakeholders of the change • Collaborative effort so little resistance is seen
Potential Weaknesses	• Little employee participation • Misunderstandings and resistance resulting from lack of communication • May promote change strategy that is inconsistent with front-line capabilities	• Not practical in large organizations • Time-consuming to reach consensus • Total consensus may not be desirable • May be too detail-oriented, lacking strategic view	• Hard to identify proper balance of top-down vs. bottom-up leadership • Diffuse accountability • May be too process-oriented
Corresponding Authors	Black and Gregersen (2002), Conger (2000), Kotter (1996), Slater (1999)	Autry (2001), Bennis (2000), Greenleaf (1970), Raelin (2003)	Atwood et al. (2003), Dunphy (2000), Kee (2003), Kelman (2005), Harmon (2007)

Leader-Centered Change Leadership

Much of the change leadership literature is based on the assumption that change initiatives emanate primarily from the top leader or leaders of an organization. While various levels of employee participation may be involved, the ultimate change vision and strategy are formulated by those at the organization's helm and trickle down through the various levels of hierarchy in a top-down approach. In this model, the success or failure of the change initiative is solely dependent upon the actions of the leader.

Charismatic leaders who initiate changes based on their personal characteristics and inspire others to follow their vision fall into this category of change leadership. A prime example of charismatic leadership is the legendary General Electric CEO Jack Welch. According to Welch, "leaders are people who 'inspire with clear vision of how things can be done better'" (Welch quoted in Slater 1999, 29).

Strengths of Leader-Centered Leadership

One argument for the leader-centered framework is the assumption that the leader is in the best position to plan for an organization-wide change effort. Top leadership has the power to use the organization's resources for the change, the ability to see the system holistically, and the authority of being in a leadership position, which legitimizes the change effort in the eyes of employees (Conger in Beer and Nohria 2000).

Kotter argues in his book *Leading Change* that top leadership is in the unique position of effecting change. Kotter articulates eight steps that he deems necessary to lead change successfully, including creating a sense of urgency for change, communicating the change vision, creating small wins, and embedding the change into the organization's culture. Although these steps involve employee participation and involvement along the way, they are ultimately the responsibility of top management (Kotter 1996).

According to other change leadership authors, top leadership is also best positioned to overcome resistance to change from lower level employees by changing employees' "mental maps," or their current understanding of the status quo, so they are more willing to embrace the change effort (Black and Gregersen 2002). The primary goal is not to involve employees in the vision-setting stage of the change process, but instead to invite their participation in the implementation stage of the change so resistance can be mitigated.

An additional strength of leader-centered change is the efficiency it provides in decision-making. When a decisive, timely decision needs to be made, relying on the top leader to make the call can be the quickest course of action. While occasionally it may be beneficial to have input from employees in decision-making, there may not be time for such extended interaction when making a decision for change. Leaders often need to adapt to a new course quickly and effectively.

Potential Weaknesses of Leader-Centered Leadership

Although the leader-centered change strategy has many benefits, it also has several drawbacks. The first consideration is whether the organization's culture will accept or reject the change effort. Often, organizational cultures are resistant to change and can thwart the process, through both direct and indirect means. If top leadership simply tries to push change down the ranks, the employee culture may resist and successfully sabotage the effort.

Another drawback to the leader-centered approach is the potential lack of communication between top management and those actually implementing the mechanics of the change. Kotter contends that communicating the change through repeated announcements or meetings is important to help people become familiar with the change process (1996). However, any change effort pushed from the top down has the potential to be misconstrued by those not involved in the planning. They may not have the background or full understanding of why a change is necessary and may therefore resist the change. Such a scenario is not conducive to the type of "buy-in" so many change authors (e.g., Kotter 1996) say is critical for effectively overcoming resistance and orchestrating change.

Related to the problem of buy-in is the sometimes faulty assumption that top leadership knows the one and only successful change path. However, it is often mid-level managers and frontline employees who will be charged with implementing the change effort. These hands-on individuals have experience and knowledge of details related to implementing the change that top leadership may not. If frontline workers are not included to some degree in the planning process, leaders may miss important ideas for implementing the change.

Follower-Centered Change Leadership

In contrast to the top-down approach of the leader-centered model, the follower-centered leadership framework outlines how change is accomplished from the bottom up. In this model, change is initiated from any level within the organization. Top leadership works to bring frontline change issues to the forefront and then steps back and allows lower level employees to control the change process. The idea of servant leadership is conducive to this model (Greenleaf 1977; Autry 2001).

One role of a servant leader is to delegate authority and power to subordinates in order to improve the employees' leadership skills and abilities (Northouse 2004). In the change process, a servant leader defers to employees' ideas and approaches in implementing the change. While this process may not lead to the exact change the leader seeks, the change that does occur is more likely to be supported throughout the organization.

Strengths of Follower-Centered Leadership

One major advantage of the follower-centered approach is its ability to lower resistance to change and encourage the feeling of empowerment among those being asked to implement the change. This deep level of involvement can lead to a consensus for change. Raelin's idea of "leaderful organizations" (2003) is a good example of this strategy. To be leaderful is to distribute leadership roles, including the powers of decision-making, goal-setting, and communicating, throughout the entire group or team working on a change process. The focus is on fostering group dynamics that help individuals feel valued and part of the entire change effort.

Bennis argues that our society places too much emphasis on individual leadership capabilities and overlooks the value of considering everyone's role in the organizational system. He labels top-down change management "maladaptive" and "dangerous" (Bennis in Beer and Nohria 2000, 120). For Bennis, successful organizations are those whose leaders focus on followers and encourage the expression of their opinions on organizational operations, including change processes.

By encouraging involvement and collaboration, the follower-centered approach offers the potential for increased intra-organizational communication. If everyone in the organization is a part of the change effort, then there is likely to be increased communication and collaboration, although it will take more coordinating effort from leadership to achieve this increase.

Potential Weaknesses of Follower-Centered Leadership

The main drawback of the follower-centered approach is its lack of timeliness in fostering decisions. In today's fast-paced world, there is often insufficient time to devote to such a labor-intensive change process as the follower-centered framework requires. Developing a group to the level of a "leaderful organization" as Raelin suggests would take more time and resources than most organizations have to spare. Additionally, the emphasis on consensus building is not realistic or even desirable in all cases. Often, people cannot completely agree on a certain issue, yet a decision needs to be made to move forward.

Furthermore, while this approach may work well in a small team of six to eight people, it is not likely to be achievable or effective in a government agency with over 10,000 employees or a large nonprofit agency, such as the Red Cross. The logistics of organizing such a high level of collaboration and leadership sharing in such a huge organization are hard to fathom. Additionally, there are often legitimate reasons, such as security concerns, for restricting information within the organization.

The last major challenge to the follower-centered approach is its potential lack of strategic thinking. While those on the front lines will often know implementation details better than top management, they may not be privy to the full picture of what the change process needs to achieve on all levels. They may understand their particular team or department well, but they may not understand the full impact of how their piece fits into the larger organizational change puzzle. Also, because of the potential lack of the "big picture," follower-centered change groups may not have the extra-organizational contacts necessary to make a change initiative successful.

Change-Centric Leadership

The leader-centered and follower-centered approaches (top-down versus bottom-up) do not offer much middle ground. Based on our research and case studies, we believe that change-centric, transformational stewardship presents an alternative and more successful approach. This model does not focus on which level of the organization should institute the change effort. Instead, what matters is finding the proper balance of top-down and bottom-up management that leads to a successful change effort.

The focus of change-centric leadership is on the successful change effort itself, not on assigning inflexible leadership roles. This is not to say that leadership is unimportant. On the contrary, the leaders of an organization serve as facilitators of change. They should strive to be cognizant of when change efforts require more initiative from the top and when the success of change efforts may hinge on allowing more employee participation and formulation of the change vision and plan. Dialogue among all levels of leadership is encouraged, but not to the extent of hindering the decision-making process.

Sometimes the top leaders in an organization will need to make change decisions, especially when external environmental pressures and resource constraints do not allow for more employee involvement. However, because change efforts in the public and nonprofit sectors are often completed over a longer time frame, more participation from lower ranks can be cultivated.

Strengths of Change-Centric Leadership

One of the major strengths of change-centric leadership is its ability to address the buy-in and resistance problems associated with the leader-centered model. As a result of the interaction between top leadership and lower levels of employees, employees can feel more like a part of the process instead of merely following orders. This approach will ultimately lower resistance and increase a feeling of ownership for those involved with the change process at all levels.

The change-centric leadership approach we advocate is not the same as "situational" leadership—where the focus is more narrowly on the competence and commitment of the followers—but is a more whole systems approach. By "whole systems" we follow Atwood et al.'s (2003) notion of a comprehensive approach that requires leaders to build trust and collaboration among affected interest groups, users, communities, and potential partners and stakeholders. In this approach, the leader is not working in a vacuum for change: "leaders need to develop coherent frameworks within which people can decide what should remain the same and what should change" (p. 61). Numerous stakeholders are involved in the change process, and the leader facilitates the interaction among internal and external stakeholders regarding change initiatives.

Dunphy provides further support for our definition of change-centric leadership. Theories about the source of change leadership are based on the false assumption that "unitary leadership" is present in every organization (Dunphy in Beer and Nohria 2000). Dunphy argues that more than one leadership movement is often present in an organization, which could result in multiple change efforts being promoted at the same time. These movements could also come from various levels in the organization.

According to Dunphy, an organization that is attempting to change needs to have strategic goals from top management as well as tactical involvement by informed and knowledgeable members of the organization at all levels. Change-centric leadership offers a framework for dealing with multiple change initiatives from varying levels within the organization through facilitation and open discussion.

The idea of change-centric leadership is also supported by the existing literature on leading through stewardship. Stewardship involves creating a balance of power in the organization, establishing a primary commitment to the larger community, having each person join in defining purpose, and ensuring a balanced and equitable distribution of rewards. Stewardship is designed to create a strong sense of ownership and responsibility for outcomes at all levels of the organization (Kee 2003).

Steven Kelman, former director of the Office of Federal Procurement Policy within the Office of Management and Budget, presents a prime example of change-centric leadership in his book *Unleashing Change*. Kelman recounts his firsthand experience leading procurement reform efforts during the first Clinton administration. Although Kelman saw a need for reform, he did not push a change agenda down through the ranks. Instead, he sought information and found that many of the frontline procurement officers were also calling for change in the system. Kelman refers to these individuals as the "change vanguard" (2005).

Kelman used the power of his position to unleash the change effort that was fermenting at the lowest levels. In this instance, he served as a facilitator of the change effort; he was a leader pushing for change while simultaneously helping those in the change vanguard see their initiatives succeed. Procurement reform is widely viewed as one of the success stories of the Clinton administration's "Reinventing Government" efforts (Kettl 1998).

Potential Weaknesses of Change-Centric Leadership

Although the change-centric framework provides middle ground to the top-down, bottom-up dichotomy, its implementation poses some potential challenges. The first deals with the tough questions of how much facilitation is needed and in what context. It is easy to say that a combination of leadership from the top and involvement from lower level employees is ideal in a change environment, but how much of each should be sought? As with most complex matters, the unsatisfactory answer is: it depends. Many issues, such as available time and resources, the skill level of those implementing the change, past experiences with organizational change, and technology that may aid the change process will influence how much control the change-centric leader should exert in any given change program. The more experience a leader has in overseeing change, the greater the chance that he or she can be a successful change-centric leader, providing the right balance of facilitation and control.

Another potential drawback to change-centric leadership is that those facilitating the change process may focus too much on the process of involving others in the plans rather than on the change itself. The danger is that the change-centric leader could become too process-oriented and lose sight of how to achieve the long-term change objectives. The leader must balance the competing demands of engaging in a collaborative process and guiding those involved toward the end goals—and not get lost in the process of change.

A final challenge of this model is the potential for ambiguous accountability. With so many people at different levels within the organization involved in the change effort, it may be easy for individuals to assume that someone else has responsibility for a task that may fall under their reach. To avoid confusing questions of who is accountable for what, clear tasks and measures need to be identified early in the process so that everyone knows exactly how he or she will contribute as the change progresses.

TRANSFORMATIONAL STEWARDSHIP: ATTRIBUTES OF CHANGE-CENTRIC LEADERS

We believe that for public and nonprofit leaders to be successful, change-centric leaders must become transformational stewards of their organizations (Kee, Newcomer, and

Davis 2007). Transformational stewardship, in the broadest sense, can be thought of as a leadership function in which those exercising leadership (those with "legitimate" authority as well as others throughout the organization exercising a leadership role) have developed certain attributes that provide a foundation for their actions. These attributes reflect leaders' personal outlook or attitude (their inner-personal beliefs or values), how they approach a situation (their operational mindset), and how they involve others in the function (their interpersonal abilities/interactions with others).

The dominant advice in the literature on change management is that public and nonprofit sector leaders (much like their private sector counterparts) must "overcome" resistance to change, through a variety of top-down approaches designed to influence the agency's stakeholders (see, for example, Kotter 1996). Atwood and colleagues (2003) refer to this—in its extreme version—as "Mad Management Disease," the notion that if leaders can just impose enough controls, supply the "right vision," and develop the appropriate "carrots and sticks," they will successfully overcome the change resisters. However, our research finds that success with public and nonprofit sector changes depends on much more than compliance through rewards and punishments (even though reinforcement is an important aspect of successful change).

We believe that, rather than relying on top-down controls, public and nonprofit sector change leaders must employ a model of change leadership that engages other stakeholders in a "whole systems" approach to the change process. Rather than focusing on which level of the organization should institute the change effort, transformational stewards develop a variety of collaborative processes to find the proper balance of strategic leadership and involvement by informed and knowledgeable members and stakeholders at all levels of the organization.

Table 2.2 provides an overview of the key attributes of transformational stewards. Table 2.3 summarizes the supporting evidence in the research literature for those attributes.

Inner-personal Leadership Beliefs or Values

We believe that the most important personal leadership attributes are not ones we are born with, but those we develop throughout our lives. These attributes provide us continuing guidance on how to act in a particular situation, in essence becoming inner-

TABLE 2.2: Attributes of Transformational Stewards

Attribute	Description
INNER-PERSONAL BELIEFS OR VALUES	
Ethical	Maintain high standards of integrity for themselves and their organization, recognizing that change issues may pose ethical dilemmas.
Reflective/ Learning-oriented	Able to step back from the situation and consider alternatives; learn from success and failures; self-aware; tolerant of other views.
Empathetic	Demonstrate concern for those who might be affected by the change initiative, both within and outside the organization.
Visionary/Foresight	Able to look beyond the current situation and view the change relative to the big picture for the mission and the organization, creating a vision for the future.
Creative/Innovative	Take a pragmatic approach to the organization's change needs; open to new ideas of what is possible; use intuition and inspiration; willing to take risks; not tied to past dogmas.
OPERATIONAL MINDSET	
Trustee/Caretaker	Act in trust for others—the public in general and future members of the organization.
Mission-driven	Fiercely and courageously pursue the organization's mission; create a "common purpose" for the change.
Accountable	Measure change results in multiple ways, in a transparent fashion, and share with those who contribute to the organization's success.
Integrative/Systems Thinker	Understand forces for change and interrelationships; able to find integrative, rather than polarizing, solutions.
Attention to Detail	Able to distinguish between details that impact people and the "red tape" that slows change.
Comfortable With Ambiguity	Able to balance conflicting organizational objectives and priorities—continuity and change, efficiency and equity, etc.
INTERPERSONAL ABILITIES/INTERACTIONS WITH OTHERS	
Trust Builder	Develop community and maintain trust with the members of their agencies, constituents, and principals (legislatures, boards of trustees, political leaders).
Empowering	Decentralize authority and real decision-making throughout the organization so others can become co-leaders and stewards of change in fulfillment of the public interest.
Democratic	Work with others in an inclusive fashion and involve stakeholders in decisions about what constitutes the public interest.
Power Sharing	Rely less on positional authority and more on persuasion, moral leadership, and group power to achieve change goals.
Coalition Builder	Recognize the importance of building coalitions with others within government and in the nonprofit and for-profit sectors to facilitate change.

SOURCE: Adapted from Kee, Newcomer, and Davis (2007).

TABLE 2.3:　Attributes of Transformational Stewards—Supporting Authors

Attribute	Selected Supporting Authors
INNER-PERSONAL BELIEFS OR VALUES	
Ethical	Burns 1978; Ciulla 2004; Fairholm 2000; Johnson 2005; Thompson 2000.
Reflective/ Learning-oriented	Greenleaf 1977; Senge 1990; Thompson 2000; Wheatley 2005.
Empathetic	Autry 2001; Coles 2000; Goleman 1998; Thompson 2000.
Visionary/Foresight	Bass and Avolio 1994; Bennis and Nanus 1985; Burns 1978; Fairholm 1997; Follett in Graham 2003.
Creative/Innovative	Bennis 2000; Dunphy 2000; Harmon 2007; Kee and Setzer 2006; McSwite 2001; Thompson 2000; Vaill 1996.
OPERATIONAL MINDSET	
Trustee/Caretaker	Block 1993; Denhardts 2003; Diver 1982; Kass 1990; Kee 2003.
Mission-driven	Block 1993; Kee and Black 1985; Follett in Graham 2003; Matheson and Kee 1986.
Accountable	Behn 2001; Block 1993; Demming 1986; Harmon 1990, 1995; Moe 2001; Romzek and Dubnick 1987; Vaill 1989b.
Integrative/Systems Thinker	Atwood et al. 2003; Follett in Graham 2003; McSwite 2001; Senge 1990; Thompson 2000; Vaill 1996.
Attention to Detail	Addington and Graves 2002; Block 1993; Moe 1994; Terry 1995.
Comfortable With Ambiguity	Depree 1989; Harmon 2007; Kee and Black 1985; Thompson 2000; Vaill 1989a.
INTERPERSONAL ABILITIES/INTERACTIONS WITH OTHERS	
Trust Builder	Fairholm 1994, 2000; Greenleaf 1977; Mitchell and Scott 1987; Phillips and Loy 2003.
Empowering	Denhardts 2003; Follett in Graham 2003.
Democratic	Autry and Mitchell 1998; Follett in Graham 2003; Hill 1994; Kee 2003.
Power Sharing	Behn 2001; Harmon 2007.
Coalition Builder	Kelman 2005; Phillips and Loy 2003.

SOURCE: Adapted from Kee, Newcomer, and Davis (2007).

personal guides to our actions. The most vital attributes for transformational stewards are ethical conduct; a reflective, continuous learning attitude; empathy toward others; the foresight or vision to lead an organization toward a preferred future; and a propensity toward creative and innovative actions.

Ethical

An overriding inner-personal attribute is integrity or ethical values and standards. Transformational stewards must maintain a high level of standards for themselves and their organizations, which will allow leaders and followers to elevate the organization to a higher plane. Leadership scholar James MacGregor Burns (1978) posits that moral values lie at the heart of transformational leadership and allow the leader to seek "fundamental changes in organizations and society" (Ciulla 2004, x).

Similarly, those arguing for a servant-leadership approach (often aligned with the concept of stewardship) argue for the importance of "core ethical values, including integrity, independence, freedom, justice, family and caring" (Fairholm 1997, 133). Ethics and moral standards have their roots in principles we learn throughout our lives, either from parents and mentors or from our own inquiries into what constitutes just action.

Reflective/Learning-oriented

Wheatley suggests that: "Thinking is the place where intelligent actions begin. We pause long enough to look more carefully at a situation, to see more of its character, to think about why it is happening, and to notice how it is affecting us and others" (2005, 215). Transformational stewards are willing to step back and reflect before taking action. They take the time to understand and to learn before and during the acting.

Thompson argues that "Beyond a certain point, there can probably be no personal growth, no individualization, without the capacity for self-reflection" (2000, 152). While continuous learning is critical for organizations (Senge 1990), it is equally important for individuals. Self-reflection, including personal awareness and continuous learning, is not always easy or calming—just the opposite, "It is a disturber and an awakener" (Greenleaf 1977, 41). Transformational stewards must be awake to new approaches to problems, new understandings of relationships, and potential consequences of actions and impacts on others. Only then they can lead with confidence.

Empathetic

A transformational steward demonstrates concern for others, both within and outside the organization. Organizational change involves potential winners and losers. If leaders are seen as acting primarily in their self-interest, transformation of the organization can be derailed. However, if leaders show a genuine concern for others and address potential losses, they may find the path easier. Empathy is an attribute that is a product of both our nature and how we are nurtured; understanding its importance can provide us with an incentive to pay more attention to the needs, views, and concerns of others.

Empathy is more than just being a "good listener," although that is an important skill. Leaders must both hear and understand. Thompson explains: "If by that we mean only that we have learned certain skills and techniques that make the other person *feel* heard, we have still largely missed the point. To empathize is to both hear *and* understand, and to grasp both the thoughts the other person is trying to convey and the feelings he or she has about them" (2000, 181). Transformational stewards *participate* in other people's feelings or ideas, leading to a broader understanding of the situation and potential courses of action.

Visionary/Foresight

A transformational steward is able to look beyond the current situation and see the big picture and the organization's potential. While this is true throughout the organization, as a leader progresses in an organization and assumes more responsibility, he or she requires greater vision and foresight (Follett in Graham 2003).

Mary Parker Follett refers to the need for leaders to "grasp the total situation.... Out of a welter of facts, experience, desires, aims, the leader must find the unifying thread...the higher up you go the more ability you have to have of this kind. When leadership rises to genius it has the power of transforming, transforming experience into power" (Follett in Graham 2003, 168–169).

While vision is necessary to transform an organization, it is equally necessary for a good steward. Failure to fully assess potential gains and risks for an organization will lead to a waste of resources and an inability to achieve the full potential of the organization. Follett continues:

I have said that the leader must understand the situation, must see it as a whole, must see the inter-relation of all the parts. He must do more than this. He must see the evolving situation, the developing situation. His wisdom, his judgment, is used, not on a situation that is stationary, but on one that is changing all the time. The ablest administrators do not merely draw logical conclusions from the array of facts of the past which their expert assistants bring to them, they have a vision *for the* future.

(169, emphasis added)

Creative/Innovative

Transformational stewards do not wait for a crisis to innovate and create; they attempt to build an environment that values continuous learning and in which workers constantly draw on current and past experiences to frame a new future for the organization. Vaill (1996) acknowledges that "creative learning" is seemingly a contradiction in a world of institutional learning where people who "know" transfer knowledge to people who do not know. However, in a change environment there often is no "body of knowledge" to transfer; thus, it is up to the transformational steward to create or facilitate creation of the knowledge. This requires a pragmatic, inquiring mind that is willing to explore options, open to new ideas, and not bound by rigid dogmas.

Transformational stewards are leaders of action; their processes involve extensive interaction and relationships with others in the organization and with concerned stakeholders outside the organization. They look for linkages and interconnections. Aware that there are limits on what can be known, they are willing to be tentative, to be experimental in deciding and taking action (McSwite 2001; Harmon 2007). Just as an artist might not always know what the final product will look like, transformational stewards must be open to the unknown, willing to surprise themselves, and able to recognize that "in that surprise is the learning" (Vaill 1996, 61).

Operational Mindset

The "style" approach or theory of leadership focuses on how leaders interact with followers and stresses the need for leaders to balance "concern for people" with "concern for production or results." The Blake and Mouton Managerial Grid is one of the best known tools reflecting this approach (1985). We believe that the operational mindset of a transformational leader includes but goes beyond simply balancing people with results, and includes a number of attributes of both transformational leader and steward.

Trustee/Caretaker

Transformational stewards recognize that they hold their position and use organizational resources for others and the public interest, not for self-aggrandizement. They take responsibility for the public in general, both current and future generations, as well as future members of the organization. Thus, the broad concept of "the public interest," while not always easy to define, must be a constant touchstone for the leader.

Public and nonprofit servants, whether elected, appointed, or part of the civil service system, are only temporarily in charge of their resources and responsibilities. They hold them in trust for the public—hence they serve the public and must act in the public interest, not for personal self-interest. "Public managers are, after all, public servants," argues Colin Diver (1982, cited in Moe 1994). "Their acts must derive from the legitimacy, from the consent of the governed, as expressed through the Constitution and laws, not from any personal system of values, no matter how noble" (404).

A public steward must be willing and able "to earn the public trust by being an effective and ethical agent in carrying out the republic's business" (Kass 1990, 113). Because ethical considerations may conflict with efficiency criteria, Kass believes that stewardship requires that efficiency and effectiveness (the traditional measures of administrative success) be "informed by and subordinated to the ethical norms of justice and beneficence" (114).

Mission-driven

Transformational stewards fiercely and courageously pursue the mission of their organization. In most cases, they act as agents of those who established that mission—the legislature, a board of directors, the chief executive, or the courts. Sometimes, conflicting goals and agendas require public and nonprofit servants to arbitrate.

Behn poses the question "What should public managers do in the face of legislative ambiguity: ask for clarification, or provide it?" He answers it by saying that public managers must courageously define their responsibilities (1998, 215). It may be in the legislature's interest to be ambiguous; moreover, "the political process itself creates a diffusion of power and responsibility that makes articulation of central values difficult" (Kee and Black 1985, 28). Thus, the transformational steward must seek to find the common purpose, values, and aims that drive the organization.

Public stewards can find this common purpose by engaging people in their agencies, citizens, and other stakeholders who will assist them in defining the organization's mission or core values—in effect, determining the public interest. Follett notes that the "invisible leader" becomes the "common purpose" and that "loyalty to the invisible leader gives us the strongest possible bond of union" (Follett in Graham 2003, 172).

At other times, the organizational mission is clear, but the organization may have multiple means of achieving the mission; its leaders must weigh how those means will affect the organization, its mission, and the larger public interest. "Legislation, public scrutiny, and constitutional checks and balances all create legitimate legal and political limitations on the freedom of public managers to act. Yet within the constraints, there is considerable room for experimentation and action" (Kee and Black 1985, 31). Unless proscribed or prescribed to act in a certain fashion, the transformational steward (with the people in the organization) has considerable latitude in pursuing the change mission.

Accountable

Transformational stewards measure their performance in a transparent fashion and share those results with the public and those who can affect the organization and its success. This is consistent with efforts at the federal level to get agencies to articulate and measure progress toward their performance goals (e.g., the Government Performance and Results Act) and to enhance public accountability (e.g., the Sarbanes-Oxley Act).

Transformational stewards support processes such as performance-based budgeting, balanced scorecards, and other efforts to measure program results in an open fashion and to subject those results to periodic review and evaluation. Measurement is not important for the sake of measurement or for the creation of short-term output measures, but for the sake of legitimate feedback and program revision aimed at achieving the agency mission. "Stewardship asks us to be deeply accountable for the outcomes of an institution…." (Block 1993, 18).

An open process ensures public accountability and allows others to see how the organization and its stewards are defining and fulfilling the public interest. This, by necessity, must be a multifaceted process, as Vaill (1989a) suggests, that considers a variety of important values, not simply economic ones that might drive a bottom-line mentality. An open process provides a natural check on how transformational stewards define and lead progress toward achievement of the organization's mission. Finally, transformational stewards, throughout the organization, take responsibility (legal, professional, and personal) for the results (Harmon 1990, 1995).

Integrative/Systems Thinker

Thanks largely to Peter Senge's groundbreaking book *The Fifth Discipline* (1990), systems thinking has become one of the most important concepts in the field of leadership. But systems thinking is not always an easy concept to grasp or apply. Vaill (1996) notes that continuing evidence demonstrates an absence of systems thinking: our tendencies to think in black and white; to believe in simple linear cause-effect relationships; to ignore feedback; to discount relationships between a phenomenon and its environment; and to ignore how our own biases frame our perceptions. Vaill sees the core idea of systems thinking in the balancing and interrelating of three levels of phenomena that all move dynamically in time: first, the "whole," or the phenomenon of interest itself; second, the inner workings of the whole—the combining and interacting of the internal elements that produce the whole; and third, the world outside the whole that places the phenomenon in its context (1996, 108–109). Vaill argues that the key to learning systems thinking is "understanding oneself in interactions with the surrounding world" (1996, 110).

Attention to Detail

Transformational stewards know that details do matter (Addington and Graves 2002). Details are often the way in which government programs ensure important democratic values, such as equitable distribution of public benefits or access to public programs. Process "red tape" is often the means by which we ensure adherence to procedural imperatives; however, it should not be used as a cover or an excuse for lack of performance. Rather, transformational stewards need to distinguish between those processes designed to achieve certain public purposes and those designed primarily to impose excessive control. With the latter, transformational stewards might seek waivers, exceptions, etc., to enable the organization to manage itself better to accomplish its mission.

Comfortable with Ambiguity

Transformational stewards recognize that conflicting organizational objectives and priorities often require a careful balancing act: continuity and change; efficiency and equity; and so on. Public and nonprofit leaders, like their private counterparts, live in an era of "permanent white water," bombarded by pressures from both within and without the organization (Vaill 1996). Transformational stewards recognize that their "solutions" are among many plausible alternatives and must be pragmatically reassessed and adjusted as conditions change.

Interpersonal Abilities/Interactions with Others

Leadership theories increasingly stress the importance of the leader's interaction with others. For example, the "situational" approach characterizes the leader's role along a "supportive" and "directive" matrix, based on the development level of the followers (Hersey and Blanchard 1993). Leaders delegate, support, coach, or direct, depending on the capacity of the followers—specifically with regard to the job (competence) and psychological maturity (commitment) of the followers.

Transformational stewards often approach their interactions with others differently than many leadership theories prescribe. The chief goals for transformational stewards are engaging, empowering, and engendering trust in employees throughout the organization, and building coalitions with other organizations and stakeholders that are important to the success of the change.

Trust Builder

Transformational stewards build program success through developing and maintaining trust—with the members of their organizations, their constituents, and their principals. Leadership is mainly about developing trust, with leaders and organization members accomplishing mutually valued goals using agreed-upon processes. "Leaders build trust or tear it down by the cumulative actions they take and the words they speak—by the culture they create for themselves and their organization members" (Fairholm 2000, 91).

Developing trust is about engaging the organization's employees, building community—"the creation of harmony from, often diverse, sometimes opposing, organizational, human, system and program functions" (Fairholm 2000, 140). Public stewards also must build trust with the citizens they serve and the principals (executives and legislatures) to whom they report. Nonprofit stewards must build trust with their board of directors, their donors, and the community they serve.

Mitchell and Scott (1987) insist that stewardship "is based on the notion that administrators must display the virtue of trust and honorableness in order to be legitimate leaders" (448). Trust is ephemeral—hard to gain, easy to lose. Trust encourages the involvement of citizens and often leads to grants of discretion from principals.

Empowering

Closely related to trust is the concept of empowerment. Trust demands empowerment of an organization's employees and, where possible, decentralization of authority—real decision-making—throughout the organization. Follett, writing in the 1920s, put it this way: "Many are coming to think that the job of a man higher up is not to make decisions for his subordinates but to teach them how to handle their problems themselves, teach them how to make their own decisions. The best leader does not persuade men to follow his will. He shows them what is necessary for them to do in order to meet their responsibilities…the best leaders try to train their followers themselves to become leaders" (Follett in Graham 2003, 173).

Developing leaders for a common purpose is a key function of transformational stewardship. Stone (1997) makes a useful distinction between the market and the "polis." In the market, economic principles and incentives are the norm. In the polis, the "development of shared values and a collective sense of the public interest is the primary aim" (Stone 1997, 34). To the extent that leaders empower others (employees and citizens), they become co-leaders and stewards in fulfillment of the public interest. This is a fundamental role and opportunity for transformational stewards throughout the organization.

Democratic

Becoming co-leaders and stewards in fulfillment of the public interest, as Stone suggests, requires transformational stewards to engage in democratic processes that ensure the widest possible involvement of others in defining the public interest and in acting on that definition. Harmon suggests a "unitary" or "process" conception of democratic governance based on the notion of "collaborative experimentation" (2007, 71). Decisions would use criteria that are local, context-specific, and flexible, rather than relying on inflexible decision rules.

Harmon suggests starting with a generic question, "How shall we live together?" This would be followed by a more context-specific, "What should we do next? (140). As public servants, we promote democratic governance by focusing on what kind of government (or nonprofit organization) can best contribute to the development of its citizens; it is that development that leads to mutual collaboration among citizens, public officials, and public and nonprofit administrators in "both defining and contending sensibly with problems of shared concern" (159).

Power Sharing

Transformational stewards rely less on positional authority for their power and more on personal power sources, persuasion, and moral leadership to effect change (Hill 1994). Beyond personal power, transformational stewards rely on "group power." Follett claims that "it is possible to develop the conception of *power-with,* a jointly developed power, a co-active, not a coercive power." And "the great leader tries…to develop power wherever he can among those who work with him, and then gathers all this power and uses it as the energizing force of a progressing enterprise" (Follett in Graham 2003, 173, emphasis added).

Coalition Builder

Transformational stewards recognize that they cannot fully meet the organization's mission with their given resources (people, dollars, etc.) without involving others. They know that horizontal relationships and coalition building with other organizations within government, in the nonprofit sector, and in the for-profit sector are essential for their success. Such coalitions might be critical for the organization's successful transformation or vital when the organization is faced with a crisis (such as Hurricane Katrina). Coast Guard Admiral Joel Whitehead refers to the importance of developing "pre-need" relationships, noting that this is one of the Coast Guard's fundamental principles—a recognition that they cannot do everything and must rely on others as partners in achieving their organizational mission (Whitehead 2005).

EVIDENCE FROM THE CASE STUDIES

Our six case studies, which are described in more detail in Chapter 4, reinforce the importance of the leadership role in organizational change and illustrate many of the attributes that we have identified as important for transformational stewards.

Leadership and Employee Involvement

A major strength of transformational stewardship is that leaders at all levels of the organization are empowered to address the buy-in and resistance problems that are often associated with change initiatives. In the case study of the Veterans Health Administration (VHA), leadership was important both at the top and throughout the organization. Dr. Kenneth Kizer was specifically hired as Under Secretary for Health to make changes in a tense environment where the very survival of the veterans' healthcare system was in question. Kizer is described by others as a strong visionary leader and a committed change agent; his political leadership skills proved critical to gaining the external support needed to move the agency "from a hospital system to a healthcare system."

Kizer's VHA strategy was to get everyone to recognize that they were on "a burning platform" that needed immediate and systemic change. Kizer "created a lot of positive energy" and sought to tap into the priorities for change of key VHA staff. One interviewee noted that "you can't take people somewhere they don't want to go." Kizer used a core group of 22 regional leaders to create a change vanguard to guide the plan and achieve ownership of the change at the local level.

While noting that you cannot shift accountability from the head of the organization and that "at the end of the day it is not an absolute democracy," one interviewee commented that it was important for Kizer and his successors to create a sense of shared leadership, common vocabulary, and collective accountability among all the key stakeholders; they accomplished this through widespread collaboration and sharing of mutual concerns. Performance metrics (developed through collaboration) and performance contracts with VHA managers were used to engender accountability throughout the organization.

Admiral Patrick Stillman, the Program Executive Officer of the Coast Guard's Deepwater Program, incorporated the "system of systems" vision in the Deepwater mission, emphasizing "interoperability of systems" and "increased operational readiness, enhanced mission performance and a safer working environment." As Program Executive Officer, Stillman had to translate the broader systems concept into measurable outcomes, while overcoming considerable skepticism among the rank and file regarding the Deepwater approach. One of Stillman's strengths, according to those interviewed, was his ability to communicate the vision and foster a sense of inclusiveness and joint responsibility.

Admiral Stillman was described as having a strong sense of Coast Guard history and legacy, a sense of Washington, D.C., "beltway" politics, and good speaking skills that enabled him to motivate his staff. One interviewee commented: "He could operate in a political environment without giving in to the pressure; he was open to ideas and teaming with others and had the philosophy that 'you get a lot done if you don't care about who gets the credit.'" Stillman demonstrated a good balance between advocating for the change and allowing ideas to percolate up through the organization.

In the Fairfax County human services delivery case, the vision was set by the County Board of Supervisors. It was left up to the new Department of Systems Management for Human Services (DSMHS) to give substance to that vision.

Fairfax County hired a change-centric leader, Margo Kiely, to initiate the change. Kiely exhibited many of the attributes of transformational stewardship, and her leadership was viewed as critical even by others who had unsuccessfully sought the department directorship. The new director won them over with an open, collaborative leadership style that the change team worked to cultivate throughout the organization. Kiely fostered a culture of learning and sharing, where suggestions from staff were welcomed; many of those suggestions were pursued and decisions not to implement others were explained.

Other methods Kiely used to engage staff included:

- Developing a "learning opportunities program" to provide continuous staff improvement

- Using a "collaborameter" to assess the readiness of groups to collaborate
- Planning through charrettes, which involve the collaboration of all project stakeholders at the beginning of a project to develop a comprehensive plan or design
- Developing a "common vocabulary" for the change effort
- Sharing frequent and descriptive updates and disclosing the reasoning behind high-level decision-making.

Kiely recognized a constant need for the redesign team and top managers to work closely with other leaders and support teams to ensure that information about the change reached everyone. She took a very pragmatic approach to designing solutions and was able to adjust goals as conditions changed (such as the budget shortfall).

Mary Funke's leadership of N Street Village (NSV) also demonstrated many of the attributes of transformational stewardship. Her strong faith provided an ethical foundation for all her actions. She demonstrated great empathy when making changes to staff or to benefits for NSV's clients. While the vision of excellence began with her, her involvement of the staff and the board in detailed strategic planning helped everyone assume ownership.

Funke encouraged continuous learning, providing staff training funds even when cutting the total budget. She built coalitions with potential donors and encouraged staff to pay attention to the details of both fundraising and client services. As for personal characteristics of change leadership, Funke cited integrity, high expectations, empathy, a sense of humor, and an optimistic outlook as important.

Generating Support from Key Senior Leaders and Middle Management

Our case studies revealed that one of the major implementation challenges for leaders is communicating with and gaining the support of program leaders within the organization. Sometimes support from senior leadership and middle management is taken for granted; failure to adequately address these important groups can derail a change effort. Middle managers often provide the key link between the leadership vision and the rank-and-file in the organization.

In the case of Fairfax County, the DSMHS director recognized a constant need for the redesign team and top managers to work closely with other leaders and support teams to ensure that information about the change was vetted by everyone. Despite the efforts to incorporate buy-in and collaboration, resistance still existed and had to be managed. One interviewee volunteered that, if she faced the option of undertaking the change process all over again, she would incorporate mid-level managers to act as change champions to help with staff buy-in and thereby facilitate a quicker process of change.

Leadership also is widely fostered throughout the Coast Guard and at the Coast Guard Academy. Several interviewees noted that the majority of Coast Guard leaders come from the small Coast Guard Academy "society," which creates a great deal of positive collegiality that may, in some ways, make it more difficult to initiate changes. Coast Guard officers, given this bond, constantly ask themselves, "How will this [change] be perceived by my peers?" Such trepidation may have led to more delays than necessary as various factions weighed in during the Deepwater planning process.

While Deepwater has had the backing of the top Coast Guard leadership, some other senior leaders in the Coast Guard remain opposed to the program. Opposition may fade as new assets are delivered, yet one pessimistic interviewee suggested that it might take a new generation to support fully the systems concept embedded in the Deepwater program.

Leadership Development

Continually strengthening organizational leadership is important to enhance the overall change capacity of an organization. In the Fairfax County case, in addition to involvement in the change effort itself, the director of DSMHS developed a variety of training opportunities for her employees. Also, the Fairfax Deputy County Manager had the idea of creating a "university" that would train workers in change- and transformation-related skills. Although this specific idea was not followed through because of budget constraints, it demonstrates the extent to which change-centric leaders think about long-term organizational development.

Transformational stewards look out for the long-term leadership of the organization. N Street Village director Funke is already training a potential successor. In contrast, one of the weaknesses cited in the Hillel transformation was the failure to develop widespread leadership throughout the organization, raising questions about whether the reforms would last after the change in national leadership.

The Coast Guard and other federal military branches include leadership development as part of their employee appraisal and development processes, providing an ongoing source of new leadership. However, strategic and funded leadership development is not widespread in all public agencies and is often lacking in nonprofit organizations. The lack of leadership succession planning constitutes a major challenge as public organizations begin to face a wave of retirements in the coming years (Newcomer et al. 2006).

TRANSFORMATIONAL STEWARDSHIP: A BALANCING ACT

To initiate change successfully, transformational stewards must balance a number of competing interests. In particular, they must work within structural bureaucratic limitations, satisfy (to the extent possible) the diverse, complex interests of stakeholders, and maintain appropriate political and board accountability. At they same time they must consistently move forward with a practical change agenda that enhances agency effectiveness. Leadership development approaches have traditionally sought to address the need for this balance by providing general collaboration, negotiation, and ethics training. We feel that a more complete understanding of the requirements and mechanics of change illuminates the need for a much richer array of skills and experiences.

Is a transformational stewardship approach the "best" approach to change? Because the extent and nature of change risks vary, leaders need to rely on those sources of power and influence that are best able to balance corresponding risks and opportunities. While in some cases the nature of the risk might suggest a leader-centered or follower-centered approach, in most cases, leaders will need to adjust their leadership approach to the nature of the risk—maintaining a balanced approach. Ultimately, this will likely entail transformational stewardship that encompasses both leader- and follower-centered approaches and relies primarily on building community and mutual trust with the various stakeholders in the change effort. Kelman's experience with procurement reform in the federal government (2005) and our cases involving Fairfax County, VHA, and N Street Village demonstrate that this approach to leadership can work.

Public and nonprofit sector change initiatives involve multiple stakeholders and often high degrees of complexity. Thus, we believe that a transformational steward will best be able to mitigate the unique combination of the sociopolitical environment, stakeholders, resources, and types of risks that arise during public and nonprofit sector change efforts.

PRACTICAL TIPS FOR THE CHANGE LEADER

- Tap into the desires for change that already exist in your organization.

- Create a sense of urgency, shared leadership, common vocabulary, and collective responsibility for success.

- Rely on mutual trust and community, drawing upon both your own and the followers' power to achieve the needed change.

- Balance top-down advocacy for change with bottom-up ideas and feedback.

- Foster a culture of learning and sharing.

- Empathize with and assist those who may be harmed by the proposed change.

- Develop leadership throughout the organization.

SUGGESTED READINGS ON TRANSFORMATIONAL STEWARDSHIP

James MacGregor Burns, *Transforming Leadership*. New York: Atlantic Monthly Press, 2003.

Burns won the Pulitzer Prize for *Leadership* (New York: Harper and Row, 1978), and this book represents his latest thinking on the subject of transformational leadership. He focuses on how leaders can evolve from being "transactional" deal makers to dynamic agents of major social change who can energize and empower their followers. Burns provides an historical view of the evolution of American thinking on leadership. He includes such important topics as followers as leaders, moving from engagement to empowerment, the use of power, the importance of "transforming values," and how to put leadership to work on the world's most difficult problem—global poverty.

Robert K. Greenleaf, *Servant Leadership: A Journey into the Nature of Legitimate Power and Greatness*. New York: Paulist Press, 1977, 2002 (25th anniversary edition).

Greenleaf has changed leadership thinking from the leader's actions over others to the notion of service as the hallmark of effective leadership. He argues that leaders must become attentive to the highest priority needs of followers; in doing so, they will make their organization successful. Greenleaf lays out the concept in a convincing, practical style, with case studies from business, education, foundations, and charities. The 25th anniversary edition contains a thoughtful foreword by Stephen Covey. A complementary book that applies the servant-leadership concepts to everyday management situations is James Autry's *The Servant Leader: How to Build a Creative Team, Develop Great Morale, and Improve Bottom-Line Performance* (New York: Three River Press, 2001).

Peter Block, *Stewardship: Choosing Service over Self-Interest*. San Francisco: Berrett-Koehler Publishers, 1996.

Supportive of Greenleaf's notion of servant leaders, Block's concept of "stewardship" calls for rethinking the role of the leader from that of "patriarchy" to "partnership," which involves the redistribution of power, purpose, and wealth within the organization. Block uses business case studies; however, the concepts are equally (perhaps even more) important for public and nonprofit leaders. Block calls for a radical reengineering of work processes that support a decentralized decision-making and production structure.

Pauline Graham, editor. *Mary Parker Follett: Prophet of Management.* Washington DC: Beard Books, 2003 (first published in 1995).

The author brings together the writings of Mary Parker Follett, an organizational theorist of the early 20th century whose views on leadership, authority, delegation, empowerment, and constructive conflict have served as the foundation for many of today's leadership scholars. Follett's concepts (such as "power with" instead of "power over" and "integration") continue to provide fresh insights for addressing today's leadership dilemmas.

CHAPTER THREE

A Model for Leading Change Initiatives

Transformational stewards are leaders in the public and nonprofit sectors. They have the attributes necessary to implement significant transformations in the increasingly complex networks that deliver public services. Having the right traits and skills, however, is not enough.

Our literature review and case studies demonstrate that change leadership also requires that a variety of leadership functions be undertaken within the organization. Some of these actions will be undertaken by the "leader" at the top; some must be initiated by leaders throughout the organization. The key is that change leadership is exercised throughout the organization.

In this chapter we identify key change leadership responsibilities and present a model to assist leaders in diagnosing and implementing change initiatives in the public interest.

CHANGE LEADERSHIP RESPONSIBILITIES

The lifecycle of instituting change in the public sector begins when a legal mandate or drastic change in the immediate environment occurs, or when organizational leaders choose to undertake major changes. Whether a change is imposed or is undertaken from within, the lifecycle evolves from an initial assessment to a reinforcement of the change initiative.

The four critical leadership functions or responsibilities we have identified in this lifecycle are (1) *diagnosing change risk and organizational capacity;* (2) *strategizing and making the case for change;* (3) *implementing and sustaining change;* and (4) *reinforcing change by creating a change-centric, learning organization.* Effective change leaders must have the capability to make a compelling case for the change being undertaken, and to manage change risk in a manner that protects the agency and the agency's many stakeholders. Figure 3.1 provides an overview of leadership responsibilities for change in the public and nonprofit sectors.

The leadership responsibilities for change do not usually occur in chronological order; in reality, the responsibilities are not linear but interactive as leadership effectiveness in one area affects the others. For example, effective diagnoses of the change risk and organizational capacity will assist the leader in strategizing and making the case for change; creating a more change-centric organization strengthens the leader's abilities in the other three areas.

Diagnosing Change Risk and Organizational Capacity

The leadership is primarily responsible for assessing the risks of change and the organization's capacity for change prior to initiating a change, even if that change is imposed

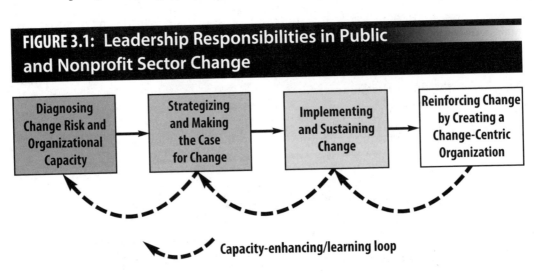

FIGURE 3.1: Leadership Responsibilities in Public and Nonprofit Sector Change

Diagnosing Change Risk and Organizational Capacity → Strategizing and Making the Case for Change → Implementing and Sustaining Change → Reinforcing Change by Creating a Change-Centric Organization

Capacity-enhancing/learning loop

from outside the organization. Key activities in this area include the following:

- Determining change drivers—what is mandating the change
- Analyzing change complexity, stakeholder perceptions, the sociopolitical environment, and organizational capacity
- Facilitating identification/realization of common interests and objectives
- Setting and managing specific change objectives and measures
- Anticipating the overall scope required for integrated total systems change
- Accomplishing change within the capacity limitations of the organization and with a maximum return on resources
- Developing change implementation mechanisms and risk mitigation plans
- Identifying and initiating discussions with potential partners in the change to enhance organizational capacity.

Strategizing and Making the Case for Change

Change initiatives begin with someone, usually a leader—whether at the top or within the organization—articulating a need for change. Effective leaders must constantly scan their external sociopolitical environment and internal organizations for potential drivers of change. Once the need for change is clear to the leaders, they must provide a compelling case for that change to their organizations.

Effective leaders are more than just "goal directed"; they are "vision directed." Change leaders must have a vision for change that "grabs" the attention of both the internal and external stakeholders of the organization. This cannot be a dreamlike fantasy, but must reflect a possible, achievable action in the "harsh reality" of the current situation (Bennis and Goldsmith 2003).

The central theme of most change management literature is the need for stakeholder buy-in. This is especially important with those stakeholders who have the ability to influence others and garner additional support for the change. The following are important actions to take when making the case for change to stakeholders:

- Establish a sense of urgency for the change through environmental scanning and conveying to stakeholders both evidence to support the reason the change is necessary and the possible risks associated with not implementing the change (Kotter 1996).

- Establish a vision for the change effort that can be communicated to stakeholders and executed. This should be followed by communication of the vision to all stakeholders, along with processes for them to express their feelings and concerns and ask questions for clarification.
- Establish a coalition of stakeholders (i.e., a change vanguard) who support the vision for change and will inspire and encourage other members of the organization to get on board with the effort and "act on the vision."

Because organizational transformation is most successful with the support of those inside the organization, a sense of urgency accompanied by explicit understanding of why the change is imperative will motivate individuals to get on board and support the effort.

Implementing and Sustaining Change

The leadership tasks do not end with creating a clear vision, strategy, and case for change. Implementing and sustaining change require a constant effort, including the following:

- Establishing transparency, engagement, and collective ownership
- Developing communication and collaboration strategies with stakeholders
- Developing a common vocabulary for all those involved in the change
- Appreciating, understanding, and addressing resistance
- Aligning organizational capabilities (e.g., personnel, processes, structures) with the change
- Developing a system that measures performance of the change
- Celebrating the successes of the change initiative
- Partnering to implement transformation successfully.

These activities must be planned for during the diagnosis and strategy phases and followed through during the implementation and sustaining phases.

Reinforcing Change by Creating
a Change-Centric, Learning Organization

Change leaders must constantly reinforce an organizational climate that is conducive to change. To facilitate resilience and productivity in their organizations, leaders have an ongoing responsibility for strengthening their own skills and the vitality of their organizations—to make their organizations more change-centric for the future. This need for constant renewal involves the following:

- Facilitating organizational learning, improvement, and innovation
- Establishing an environment of collaboration, information sharing, and stewardship
- Establishing change implementation management practices, structures, and strategies
- Creating a variety of feedback procedures to foster a learning environment
- Developing transformational stewards throughout the organization
- Developing a transformational ethic as part of the organization's culture.

A MODEL FOR LEADING CHANGE IN THE PUBLIC INTEREST

Each of the four stages of leadership responsibilities is important. Effective change leaders need to analyze and address the factors affecting the change initiative throughout the change cycle. We present a "Leading Change in the Public Interest" model to assist change leaders in diagnosing, implementing, sustaining, and reinforcing change initiatives (see Figure 3.2). The model comprises the four processes or phases (diagnosing, strategizing, implementing, and reinforcing) as well as four factors that we believe change leaders should continually monitor as they proceed:

- *Change complexity:* the magnitude, scope, and fluidity of the initiative
- *Stakeholders:* those individuals and organizations that perceive they have a role in, or are affected by, an organizational change, including both internal and external stakeholders
- *Sociopolitical environment:* the context in which the change takes place.
- *Organizational capacity:* the organization's ability to initiate and sustain a major change effort, which involves leadership throughout the organization, the organizational culture, change implementation mechanisms, and performance measurement.

At the heart of all efforts must be a continuing focus on the public interest.

FIGURE 3.2: A Model for Leading Change in the Public Interest

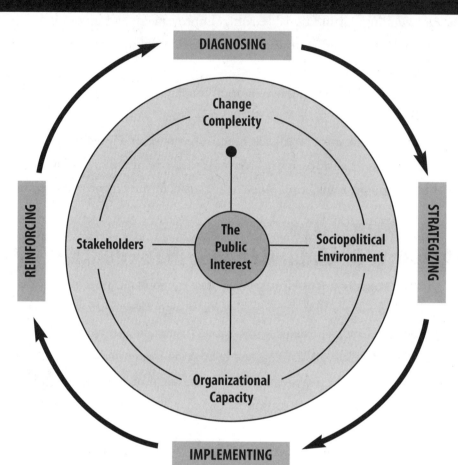

Change Complexity

We believe that *change complexity* should be the initial focus for evaluating the risk associated with a change effort. Change complexity must be assessed and anticipated both in advance of a major change and during the change process itself. A change that is too complex, is opposed by many stakeholders, and is undertaken where the organization lacks strong capacity will likely fail.

Change leaders and managers should assess numerous aspects of complexity, both to assess how pertinent or significant they are to the change effort and to determine how well prepared the organization is to address the implications of the complexity level. Assessing complexity in advance of initiating a change increases the likelihood of a positive result, although in an unpredictable, turbulent environment additional challenges to implementation also may emerge.

While there may be many ways to analyze the complexity of a change initiative, we believe that complexity can be assessed effectively by focusing on the *magnitude, scope,* and *fluidity* of a change effort. In other words, how big an impact does the change have on the organization as a whole, how deeply does the change affect the organization, and is the change initiative itself likely to be amendable in response to unexpected changes in the sociopolitical environment? We have created a checklist of questions to guide leaders and managers in assessing the complexity of a change effort, focusing on the magnitude, scope, and fluidity of the change (see Table 3.1).

TABLE 3.1:   Complexity Checklist

Magnitude

To what extent:

Are many organizational units and employees affected by the change?

Are the organizational units affected by the change widely dispersed geographically?

Are partnerships with external stakeholders and organizations required to implement the change?

Scope

To what extent:

Are the organization's policies and procedures affected?

Will employees be required to acquire new skills?

Does the change initiative intrude on or alter the current routines of employees?

Is revision (or replacement) of information systems technology required to support the change initiative?

Fluidity

To what extent:

Is the organization undergoing significant changes in mission or responsibilities as a result of changes in the external environment that will require the change initiative itself to adapt?

Is the change initiative prescribed in a rigid manner (without discretionary flexibility)?

Is the external environment likely to change in ways that may affect implementation of the change initiative?

If leaders of the organization systematically assess complexity by answering these questions, they will enhance their ability to anticipate and cope with obstacles. Failure to comprehend the nature of a change initiative up front can lead to problems during the implementation phase of the change initiative.

How should leaders strategize when the responses to the questions reveal a highly complex change initiative? In the short run, leaders can reduce the complexity of a change initiative by reducing the magnitude or scope by scaling down the change effort, starting with a pilot project or phased approach to the change, or engaging a partner (with more capabilities) in the change effort. Building a more change-centric and capable organization can strengthen the organization's ability to implement more complex changes over the long term.

Magnitude

We define *magnitude* as the overall size, extent, and coverage of a change in relation to the organization. Magnitude generally refers to the number of people or stakeholders potentially affected by the change effort, both within and outside the organization. Magnitude also refers to how many locations or divisions within the organization stand to be affected by the proposed change: The more locations and divisions affected, the more complex the change. In addition, magnitude captures the number of people who must be brought on board to support the change and the need to develop partnerships with other organizations to facilitate the change.

When analyzing the magnitude of a change, it is critical to understand that the importance of the number of stakeholders affected by the change is directly related to how the internal and external stakeholders perceive that the change will alter their daily functioning and their overall satisfaction with the organization. It is also important to gauge how employees view their roles or positions within the organization relative to the change—are they likely to be enhanced or threatened?—because this will have a significant impact on their contributions to the change process.

If stakeholders perceive their own participation in the change effort as a threat to their work, they are less likely to support the overall effort. In some cases, stakeholders who feel particularly threatened may attempt to sabotage the process entirely. On the other hand, stakeholders who perceive that their positions will be enhanced by the change may prove to be valuable allies during the change process.

To gauge the magnitude of a change fully, it also is necessary to assess how the change will affect external stakeholders of the organization. The greater the number of external stakeholders affected, the more complex the change. The first task is to understand and identify the number of external stakeholders likely to be affected and their potential impact on the change effort. In most cases, it is vital to have the buy-in of key outside actors, especially those who have the ability to influence others, either in support of or in opposition to the change. In some cases, it may be necessary to partner with outside organizations to implement the change, adding further complexity to the change initiative.

Scope

The *scope* of a change initiative refers to the potential impact of the change on the organization's current culture, structures, policies, strategies, processes, and behaviors. This aspect of the complexity of a change reflects how deeply the change is going to affect the organization's most essential operational elements. For example, the change may require the use of new technology, different skills, or modified responsibilities. The more systems and structures that need to be modified, the greater the scope of the change and the greater the potential for resistance to the change.

Fluidity

Fluidity, or the adaptability of the change initiative to the shifting nature of the environment, is the third key aspect of the complexity of a proposed change effort. The organization's ability to adapt and alter processes may depend upon the degree to which the environment is changing during the transformation, thus affecting how the change initiative itself evolves. Change initiatives within organizations are likely to evolve in response to both external and internal factors.

Throughout the planning and implementation process, the change agents may need to shift their focus and revise the planned strategy or tactics. When new external or internal impediments arise, momentum in achieving progress toward implementing changes in processes or systems may suffer. The consequence of not adequately assessing the internal and external environments that will interact with a change initiative is that the leaders of the change may not be ready to adapt and refocus their efforts.

Stakeholders

Stakeholders are the individuals and organizations that perceive that they have a role in, or are affected by, an organizational change. *Internal stakeholders* are the employees located within an organization undergoing change. *External stakeholders* are located outside the organization undergoing transformation, usually including Congress, the executive branch, private interest groups, other governmental or nonprofit organizations, and citizens. Private contractors to public and nonprofit sector organizations are also considered external stakeholders.

The key elements to be assessed regarding stakeholders are (1) the degree of diversity among the stakeholders, in terms of profession, worldview, and mission orientation; (2) the perceptions of stakeholders regarding their potential gain or loss from the change initiative; and (3) the existence (or lack) of collaborative networks among stakeholders to facilitate communication among them and between leaders and important stakeholder groups.

Diversity of stakeholders, based on group values, professional training, and commitment, can increase the challenges to leading change. For example, management of homeland security and public emergency issues requires collaboration among stakeholders from many different professions (Klein 1999). Direct contact and communication with all stakeholders involved in a change process are key to ensuring successful change efforts. When collaborative networks are available to facilitate communication during change initiatives, planning and implementation become much easier.

To assist change leaders and managers, we have developed a set of questions that will help gauge the role of stakeholders in change initiatives. If organizational leaders can confidently answer the questions in Table 3.2, they have a good understanding of the perceptions, diversity, and collaboration processes involving stakeholders. In addition, they will be able to diagnose potential problems and to take actions to ensure stakeholder buy-in and support during implementation. If leaders do not know the answers or find that the extent of their knowledge and preparation is minimal, stakeholders may not be managed effectively as change is implemented, heightening the risk of implementation weaknesses or failure. (Chapter 5 provides change leaders with approaches to strengthening communication and collaboration with stakeholders.)

TABLE 3.2: Stakeholder Checklist

Diversity

To what extent:

Are the key stakeholders diverse in terms of their professions or worldviews?

Have leaders adopted a common language for implementing the change that is familiar to most or all stakeholders?

Are efforts being made toward building trust regarding the change initiative?

Perceptions

To what extent:

Do stakeholders feel intensely that the proposed change will adversely affect them?

Are resistant stakeholders likely to negatively affect timelines or the overall success of the change?

Is the change initiative likely to gain the support of stakeholders who perceive they will gain from the change?

Collaborative Networks

To what extent:

Are explicit, multidirectional, regular communication and collaboration structures and processes in place to facilitate the sharing of accurate information and feedback?

Are organizational performance plans and individual performance appraisals used as tools for communicating about and collaborating on planning and implementing changes in operations?

Are conflict resolution techniques available to address disagreements or misgivings about the change initiative?

Are stakeholder interests managed through a network of key stakeholders and program managers, rather than through a separate function (e.g., public affairs)?

Sociopolitical Environment

The *sociopolitical environment* is the context in which the change takes place. This includes legal and policy mandates and constraints, economic and fiscal conditions, and the levels of support and trust the agencies receive from key political actors and the general public.

External demands on public organizations include legal and regulatory constraints and initiatives, catastrophic events (such as 9/11) that expand agency requirements, and political and citizen support that may influence what is possible. Critical external actors can be supportive, express opposition, or remain neutral regarding an organization and its change initiative. A public organization's credibility or image, its legal flexibility, and its budgetary resources are a function of both the external environment and the internal capabilities of leadership.

Change leaders must assess the environment to identify potential opportunities and problem areas, as well as their organization's capacity to respond to environmental factors. In assessing organizational capacity, leaders must first determine whether the organization has an ongoing process for monitoring the external environment to identify potential problem areas and opportunities that may affect the change initiative. Second, leaders must determine whether the organization has developed structures and processes that can influence the external environment (to the extent possible) to support the change initiative.

Two approaches to addressing the sociopolitical environment are environmental scanning and SWOT (strengths, weaknesses, opportunities, and threats) analysis. Environmental scanning is "the internal communication of external information about issues that may potentially influence an organization's decision-making process. Environmental scanning focuses on the identification of emerging issues, situations, and potential pitfalls that may affect an organization's future" (Albright 2004). Information gathered through environmental scanning is provided to key leaders and managers within the organization and is used to guide future plans and change efforts.

SWOT analysis generally involves a group planning exercise that may include both internal and external stakeholders, to ensure that all views are available to the organization. Both SWOT analysis and environmental scanning are used to evaluate an organization's strengths and weaknesses in response to external opportunities and threats. Successful change organizations are adept at both analyzing and reacting to their sociopolitical environments.

Based on our research, we have developed a list of issues that change leaders should consider when assessing the impact of the external environment on a change effort and the capacity of the organization to address the changing environment. These issues are listed in Table 3.3.

TABLE 3.3: External Environment Checklist

Assessing the Sociopolitical Environment

To what extent:

Does the organization enjoy a positive image among policymakers, the general public, and the media?

Do government policies and procedures support the proposed change?

Is the organization likely to receive any additional resources needed to accomplish the change?

Have changes in legislation that are necessary for the change initiative been identified?

Do policymakers and citizens support the proposed change?

Structures that Monitor and Interact with the External Environment

To what extent:

Does the organization have in place mechanisms to scan the external environment for potential threats or opportunities?

Are conflict resolution procedures in place for the organization to use when facing opposition from key external stakeholders?

Has the organization prepared options if the resources requested to implement the change are not forthcoming?

Does the organization have an effective liaison with the legislature?

Does the organization have structures in place to generate support from the public?

Change leaders and agents who continually and effectively monitor their external environment and understand how that environment affects their organization are more likely to find methods to mitigate obstacles or constraints imposed from outside as they plan and implement change initiatives.

Organizational Capacity [1]

An organization's internal capacity or capability to initiate and sustain a major change effort involves a number of aspects and is affected by both human and material resources.

Kaplan and Norton (2005), for example, argue for the importance of "organizational capital," consisting of leadership, culture, alignment, and teamwork in change efforts. McKinsey's Capacity Assessment Grid for nonprofit organizations includes aspiration (vision and mission), strategy, organizational skills, human resources, systems and infrastructure, organizational structure, and culture (McKinsey 2007).

In our analysis of organizational capacity, we have identified and defined the following key elements as necessary to facilitate major change and transformation:

1. *Organizational leadership,* both at the top and throughout the organization (discussed in Chapter 2, Transformational Stewardship in the Public Interest)

2. An *organizational culture* that values and supports change initiatives, reinforcing change-centric behavior (discussed in Chapter 6, Creating a Change-Centric Culture)

3. *Change implementation mechanisms*—strategies, policies, procedures, structures, and systems that support and are aligned with a change initiative (discussed in Chapter 7, Building Change Implementation Mechanisms)

4. *Performance measurement*—the use of performance data to inform key

---

[1] The terms "organizational capacity" and "organizational capability" often are used interchangeably, although sometimes there are nuanced differences. Thus, when considering whether an organization is capable of performing certain tasks, the critical factors are often employee skills, processes, and resources. In contrast, we view organizational capacity in a broader sense to include organizational culture and infrastructure. Capacity also is the term most used when assessing nonprofit organizations, and thus the term organizational capacity seems the more accurate in terms of our discussion.

stakeholders about why and where change is needed, to focus on aspects of programmatic performance likely to be affected by the change, and to reinforce and reward desired outcomes of change efforts (discussed in Chapter 8, Measuring Change Performance).

Within each of these areas, our model suggests that change leaders should go through the four-step process of diagnosis, strategy, implementation, and reinforcement to (1) better understand and mitigate the risks of the proposed change and (2) develop approaches to enhance the long-term change capacity of the organization.

Organizational Leadership

Effective leadership throughout the organization is essential to successful change initiatives. Transformational stewards, or change-centric leaders, create a strong sense of ownership and responsibility for change outcomes at all levels of the organization. Organizational leadership is critical in the processes of making the case for change, assessing risk and initiating change, implementing and sustaining change, and continuing to encourage employees throughout the organization to become change-centric. Each of these areas is important and should be considered when analyzing the leadership aspect of organizational capacity.

One of the major implementation challenges for leaders is communicating with and gaining the support of program leaders within the organization. Sometimes support from senior leadership and middle management is taken for granted; failure to adequately address this important group can derail a change effort. Middle managers often provide the key link between the leadership vision and the actions of the rank-and-file in the organization.

Continually strengthening organizational leadership is important to enhance an organization's overall change capacity. However, strategic leadership development is not widespread in all public agencies, and the lack of funding and a plan to continually renew organizational leadership constitutes a major challenge, especially as public organizations face the expected retirement of senior leaders in the coming years (Newcomer et al. 2006).

One of the most important tasks for leaders of change is to examine whether their organization has the requisite change leadership. The questions in Table 3.4 may assist

TABLE 3.4: Organizational Leadership Checklist

Leadership Vision and the Case for Change

To what extent:

Do leaders provide a compelling vision and case for the proposed change?

Have leaders identified gaps between the vision for change and implementation realities, and developed strategies to close the gaps and strengthen the case for change?

Have leaders provided a common vocabulary to guide change?

Leadership and Employee Involvement

To what extent:

Have leaders ensured that employees see the connection between their own work and the organizational vision for the change?

Have leaders negotiated a change plan or strategy in a democratic, inclusive manner?

Have leaders identified potential sources of change resistance and developed strategies to manage them?

Generating the Support of Key Senior Leaders and Middle Management

To what extent:

Is the organization's senior leadership unified in support of the change vision?

Do mid-level managers act as change champions to help with staff buy-in and maintain a good pace for the change process?

Do leaders encourage collaborative decision-making and joint ownership throughout the organization?

Leadership Development

To what extent:

Is leadership development, particularly the development of skills in change leadership, promoted throughout the organization?

in assessing organizational leadership in the context of implementing change initiatives. (Chapter 10 provides leaders and human resource managers with approaches to strengthen change leadership development within the organization.)

If organizational leaders can answer most of these questions affirmatively—that the agency promotes widespread leadership to a great extent—it is likely that the organization's leadership capacity is sufficient to support change. Any negative answers are potential sources of concern and a call for improvement. Leadership that is lacking in sound change management skills and strategies may find it very difficult to initiate a successful change.

Organizational Culture

Organizational culture is the behavioral, emotional, and psychological state of affairs in an organization, widely accepted "as the way we do things" by all employees. Cultures that are more status quo-oriented and resistant to change may present a significant challenge in leading change efforts. Cultures that are more open and adaptive are likely to be more receptive to change initiatives.

Leaders who initiate major change initiatives must examine their organizational culture and assess whether it is likely to support the change. If the culture is resistant to change, leadership has a twofold challenge. In the short run, leaders have to address potential obstacles to change. In the long run, leaders need to devise strategies to make their culture more change-centric. Table 3.5 presents a set of questions for leaders to address when analyzing their culture. (Chapter 6 provides an approach to developing a change-centric culture.)

TABLE 3.5:   Organizational Culture Checklist

To what extent:

Does the culture support a systems view of issues and problems that is open to different worldviews or mental models?

Does the culture reinforce team learning and cross-team collaboration?

Is the culture supportive of innovation and risk-taking?

Does the culture promote creativity and change through supportive feedback, recognition, and rewards?

Are power and influence in the organization determined by personal attributes and skills rather than position?

Are employees personally committed to the organization's mission?

Are employees comfortable challenging existing traditions, norms, and values?

Do employees share ideas for improving the quality of their work?

Do organizational norms and processes support a learning culture?

Does the culture support a democratic approach to decision-making?

The more affirmative the responses to these questions, the higher the likelihood that the culture will provide a strong foundation for change efforts. If many responses are negative, leaders should pursue efforts to make the culture more change-centric during the change initiatives. At the very least, change leaders will need to address those elements of the culture that are most problematic for the change effort. Since cultural change typically comes very slowly, leaders of change will need to address those areas of greatest weakness and develop a broad strategy to gradually introduce the organization to an approach that is more welcoming of change.

Change Implementation Mechanisms

Change leaders need tools to plan, steer, implement, and evaluate organizational changes. While a number of change mechanisms may be helpful, three primary mechanisms are especially effective: (1) the use of strategic management processes to create a shared change vision and to align resources with that vision among employees; (2) the development or more effective use of specific channels (or change structures) to facilitate two-way communications about the change throughout the organization; and (3) the development of continuous improvement programs, after-action reports, and other approaches to creating a learning organization.

As leaders initiate major change, they must take a hard look at their existing strategies, processes, policies, and structures to determine whether they support the change initiative. If agencies have continuous improvement programs or other change mechanisms in place, new changes will occur much more easily. If not, the challenge is twofold. In the short run, leaders have to create a mechanism to initiate the change successfully. In the long run, leaders need to devise a strategy to make processes and structures more change-centric and to encourage their agencies to become "learning organizations."

Table 3.6 provides a set of questions that can assist leaders in assessing their change implementation mechanisms. (Chapter 7 provides advice on how to create mechanisms that support change initiatives and promote continuous learning.)

TABLE 3.6:   Change Implementation Mechanisms Checklist

Strategic Management

To what extent:

Are vision and mission statements pertinent to the change and clear to the members of the organization?

Is there flexibility to move human and financial resources to support the change effort?

Are performance measures in place to track outcomes of the change initiative?

Do employees have training and career development opportunities that enable them to support the change?

Are employee goals and objectives aligned with the change strategy?

Change Structures

To what extent:

Do change teams or other change infrastructures exist in the organization?

Are change mechanisms in place in the organization to facilitate networking among change agents?

Are information technologies available to facilitate decentralized networks?

Creating a Learning Organization

To what extent:

Are continuous improvement programs in place?

Are individuals and teams encouraged to learn from their past actions, through after-action reports and other methods of learning?

The higher the level of positive responses to the diagnostic questions, the greater the likelihood that the organization has implementation mechanisms in place that will be helpful in facilitating change efforts. If the answers to the questions reveal that processes and change mechanisms are lacking, the change risk increases and leaders must focus on building mechanisms to support the change process.

Performance Measurement

Building internal organizational capacity in performance management involves the use of a set of balanced performance measures to focus and inform management about change efforts. To assess change-related performance, performance metrics or measures should capture the implementation and intended outcomes of the change initiative. The extent to which performance measurement is institutionalized in an organization prior to a change initiative is a critical factor: The more accustomed managers are to measuring performance, the easier it will be to use existing processes to support change efforts.

To assess the extent to which performance measurement within an organization is likely to support change efforts, leaders and managers should address the set of questions provided in Table 3.7. (Chapter 8 presents an approach to building an effective performance measurement system for change efforts.)

TABLE 3.7: Performance Measurement Checklist

To what extent:

Are programmatic performance measures available to managers in the organization?

Are managers confident that the available performance measures are valid and reliable?

Do leaders in the organization support and reward the use of performance measures in managerial decision-making?

Do performance metrics capture the programmatic outcomes that will be affected by the change?

Are current performance measurement systems satisfactory (i.e., will they need to be modified, or new systems designed, to collect useful performance measures)?

Are resources available to modify current measurement systems or build new systems?

Have all appropriate stakeholders been involved in deliberations about performance measurement related to the change?

Are agreement and buy-in sufficient among critical internal and external stakeholders about how change-related performance should be measured?

Are programmatic performance measures typically used in addressing the performance of managers in the organization?

Is it feasible to tie change-related progress to performance measures for the appraisal of senior leaders in the organization?

The higher the level of positive response to these questions, the greater the degree to which performance measurement permeates an organization's culture. Preexisting processes supporting performance measurement can make implementation of change initiatives easier. The strategic use of a viable performance measurement system provides vital support in leading change.

RELATIONSHIPS AMONG RISK FACTORS

Ultimately, change risk is a function of each of the elements in the model both individually and in terms of how they interact with one another. Thus, the *complexity* of the change initiative has both direct and indirect effects on risk. The magnitude, scope, and fluidity of a change are variables that are individually important and that also interact with the organization's capacity to deal with the risks of change and the stakeholders' perceptions. If an organization's leaders are comfortable in complex, volatile situations, they may accommodate a complex change more easily. The extent to which stakeholders perceive the change as a threat may exacerbate the risk, or collaboration among stakeholders may reduce risk.

Organizational capacity, stakeholders, and *the sociopolitical environment* are also linked. Good organizational capacity and effective communication and collaboration approaches to stakeholders can reduce stakeholder perceptions of loss and enhance perceptions of gain. Leadership efforts to monitor the sociopolitical environment can lead to strategies to mitigate adverse events and to gain the support of key stakeholders.

In general, the larger the magnitude, the wider or deeper the scope, and the more fluid the environment of an organization undergoing a change, the more complex the change and the higher the risk of failure. However, the more capable or change-centric the organization, the lower the risk associated with major change and transformation efforts; strong organizational capacity can mitigate change risk.

Table 3.8 provides a summary of the major elements and risk factors involved in public sector change.

TABLE 3.8:   Risk Factors in Public and Nonprofit Sector Change

Factors	Description	Change Risk
COMPLEXITY		
• Magnitude	Overall size, extent, and influence of the change in relation to the organization	The greater the number of people and organizational entities affected, the greater the risk.
• Scope	Impact on the organization's current culture, structures, policies, strategies, and processes	The deeper the impact on organizational culture, structures, policies, strategies, and processes, the greater the risk.
• Fluidity	Adaptability of the change initiative to the changing nature of the environment	The less adaptable the change initiative is to the environment, the greater the risk.
STAKEHOLDERS		
• Diversity	Range of conceptualizations of organizational mission, orientation, and worldview as a function of the size and variety of organizational units and purposes	The more diverse the organizational viewpoints and perspectives, the greater the risk.
• Perceptions	Perceptions of gain and loss held by internal and external stakeholders and the intensity of those perceptions	The more intensely stakeholders perceive their potential loss, the greater the risk.
• Collaborative Networks	Extent to which collaborative processes and structures are in place among internal and external stakeholders	The more effective the collaboration among stakeholders, the lower the change risk. A lack of collaborative processes increases risk. Effective communication processes among diverse stakeholders reduce risk.
SOCIOPOLITICAL ENVIRONMENT		
• Legal and Policy Mandates	Laws and regulations imposing changes or constraining changes in operations	The more rigid the regulatory constraints, the greater the risk.
• Economic Trends	Resources to support change initiatives from budgets or taxes	The more vulnerable the funding, the greater the risk.
• General Political Support	Citizen trust or demands for or against change	The greater the public interest in the change, the greater (or lower) the risk.
• Interface with External Environment	Capacity of leaders and staff to integrate and accommodate external demands and forces constraining or supporting their actions	The lower the capacity of leaders and staff to deal with environmental pressures, the greater the risk.

TABLE 3.8:	Risk Factors in Public and Nonprofit Sector Change (cont.)	
Factors	**Description**	**Change Risk**
ORGANIZATIONAL CAPACITY		
• Leadership	Leadership throughout the organization relative to the change	The more change-centric leadership throughout the organization, the lower the risk. Ineffective leadership increases risk.
• Culture	Norms and routines exhibited by people who work in the organization, which signal to employees what they should do, how they should feel, and what they should think about change	The more supportive the organization's culture is of innovation and change, the lower the risk. The more resistant the culture is to change, the greater the risk.
• Change Mechanisms	Strategies, processes, policies, and structures to initiate, accommodate, and support the change	The use of strategic management and explicit change structures to facilitate change reduces risk. The lack of such structures increases risk.
• Performance Measurement	Strategic use of performance measurement to facilitate change	The more widespread the use of performance metrics, the lower the risk. Lack of a performance measurement system increases risk.

IMPLICATIONS FOR CHANGE LEADERS

We conclude this chapter with the inevitable cautionary note about models: They are necessarily simple, attempting to show high-level patterns and relationships to increase their usefulness, at the expense of precision and detail. Every change initiative is different and so is every organization. In the remainder of this book, we analyze how six organizations handled their change initiatives, discuss how our model highlights change-related risk, and offer practical steps that leaders can take when initiating change.

Uncertainties, ambiguities, and anxieties among the parties affected are always associated with change. The diagnostic instrument we provide in Appendix A is intended to assist in analyzing factors that increase the risk involved in change initiatives. Our model is designed to make it easier to envision the dynamics among change complexity, organizational capacity, stakeholders, and the sociopolitical environment. Most of these factors can be controlled at least to some degree, even when change is imposed from outside an organization. While the external environment and the complexity of the change initiative are the factors that are least controllable, continuous collaboration and communication with external stakeholders and enhanced organizational capacity can help increase the probability of successful outcomes.

As we illustrate in the discussion of the cases, the success of change initiatives depends on the degree to which leaders assess, monitor, and recalibrate organizational strategies, processes, implementation mechanisms, and structures to facilitate change. Consistent, proactive top-down and bottom-up transformational stewardship greatly enhances the potential for successful outcomes of change initiatives.

PRACTICAL TIPS FOR THE CHANGE LEADER

- Develop the case for change and a vision of that change; help the organization become vision-directed.

- Analyze the risks versus the rewards of various change strategies.

- Understand the complexity (magnitude, scope, and fluidity) of the proposed change.

- Analyze the diversity and views of stakeholders and assess the organization's current methods of communications and collaboration with those stakeholders.

- Analyze the organization's external environment, focusing on whether it is supportive or hostile to the proposed change.

- Analyze the organization's change capacity; determine its strengths and weaknesses.

- Develop a strategy for dealing with weaknesses in organizational capacity.

GENERAL READINGS ON CHANGE IN THE PUBLIC INTEREST

Janet V. Denhardt and Robert B. Denhardt, *The New Public Service: Serving, Not Steering.* Armonk, NY: M.E. Sharpe, 2003.

The Denhardts present a compelling argument that "new public management" is not the answer for the changes required in public administration. Rather, they call for a reaffirmation of democratic values, citizenship, and service in the public interest. The book is organized around seven core principles: serve citizens, not customers; seek the public interest; value citizenship and public service above entrepreneurship; think strategically and democratically; recognize that accountability isn't simple; serve, rather than steer; and value people, not just productivity. While not specifically about leading change, this book provides a strong foundation for important public values that are applicable to both the public and nonprofit sectors.

SUGGESTED READINGS ON LEADERSHIP

James M. Kouzes and Barry Z. Posner, *The Leadership Challenge: How to Keep Getting Extraordinary Things Done in Organizations.* San Francisco: Jossey-Bass, 1995 (paperback), 2002 (3rd edition).

Kouzes and Posner's popular book on leadership continues to have a wide following, and the authors have written related books, workbooks, and leadership assessment instruments based on their findings. They present five practices of exemplary leadership: modeling the way (finding your voice and vision); inspiring a shared vision; challenging the status quo (experimenting and taking risks); enabling others to act (collaborating and empowering); and encouraging the heart (providing recognition and creating a spirit of community). With numerous illustrations from leaders the authors interviewed, the book provides a strong foundation for any type of leadership, including change leadership.

Craig E. Johnson, *Meeting the Ethical Challenges of Leadership: Casting Light or Shadow,* 2nd edition. Thousand Oaks, CA: Sage Publications, 2005.

In this widely used leadership text, Johnson emphasizes the ethical responsibilities of leaders to provide "light" for their organizations, contrasted with potential "shadows" of power, privilege, deceit, inconsistency, broken loyalties, and irresponsibility. While providing a strong academic and normative foundation, Johnson uses mini-case studies and examples from contemporary movies to illustrate various leadership and ethical dilemmas.

Montgomery Van Wart, *Dynamics of Leadership in Public Service.* Armonk, NY: M.E. Sharpe, 2005.

Van Wart provides a comprehensive discussion of various leadership theories and their application to public service, which would be valuable for both public and nonprofit leaders. The book is somewhat academic but provides many useful tables and checklists for students of leadership.

Gary Yukl, *Leadership in Organizations,* 6th edition. New York: Prentice Hall, 2005.

Yukl's book is regarded as one of the most comprehensive surveys of major theories and research on leadership and managerial effectiveness in organizations. Yukl balances leadership theory and research with practical applications and offers suggestions for improving skills. He also addresses controversies and differing viewpoints about leadership effectiveness. Other topics include charismatic and transformational leadership, influence processes, leading teams, and leading change.

CHAPTER FOUR

Case Studies of Transforming Public and Nonprofit Organizations

During 2005–2007, we conducted a two-year study of change and transformation in the public sector (Kee and Newcomer 2007). The four cases we examined in the study exhibit a range of change complexity issues within local, state, and federal government agencies. With the cooperation of the agencies, we conducted more than 100 in-person and telephone interviews and examined relevant historical and current documents, websites, and legislation. We also examined two cases dealing with nonprofit organizations, one through personal interviews and the second by reviewing a case study conducted by a New York institute. For each of the cases, we analyzed issues concerning the complexity of the change, the perceptions and involvement of stakeholders, the external environment, and the capabilities of the organization initiating the change. The six case studies illustrate a variety of important issues for leaders seeking to transform their organizations.

The first case involves a local government agency, the Department of Systems Management for Human Services (DSMHS), which was given the responsibility of facilitating the coordination of human services delivery in Fairfax County, Virginia. DSMHS implemented a central system for matching the human services needs of county residents with services available in the county from both public and nonprofit agencies.

Two cases involve the federal government. In the first federal case, the United States Coast Guard (USCG) initiated a major change to address the consequences of its aging "deepwater" assets—those that operate beyond 50 miles from the U.S. shore, including ships, aircraft, and other infrastructure. Aging ships and aircraft threatened the Coast Guard's ability to meet vital and expanding mission requirements. USCG leadership developed two key strategies to address its needs. First, leaders planned to design and build each new deepwater asset (ships and aircraft) to function as part of a coordinated, interoperable system, which would enhance the overall capability of the Coast Guard's collective assets. Second, recognizing the agency's lack of experience and organizational structure needed for a procurement of this scale and magnitude, USCG leaders decided to use a public-private partnership to lead the acquisition strategy. This was a novel approach in organizational change that also was a first for the Coast Guard.

The second federal case involves the Veterans Health Administration (VHA), a federally funded, centrally administered healthcare system for veterans. By the mid-1990s, VHA struggled with a poor public image. The system had multiple hospitals with empty beds and doctors who infrequently practiced their special disciplines. While most healthcare systems were increasing the number of procedures undertaken at out-patient clinics, VHA was still requiring hospital stays for routine procedures. There was even discussion in Congress of closing the system or privatizing it. Faced with external pressure to change the entire healthcare delivery system, in 1994 President Clinton appointed a new leader, Ken Kizer, to transform the VHA system.

The final public sector case involves a complicated intergovernmental initiative, REAL ID, a new federal government requirement imposed on the states. The REAL ID Act of 2005 requires that all state-issued driver's licenses and identification cards meet new minimum security standards. The act specifies technologically complex, nation-wide personal identification and fraud-proof specifications with which state motor vehicle agencies are expected to comply. Our research focused on how various stake-holders reacted to the law and developed strategies to deal with the federal mandate.

The REAL ID study represents an externally imposed, or involuntary, organiza-tional change for state motor vehicle agencies, and it differs from the other cases because the implementation phase has not yet occurred. Nevertheless, REAL ID is a prime example of how state governments are responding to an extensive, post-9/11 federal mandate for change in the way they deliver public services. The REAL ID case also presents a rich opportunity to illustrate how pre-implementation strategizing and planning efforts by affected stakeholders can enhance organizational capacity to undergo change.

The two nonprofit sector cases involve a social services organization and a religious service organization. N Street Village (NSV) was founded in 1973 by the Luther Place Memorial Church in Washington, D.C. NSV focuses its efforts on homeless women, as fewer programs are available to women than men in the D.C. metropolitan area. By the mid 1970s, the church, in cooperation with other faith-based organizations, had turned over its block of townhouses on N Street to a wide variety of services, including temporary housing, a medical clinic, and a food and clothing distribution center.

In the late 1980s the church led an interreligious and community-based effort to pursue and enhance NSV's mission and programs. Among the new services NSV offered were affordable rental housing for individuals and families. By early 2004, however, the financial strain of subsidizing the affordable housing, along with a general lack of solid management, reliable data, and accountability structures at NSV, resulted in a cash flow shortage and low staff morale. These factors, compounded by the exit of an ineffective executive director, created the need for major change—an effort initiated in 2004 by the newly hired executive director, Mary Funke.

The second nonprofit case involves Hillel, widely recognized as the premier organization serving Jewish college youth. The organization's mission is "to enrich the lives of Jewish undergraduate and graduate students so that they may enrich the Jewish people and the world." However, 20 years ago, financial crisis, poor reputation, and weak governance threatened the viability of Hillel as a sustainable and effective nonprofit organization.

Richard Joel, a newly appointed national leader, led Hillel through a seven-year transformation that enabled the Jewish campus outreach organization to reach unprecedented levels of achievement. Despite this leader's phenomenal ability to achieve stakeholder buy-in and adapt to the external environment, the change was quite risky; not only was it enormously complex, but it challenged Hillel's decentralized, rabbinical culture.

In this chapter we apply our model to analyze these six cases of large-scale change. In each case we focus on how the sociopolitical environment, the complexity of the change initiative, stakeholder involvement, and organizational capacity posed challenges to leadership. In many cases, effective leadership was critical in addressing and overcoming the challenges; in some cases, challenges remain.

FAIRFAX COUNTY HUMAN SERVICES MANAGEMENT TRANSFORMATION

The Fairfax County Department of Systems Management for Human Services (DSMHS) facilitates the coordination of human services delivery in the county. Through extensive communication and information sharing, DSMHS staff promote collaboration between the organizations that provide services to the community and county residents.

The organizational and cultural challenges of implementing a coordinated approach to providing human services to the community were enormous. The redesign and implementation teams had to gain the support of social workers within DSMHS, staff of other county agencies, and members of community nonprofits. The cooperation of these nonprofit service providers was especially critical to creating a meaningful multiservice access point for citizens.

The Fairfax County initiative demonstrates the importance of effective leadership for a major change effort, not just at the top but throughout the organization. While it is difficult to break through the "stovepipe" mentality that sometimes characterizes bureaucratic structures, in this case, strong leadership encouraged effective communication and collaboration with affected stakeholders, promoted the use of performance metrics to spur change and keep everyone on track, and worked to ensure that adequate flexibility was available to accommodate unexpected resistance.

Sociopolitical Environment

Beginning in the 1980s, a rise in the number of immigrants entering Fairfax County caused a dramatic increase in the number of residents requiring social services. The county increasingly relied on a network of nonprofit social service agencies to provide those services. The demographic change and the expanding number of providers spurred county officials to commission an organizational redesign study to improve service delivery. Fairfax County officials sought to establish a more efficient central system for matching services with the needs of individuals.

While the original vision of full integration of client intake was not achieved, DSMHS has transformed the way the county delivers social services through the implementation of Coordinated Service Planning (CSP). CSP consists of a call center to receive inquiries from prospective human services clients. DSMHS staff prioritize the urgency of the requests and direct residents to governmental and nonprofit agencies that can deliver the services they need.

Complexity of the Change Initiative

Our research indicated that stakeholders were not fully aware of the complexity involved in the redesign proposal, despite the initial strategic planning process and the engagement of consultants and high-level county officials in the effort. While many on the oversight committee and redesign team, as well as other staff providing input, wanted to create a department to consolidate services, many sensed a lack of clear direction from top county officials. There was uncertainty about the effect of a redesign on various programs supported by state funds as well as which parts of each Fairfax County human services agency would be subsumed into the new entity. Across the agencies, perceived issues about the redesign plan translated into fears about losing turf and control.

Stakeholders were unclear about numerous aspects of the proposed change, including:

- The number of county departments that would lose some of their traditional functions
- The specific functions that would be transferred to the new unit
- The extent to which funding sources should be reallocated from different county human services programs
- The likelihood that social workers would accept a more integrated and holistic approach to client intake and referral involving telephonic rather than face-to-face client interaction.

County officials opted for a less sweeping integration, partly because the budget was cut, but also in response to some strong resistance from key stakeholders to total consolidation. The establishment of the CSP unit reduced the complexity of the change, yet achieved a key goal—a sharper focus on client needs.

Stakeholders

The redesign team initially identified a diverse group of stakeholders in both state and local governments, including human services workers, county residents who use human services, and other agencies and nonprofits that provide services to Fairfax County residents. The redesign plan had to be completed in just over nine months, perhaps leaving insufficient time to fully develop trust among the diverse internal stakeholders and to assess all stakeholder perceptions. Interview responses from nonprofit volunteers, however, indicated that the redesign team did succeed in involving them and their organizations in the planning and implementation processes.

Part of the original redesign plan was to build an online system accessible to all social workers. Although client confidentiality issues prohibited full implementation of a shared online database, DSMHS leaders took a number of other steps to improve communications. Regional managers now attend staff meetings to provide updates on performance and other regional and agency activities, and they encourage staff learning opportunities and quarterly meetings with community groups.

Organizational Capacity

DSMHS underwent a successful, large-scale change in part because of strong, widespread leadership, spearheaded by a change-centric leader, Margo Kiely, whom the county hired to implement the transformation plan. In addition to leadership, other key organizational capacity issues involved culture, performance measurement, and implementation processes.

Kiely's leadership vision and style were broadly viewed as critical. Even administrators who had been passed over for the department directorship praised the new director's leadership approach. Overall, the DSMHS director and leadership team strove to shift a change-resistant attitude among some in the department by fostering a shared sense of ownership in the change process. Leaders worked to maintain a trusting, nonthreatening work environment and culture.

The DSMHS change implementation strategy included making the organization prevention-oriented, improving ties to community nonprofits, and decentralizing operations. This approach created a need for more connectivity among agencies involved in providing services to clients. DSMHS leaders established a redesign committee of creative thinkers from relevant nonprofit and for-profit partner organizations, as well as DSMHS personnel, to make sure that the best quality services were being offered in the most effective way.

A critical component of implementation was the leadership decision to adopt a metrics-based performance management system to measure the performance of individual staff and the overall organization. The system was adopted after much discussion among affected stakeholders and testing through pilot programs, office by office and region by region.

In the effort to instill a "data-driven" work culture in a gradual and collaborative way, leaders "mined" responses from follow-up staff surveys to identify ways to improve the use of metrics. In addition, they created a "process manager" position to manage the service delivery data system, freeing up supervisors to attend to their staff supervisory responsibilities instead of worrying about maintaining the performance measurement system. Interviewees observed that separating function/process from staff management facilitated internal collaboration between supervisors and their staff as well as between program and administrative functions.

INTEGRATED DEEPWATER SYSTEM: THE COAST GUARD TRANSFORMATION STRATEGY

The Coast Guard's mission is quite broad. In addition to its most visible activity, search and rescue (SAR), the agency conducts drug interdiction, alien migrant interdiction, fisheries enforcement, boating safety, overseas maritime intercept (sanctions enforcement) operations, port security and defense, peacetime military engagements, general defense operations in conjunction with the Navy, maritime pollution law enforcement, and overseas inspection of foreign vessels entering U.S. ports. Since September 11, 2001, the Coast Guard's responsibilities for homeland security and for interdiction of potential terrorists and port safety have expanded significantly. In turn, increased capability is now required of Coast Guard assets.

In the late 1990s Coast Guard leadership developed a "system of systems" approach to recapitalizing Coast Guard assets, which means that the design of any single asset must take into account every other asset with which it will operate. The whole solution or system is more effective than its individual parts as a result of enhancements to networks, integrated sensors, and far more interoperable command, control, and communications capability. The Coast Guard realized that this integration would necessitate some changes in how it purchased and acquired assets and how efficiently it used them.

Despite great leadership, the Coast Guard's system of systems strategy is risky because of its complexity, the number of stakeholders involved, and an organizational culture that has not easily adjusted to the change. The Deepwater case is still being played out. Cost overruns and congressional criticism of the project have led the Coast Guard leadership to revise its original strategy. This case demonstrates the difficulty of implementing extremely complex change initiatives with insufficient organizational capacity.

Sociopolitical Environment

At the turn of the century, the United States Coast Guard (USCG) faced a looming crisis: The majority of its mission-critical "deepwater" assets—including ships, aircraft, and communications systems—were aging, putting Coast Guard personnel and their expanding mission requirements at risk. Through the Integrated Deepwater System (IDS) program, or "Deepwater," USCG leadership planned to design and build each new asset to function as an integrated system, significantly enhancing overall capability but adding to the complexity of the undertaking. This "system of systems" approach is a far greater challenge than the Coast Guard tradition of building assets platform class by platform class (i.e., one asset at a time)

Recognizing that the agency lacked the knowledge, experience, and organizational structure needed for a procurement of the scale and magnitude of Deepwater, Coast Guard leaders decided to establish a unique public-private partnership. They selected a Lockheed Martin and Northrop Grumman consortium, named Integrated Coast Guard Systems (ICGS), to manage the performance-based procurement. Neither the government nor the private sector integrator fully appreciated the complexity of this arrangement; it was abruptly abandoned in 2007 because of cost overruns and the failure of initial assets to meet the Coast Guard's expectations.

Complexity of the Change Initiative

The Deepwater project represented an extremely complex change strategy—in magnitude, scope, and fluidity—that included a number of challenging elements:

- Nearly all Coast Guard operations and personnel were impacted by the system of systems approach to the change, and the implementation of network-centric capability significantly changed the way the Coast Guard tactically manages its assets.

- The change involved diverse groups of actors, from both the public and private sectors, whose support and collaboration were vital to the success of the change.

- During the initiation and planning phases of Deepwater, the Coast Guard did not have the internal acquisition staff to manage the proposed acquisition.

- The enormity of the change challenged the internal conventional wisdom that the Coast Guard could do its job with minimal resources.

- The change involved creating a complex partnership with a private sector systems integrator—an arrangement with which the Coast Guard had little experience.

In addition, Deepwater was being implemented in a tumultuous, post-9/11 environment. The expansion of Coast Guard responsibilities for homeland security increased capability requirements for USCG assets. The Coast Guard was integrated into the new Department of Homeland Security (DHS) with 21 other agencies, creating immense management challenges. In essence, Deepwater presented a change within a change.

Stakeholders

Overall, a majority of the interviewees feel that Coast Guard leadership did a better job of reaching out to external stakeholders—making the case for change with executive branch agencies and Congress—than they did with internal stakeholders. It appears that the internal stakeholders' perceptions of gain or loss were not analyzed or addressed in any systematic fashion; Coast Guard personnel simply "were expected to follow along." This led to some confusion and a word-of-mouth type of understanding of Deepwater, leaving operations personnel feeling that they were not an important part of the process.

Organizational Capacity

Successful change can occur only with effective leadership—and if the organization manages its human capital, its structures and processes, and its systems to support the proposed change. Our interviews and research reveal both successes and weaknesses in the USCG's implementation of Deepwater.

The Coast Guard places heavy emphasis on leadership and individual initiative both in the educational programs at the Coast Guard Academy and in the evaluation of personnel. Thus, a number of strong change leaders played integral roles in the strategy and implementation of Deepwater. Further, the external environment was very favorable because the agency is highly regarded among key external stakeholders, including Congress. Nonetheless, two key areas of potential concern were identified: the new partnership with the agency's private sector partner ICGS, and a strong Coast Guard culture that was resistant to change.

Working with a private contractor as a lead systems integrator proved to be a challenging learning experience. First, the Coast Guard's acquisition and contracting staff was not experienced enough to negotiate and monitor such a large program and therefore had to play catch-up. Second, the importance of developing metrics to measure the program's success was recognized but no performance measurement system was in place to build upon. Third, there was a growing recognition that this type of partnership is "not a marriage, but a business relationship" and that this arrangement requires a commitment to high levels of accountability among the partners. Ultimately, after some highly visible failures of new assets and pressure from Congress, the Coast Guard dissolved the arrangement.

The Coast Guard has a defined, some say deeply entrenched, culture that is a perpetual strength in meeting the agency's mission. At the same time, this culture may be a hindrance in implementing change. The Coast Guard culture appears to cultivate *individual* command initiative at the expense of more collective systems approaches to issues. This works well in a search and rescue environment, but perhaps not as well in planning for broader, systemic threats and challenges, such as the one addressed by Deepwater. The current Coast Guard leadership is addressing both the effective use of performance measurement and the culture issues as the agency moves forward on the Deepwater program without the public-private partnership.

TRANSFORMING THE VETERANS HEALTH ADMINISTRATION

VHA is a federally funded, centrally administered healthcare system that was originally established to treat veterans with combat-related injuries as well as to provide rehabilitation to those with service-connected disabilities. The need for specialized hospitals to treat veterans expanded rapidly after World War II, when nearly one million soldiers returned from war suffering from physical and emotional trauma. The newly formed specialty hospitals struggled with a staffing shortage, which led to a partnership between outside medical professionals (mostly in academic institutions) and VHA. In exchange for professional training, these medical professionals staffed VHA hospitals to serve troops returning home from war. VHA's agenda evolved into a four-part congressionally mandated mission: patient care, research, teaching, and contingency backup for the Department of Defense medical care system.

In the VHA transformation, the sociopolitical environment, effective leadership, performance management, and good communications with stakeholders were all key to the successful transformation to improved patient services.

Sociopolitical Environment

VHA was operating in a challenging external environment. Legislative restrictions constrained the legal and budgetary authority for the proposed change; moreover, resources were strained, necessitating redeployment of other agency resources to engineer a major change. Good leadership was critical to VHA's ability to align resources with the change and to receive congressional authority to implement the strategy.

After decades of declining reputation, VHA was energized by a new leader, Ken

Kizer, who was hired in 1994 to make major changes to the system. Under his leadership, VHA personnel worked to transform the agency from a decentralized, inpatient network into an integrated, patient-centered leader in the healthcare industry. While there was no specific external impetus for change, it was common knowledge that VHA's survival as a healthcare system was at stake. VHA hospitals treated too few patients, the quality and access to care for those patients were perceived to be poor, and VHA's reputation as a healthcare institution among the general public was waning.

The external healthcare environment was very different from the environment within VHA. Increased use of out-patient procedures, the computerization of records, and cost-containment efforts all provided examples of current healthcare practices that VHA could potentially emulate.

Complexity of the Change Initiative

When Ken Kizer was selected as the new head of VHA in 1994, he knew that major changes were needed in the agency's method of operations. Patient care was poor, the management system had become inefficient, and some critics in Congress questioned whether there should be a separate federal veterans' healthcare system at all. As the new leadership analyzed its options, the threat of not changing and becoming obsolete seemed riskier than making the changes that were needed. In an effort to reshape the veterans' healthcare system, prominent players within VHA started to determine how to restore its reputation, improve services, and increase the numbers of patients using VHA services.

The changes proposed to improve VHA services required extensive coordination and collaboration among employees, physicians, and facility managers, as well as the wise redeployment of resources to align them with the change. The transformation within VHA was a complex change initiative that posed many challenging obstacles:

- VHA employees were heavily invested in the current system and the practices of each of their own hospitals; change was likely to be met with great resistance and tension among the staff nationwide.
- Employees and patients were accustomed to episodic care, which was to hospitalize, stabilize, and send the patient home. This limited contact between patient and healthcare professional did not allow for the formation

of ongoing doctor-patient relationships. Instead, treatment of the ailment at hand superseded treatment of the whole person. Implementing a continual care model presented the medical staff with a dramatically new way of handling patients.

- Changes in the delivery of care occurred at the same time that VHA was publicly criticized in the political arena. The change agents had to work to prove that these new ways of providing services to veterans would enhance both the system and the quality of care.

Stakeholders

The VHA change involved a diverse group of stakeholders. The primary stakeholders were the veterans who use or are eligible to use services through VHA. The second group of stakeholders was Congress and other government entities that funded or oversaw VHA, including the Office of Management and Budget. The political imperative was for VHA to make improvements, alter the public's perception of its value, and demonstrate that the resources invested were yielding successful outcomes. The third group of stakeholders comprised the service organizations and advocacy groups that provide additional support to veterans outside the VHA system. Service organizations provided feedback, collaboration, and consistent support throughout the entire change effort.

Academic affiliates, including medical schools and residency programs, represented another group of stakeholders. These stakeholders stood to gain from improved technology, which could in turn enhance their scope of learning. The services and benefits that VHA received in working with outside physicians and medical professionals enhanced the quality of care for veterans. Even though there was some concern over funding for research, the academic community embraced the move to a continual care approach as a positive change for both medical staff and patients.

Overall, collaboration among key stakeholders encouraged sustainable relationships based on synergy of goals and perceptions of equitable treatment. Although they recognized the difficulty of the transformation, in the end, stakeholders found that the positive results made it worth the effort needed to implement these changes. The public's perception of VHA has shifted from that of an unstable, inefficient provider to one that is capable and reliable. Stakeholders and staff now feel that they were a part of the transformation and view the change as a success.

Organizational Capacity

Change can be successful only when leadership is strong and a vision is put into action and understood by all the active participants. Interviews and research show that VHA's transformation was successful not only because of the widespread leadership and commitment demonstrated by employees, but also because of the development of an integrated system and the implementation of advanced technology.

The Veterans Integrated Service Network (VISN), a structural vehicle VHA designed and used to implement this change, produced 22 geographically defined network locations. The VISN structure, derived from a regional model of organizational management, shifted the delivery of healthcare from individual medical centers to integrated service networks that provide services to veterans in defined geographic areas. A critical aspect of the change was incorporating the use of technology called the Veterans Health Information Systems and Technology Architecture (VISTA) and the Computerized Patient Record System (CPRS). VISTA supports ambulatory, inpatient, and long-term care, and CPRS allows providers to access patients' health information and update their medical records from any VHA location.

To maintain an integrative and collaborative environment, VHA, with considerable staff input, launched a performance metrics program. This program measured six different "domains of value": quality of care, access to service, satisfaction (initially with patient care, but later expanded to include employee satisfaction), cost-effectiveness, restoration of patient functional status, and community health. Each director in VISN was accountable for his or her group's performance, and accountability was dispersed throughout the entire organization from the top directors to the frontline workers.

As a result of the use of performance metrics and increasing service levels, morale among employees improved. The use of technology and the implementation of systemwide policies and procedures have developed VHA into what is now considered one of the best healthcare systems in the United States.

VHA has expanded into the largest integrated healthcare provider in the nation, with more than 200,000 employees and an annual medical care budget of over $16 billion. The transformation of VHA's medical system included the overhaul of 157 hospitals, 134 nursing homes, 887 clinics, and more than 1300 outpatient sites where care can be provided directly to communities throughout the United States. Most important was moving VHA from an inpatient model of care with a limited number of facilities that were inaccessible to many veterans to an outpatient model of care that is accessible to all those who are eligible.

VHA healthcare resources were redistributed from hospitals to clinics to improve the performance and quality of health-related services, to increase access to care for veterans and improve the veterans' experience, and to achieve better health outcomes overall. In addition, innovative approaches were used to improve veterans' access to VHA healthcare. Internally, decision-making was decentralized and performance metrics were implemented to improve performance and increase staff accountability.

STRATEGIZING AND PLANNING FOR IMPLEMENTATION OF THE REAL ID ACT OF 2005

The REAL ID Act of 2005 (U.S. Public Law 109-13) requires that all state-issued driver's licenses and identification cards meet new minimum security standards by May 11, 2008 (later extended to December 31, 2009). While states may opt not to comply with the act, failure to do so will trigger negative consequences for state citizens because federal agencies will not accept driver's licenses or identification cards unless they meet the minimum standards.

The lead federal agency, the Department of Homeland Security (DHS), issued a Notice of Proposed Rulemaking to establish minimum standards for state-issued driver's licenses and identification cards in accordance with the REAL ID Act and solicited public comment. On March 1, 2007, DHS issued a draft rule; however, by the end of 2007, DHS had not issued the final regulations for REAL ID that will provide state-level officials full information about the technical specifications. In the interim, motor vehicle administrations (MVAs), through the American Association of Motor Vehicle Administrators (AAMVA), have been compiling cost estimates and sharing their concerns as they anticipate implementing the requirements of this new law.

Of the four public sector transformations cases, the REAL ID study represents the only imposed or involuntary organizational change.[1] The case also differs from the other studies because, as of this writing, the implementation phase has not yet occurred. Nevertheless, REAL ID is a prime example of major intergovernmental change in a post-9/11 environment.

Sociopolitical Environment

The external environment is ripe for conflict, given the involuntary nature of the legislation, the politically charged atmosphere in which it was developed, and the myriad unresolved technical and funding issues the states face. The REAL ID Act imposes highly complex policies on the states, requiring them to produce and monitor driver's licenses and identification cards that will meet specific national standards. The member organization representing the state MVAs has been actively involved in initial deliberations to plan for implementation of the law and has acted as technical advisor to members that will eventually have to implement REAL ID.

The politics surrounding the imposition of this mandate on the states is playing out differently in the 51 affected jurisdictions (the 50 states and the District of Columbia), and the different political and economic contexts will affect these individual state outcomes. Some states are beginning to implement the new regulations, but others (as of early 2008) are resisting implementation, with the Maine and Utah legislatures adopting official resolutions in opposition and a number of other states considering similar actions.

Complexity of the Change Initiative

The strategies followed by MVAs and the key interest group collaborators—AAMVA, the

---

[1] A summary of the REAL ID Act requirements most relevant to this study is found on the U.S. Library of Congress website. The act "prohibits Federal agencies from accepting State issued driver's licenses or identification cards unless such documents are determined by the Secretary to meet minimum security requirements, including the incorporation of specified data, a common machine-readable technology, and certain anti-fraud security features…." The act also requires, among other measures, "electronic access by all other States to the issuing State's motor vehicle database…."
(Available at http://thomas.loc.gov/cgi-bin/query/z?c109:H.R.418: [accessed February 21, 2008].)

National Governors Association (NGA), and the National Conference of State Legislatures (NCSL)—have had to account for many layers of complexity. These include the need for wide-ranging intergovernmental cooperation; the personal impact on more than 245 million citizens; projected nationwide implementation costs of $11 billion (estimated by AAMVA); multifaceted politics; technological challenges; and a tight implementation schedule in the face of continued uncertainty about the final regulations. Additionally, Congress stipulated a closed, rather than negotiated, rulemaking process, thus decreasing transparency surrounding deliberations over technical specifications.

Implementation will involve dozens of government, nonprofit, and for-profit organizations. Although it is understandable that a law to combat terrorism is under the purview of DHS, Congress complicated implementation by not assigning the Department of Transportation, which is the federal government's main repository of highway and driver expertise, any formal role in implementation of the REAL ID Act. Processes for securing and issuing driver's licenses and identification cards have to be revamped by every MVA in the nation. Related agencies at the local and state levels, including law enforcement and human services, also will be affected. The key stakeholders didn't begin collaborating until several months after the REAL ID law was enacted.

Stakeholders

The complexity of the change imposed by the REAL ID Act underscores the urgency of identifying stakeholders and their perceptions early in the process. AAMVA leadership needed several months to reach a working compromise with affected stakeholders; craft a consensus-based, coordinated plan; identify organizational capability needs and strengths; and implement the plan. Open, frequent communication from the beginning of the change process is ideal, but in the brief amount of time available for pre-implementation for REAL ID, open communication was time-consuming and difficult to sustain. Fortunately, the pre-Act existence of AAMVA—a coordinated network of MVAs—provided a critical vehicle for understanding and addressing stakeholder perceptions.

Organizational Capacity

Leadership, organizational culture, and implementation mechanisms are the relevant nodes of organizational capacity in this case. The primary lead has been the chair of the

AAMVA REAL ID Steering Group, Anne Witt, who exhibited an inclusive, transparent, collaborative change-centric style. The chair followed a "whole systems" approach, finding the proper balance of top-down and bottom-up direction to facilitate a successful change effort. The Steering Group at AAMVA served as a model for new implementation mechanisms at MVA offices nationwide, where "change teams" are now being established to begin to plan for REAL ID.

Two aspects of organizational culture present conflicts for implementing REAL ID. First, MVAs traditionally have included the protection of customer privacy in their mission; national security and enforcement have not been in their purview. Second, the political cultures of the state organizations are different, complicating the process of adapting REAL ID in 51 different legal, geographical, and cultural settings.

Given the imposition of the REAL ID changes on the states, partisan politics, funding issues, technological challenges, and internal organizational factors, the MVA administrators have learned some good lessons and made some smart moves to mitigate their change risk. The lack of a negotiated rulemaking process raised anxiety and uncertainty among MVAs. Clearly, it is wise for public managers to begin planning for implementation early, in a collaborative fashion, when confronted with externally imposed, sweeping changes.

■ NEW LEADERSHIP AT N STREET VILLAGE

By the late 1990s the N Street Village (NSV) mission of "empowering homeless and low-income women to claim their highest quality of life by offering a broad spectrum of services and advocacy in an atmosphere of dignity and respect" (NSV mission statement 2007) was in jeopardy because of inadequate resources. This case illustrates the importance of understanding the complexity of the change, developing appropriate strategies with affected stakeholders, and building organizational capacity for the long-run success of the organization.

Sociopolitical Environment

When Executive Director Mary Funke took office in 2004, she faced a financial crisis that was not well understood by the staff or board, but she knew she needed to take action quickly. N Street Village needed short-term fiscal adjustments to address the budget shortfall and survive the coming fiscal year, but the financial woes of the organization pointed to deeply rooted problems that would require more complex, long-term planning. Realizing the severity of the problems, the new director launched a plan to transform NSV from an organization rooted in the hopeful belief that "God will provide" to one capable of moving forward through practical mechanisms and systems.

The director began by engaging an external accountant from the Enterprise Foundation to conduct a pro bono analysis of NSV's financial situation. He delivered a realistic, but "scathing," report to the senior officers of N Street, the executive committee of the board, and the operations committee. No one on the board had been aware of the extent of the organization's troubles, and senior staff and board members lacked both the willpower and the strategic capabilities to cope with the financial management problems. The director thought it crucial that she follow the accountant's report and recommendations (in conjunction with the major elements of her own plan for addressing the problems) to build confidence in her leadership and ability to effect lasting change.

Funke's initial proposal entailed cutting $200,000 from the budget as part of a 12-month stabilization plan that involved ending one program, eliminating nine staff positions, and making other budget cuts. The board agreed with the director's plan and also established a $250,000 line of credit (recommended by the external accountant), $150,000 of which was used before the financial situation stabilized. In a more comprehensive strategic plan, Funke articulated a vision that involved creating a nonprofit "business model" and embarking on a new, aggressive fundraising and grant-writing campaign. She also included $25,000 a year in training funds for the staff.

Complexity of the Change Initiative

One major theme of the change effort—developing and implementing a nonprofit business model—was extremely complex in both magnitude and scope. The model not only required that the organization rethink its most basic management and administrative processes, but its execution affected all management, programmatic, and fundraising efforts. It included a commitment to the following (NSV Annual Report 2005):

- Performance, financial, administrative, and program accountability

- Client outcome measures
- Best principles of accounting and finance
- Up-to-date knowledge and information technology infrastructure
- Complete administrative documentation
- Effective staff, board, and volunteer communication systems.

Other challenges to implementing changes in operations included reliance on a small number of staff members for a large number of services, representation of the church on the board and the church's influence on NSV's culture, and negative spillover from the negligence of the former executive director. Moreover, a nonprofit must usually grapple with even more stakeholders and less stability in funding resources than other public organizations.

In light of these challenges, the lack of some key staff competencies, and the extent of the needed shifts in attitude and culture, Director Funke planned the change at NSV as a gradual process. She ensured a focus on fluidity—adjusting the plan as circumstances changed—which reduced complexity overall by allowing for incremental changes over an extended period.

Stakeholders

Since the new director lacked a background in social work or direct service delivery, she relied on her leadership skills and relational strengths to gain credibility with NSV's diverse group of stakeholders. She focused on sharing her vision with both internal and external stakeholders by personally involving them in a concept she called "N Street expectations for excellence." In addition to connecting with two typical external stakeholder groups in the nonprofit sector, volunteers and donors, NSV has a unique relationship with its founding institution, the Luther Place Memorial Church. Communication with both internal and external groups was vital, and the new director made a conscious effort to keep everyone well informed.

The first stages of the change effort primarily affected stakeholders within the organization: NSV's staff, regular volunteers, board of directors, and clients. On the day the changes were communicated to the organization, Funke walked the floors of NSV and personally informed the staff who would be losing their jobs of the decision she had made. She carefully explained the reasoning behind the cuts, encouraged them to emote, and offered support, including pro bono job placement services. She also talked directly to the residents who would be affected by the program cuts and asked whether they preferred to stay at N Street or be referred to another program.

To connect with the remaining internal stakeholders, Funke called an initial meeting of staff where she conveyed her vision and informed them that they would be her core implementation team—and that she was expecting a great deal of improvement in staff operations. She invited anyone unhappy with the arrangement or the vision to leave, and one staff person did decide to terminate as a result of the proposed changes.

Once internal stakeholders were familiarized with the impending changes and plan of action, the new director reached out to external stakeholders: volunteers, major donors, and members of the church. She wrote a letter to the core group of volunteers, explaining the changes and the year-one stabilization plan, met individually with major donors, and made a formal address to the church.

Funke and her director of development generally followed a philosophy of individual treatment for donors and volunteers, taking a personal interest in their lives and following up with them in meaningful ways, often in the form of a handwritten note or a freshly prepared meal. Funke iterated that it takes years to cultivate and keep donors and that the smallest actions and attention to detail sometimes make the greatest impact on individual decisions to give.

Organizational Capacity

Executive Director Funke played an enormous role in building the organization's capacity to embrace the change, and her diligence ultimately led to success and numerous organizational achievements. While some weak areas persist within the organization, NSV proved its ability to adapt to changes introduced through good planning, staff training, and performance management and accountability systems.

The director felt the staff was particularly ill-equipped to meet the challenge of the change, but she made it clear from the start that they were expected to work hard, stay positive, and adopt a new "suck it up" mentality; she reiterated that everyone had to "do what had to be done." This was an incremental process, with staff slowly gaining a better understanding of why changes were beneficial and gradually communicating their buy-in to the vision. Board members conducted an extensive self-evaluation of the board as a whole, and of themselves as individual members, to determine strengths, weaknesses, and gaps in skills needed on the board.

Funke facilitated a full-day retreat where all staff collaborated to produce a fiscal stabilization plan and initiated a SWOT (strengths, weaknesses, opportunities, threats) analysis, which gave all staff the opportunity to offer input on the vision and plan. A second retreat attended by senior management and appointed members of the board was held to rewrite the mission statement and develop a new vision statement, value statement, and five-year strategic plan.

Although implementing immediate changes necessitated a top-down approach, Funke also maintained a bottom-up management ethos throughout the change. She was sensitive to internal stakeholders' reactions and feelings; as a result, strategic goals and objectives are updated yearly, according to annual progress and stakeholder feedback. Staff members have independently written a new community statement for N Street, and they continue to play an integral role in major change decisions. They introduced a client satisfaction survey and regularly solicit input from clients about the quality of care and their overall experience at NSV.

Initially, the NSV culture was a hindrance in the proposed shift to a nonprofit business model. The staff and board were rooted in a long-established culture of grass-roots service, described as "matriarchal" in nature, and tied to the "God will provide" approach to problem-solving. The staff had no experience working under a system of accountability or maintaining comprehensive and accurate data, and they generally lacked strong management skills. Staff and board members seemed content as long as core services were being provided to the clients.

The director envisioned numerous components of the nonprofit business model. One goal related generally to policies, procedures, and practices and listed as objectives: better record keeping, updated data analysis and collection procedures, and the evaluation of administrative and client policies and practices. The goal relating to the immediate budgetary problems called for adherence to approved spending and income, a $1.5 million fundraising target, the hiring of an assistant director for development, efficient use of in-kind donations and volunteers, and a redefinition of the training subsidy program. Finally, Funke helped staff through the learning and change processes via the most far-reaching of the core goals: a strong performance management system.

Specific objectives of performance management included updating job descriptions, staff members developing their own performance objectives to serve as the basis for their performance evaluations, and identifying staff training needs (for which funds were included in the budget).

Feelings of gain were clear after N Street Village began to surpass its goals and reach new levels of achievement. Staff morale skyrocketed after NSV won the 2006 Washington Post Excellence in Nonprofit Management Award—in its first application attempt. NSV staff benchmarked other winners, worked on the application as a team, and rehearsed for the final site visit, with staff playing a large role in the presentation. Since being honored, the organization has flourished and staff feel a stronger sense of belonging. The result has been a fundamental change in organizational culture and the manner in which employees and clients "sell" N Street Village to external stakeholders.

TRANSFORMATION OF HILLEL[2]

A Christian professor, a Jewish business owner, and a rabbi began Hillel at the University of Illinois in 1923 in response to a growing number of Jewish students on college campuses who were relatively ignorant about aspects of their identity. The initial success of the organization was largely attributable to the magnetic personality and powerful preaching of Rabbi Frankel, who assumed day-to-day leadership. B'nai B'rith, which was established in 1843 as a lodge for Jews and by the 1920s was the most prominent organization in the Jewish communal world, became the parent organization for Hillel, sponsoring the B'nai B'rith Hillel Foundation in 1923. By the 1940s, Hillel had expanded across the country and served as a "synagogue on campus," providing Jewish learning opportunities, playing a role in Jewish dating and courtship, and offering a refuge to Jewish students.

---

[2] This is a summary and adapted version of a case study written by Mark I. Rosen with analysis by Amy L. Sales, *The Remaking of Hillel: A Case Study on Leadership and Organizational Transformation* (Fisher-Bernstein Institute for Jewish Philanthropy and Leadership, January 2006). Used with permission.

Sociopolitical Environment

Hillel's reputation began to erode when the organization fell out of touch with the campus environment of the 1960s, which was much more "activist" than the Hillel programming. Hillel positions were viewed as a last resort for rabbis who could not get credible positions in synagogues. Even so, the rabbis and staff loved their work, and Hillel enjoyed a strong rabbinic culture throughout the 1960s and 1970s.

Because of the intertwined structures of Hillel and B'nai B'rith, the financial woes of B'nai B'rith in the late 1970s and early 1980s had a detrimental impact on Hillel. No longer at the cutting edge of Jewish social services, B'nai B'rith was rapidly losing members and revenue because of an inability to adapt its mission. After a four-year period of ineffective leadership at Hillel, a B'nai B'rith search committee in 1988 hired Richard Joel as the new international director.

Complexity of the Change Initiative

The B'nai B'rith Hillel Foundation's transition from its traditional rabbi-led culture and decentralized structure to Hillel International's culturally based franchise model represents a highly complex transformation. Hillel had been without stable leadership for almost a year, the national office relied on the contributions of B'nai B'rith for $3 million of the $14 million annual budget, and that dependence had paralyzed efforts to provide adequate, independent leadership for the national offices. The national office was understaffed and its existing staff was underutilized. Hillel directors on campus (mostly rabbis) were not receiving enough support from the national office, and morale among staff was generally poor.

The new International Director was handed the monumental task of "both integrating and synthesizing the past and yet breaking from the past" (Rosen 2006, 34). Radical changes were necessary, but Hillel's rich history and its strong religious and intellectual values had to be carefully preserved. Richard Joel's leadership team reframed the mission of Hillel, separated the organization from B'nai B'rith, founded a new umbrella organization, implemented a national accreditation system, built a dual board structure that included a management and a leadership board, and improved fundraising capacity. During these changes, Joel was confronted by internal resistance as well as conflicting interests both within Hillel and in its external environment.

Key factors that increased the complexity of the changes required included the following:

- Changes impacted both the International Center and all local Hillels, including a fundamental shift in the organization's approach to its mission, its name, its fundraising capacity, national and local management and accountability, and external relations.

- The individual campus Hillel foundations had been functioning as autonomous units and varied widely in size, attendance, quality of programming, and leadership.

- B'nai B'rith lacked the capacity to continue funding Hillel at the same levels, yet closely guarded its hold on Hillel. The national office of Hillel had always been run as a department of B'nai B'rith and lacked essentials such as its own bank account, accounting department, and fundraising or development staff.

- Other potential sources of support, such as Jewish federations and philanthropists, refused to make donations because of the poor management and uneven quality of services among local Hillels.

Stakeholders

In 1993, Hillel broke from its parent organization, B'nai B'rith, and established a new Foundation for Jewish Campus Life to increase Hillel's fundraising capacity and to serve as an umbrella organization for all campus Hillels. Although the leaders of B'nai B'rith had kept Hillel under their administrative and financial control in the late 1980s, they did not consider Hillel a priority. The new director needed to work carefully with key B'nai B'rith officials to take advantage of their potential receptivity to change the relationship. Joel commented: "There were never any secrets kept from them. We just used the right kind of language in the right kind of way. Because…they didn't want to be responsible for losing Hillel" (Rosen 2006, 44). The role of B'nai B'rith was reduced in stages over a three-year period to allow internal stakeholders ample time to adjust to the new governance structure.

Because most of the previous directors of Hillel had been rabbis, the decision to hire Joel, a layperson, disturbed those who felt he was an outsider who would be unable to relate to the organization's values. Joel understood their concern and initiated efforts to build rapport with the local rabbis. He met with the executive committee of the professional association of Hillel rabbis and asked the members individually about their experiences at Hillel and what the organization meant to them. Joel responded with passion about his personal values and described his own vision for Hillel: "We have the power, the opportunity, and I suggest the sacred responsibility to reshape ourselves and be one of the key forces for Jewish continuity and survival in the emerging century. We are positioned to seize the moment…and command the respect, support, and partnership of the community" (Rosen 2006, 41).

Realizing that the magnitude and scope of the change would require strong leadership throughout the organization, Joel began to make difficult personnel changes at the national office and at local Hillels. He was lauded for skillful human resource management and successfully encouraging many ineffective directors to resign. Because local chapters had operated for years with little accountability to the national office, the introduction of Joel's "franchise" model upset many rabbi-directors and lay leaders. To provide an outlet for discussion, he made heavy use of boards, task forces, and commissions, providing a platform for volunteer engagement that brought diverse groups of stakeholders together to share their perceptions.

Joel brought performance evaluation to Hillel in the form of accreditation, a system he borrowed from his experience in college administration. The entire process included local feedback and was implemented using a bottom-up approach because Hillel directors felt the new accreditation system threatened their job security.

A retreat organized by a National Committee on Quality Assurance (composed of a diverse mixture of Hillel's internal stakeholders) resulted in the Everett Pilot Program for Excellence, which featured a four-stage accreditation process. Local Hillels engaged in their own self-study in the first stage and then worked with an outside Hillel team that led a site visit and delivered an action plan for the local organization. After passing accreditation, local Hillel foundations were expected to comply with other national directives, like engaging in independent fundraising and participating in new program initiatives, with support from the national office. Joel designed the programs and gave local Hillels half of the money needed for the programs (from national fundraising efforts), while the new director of development taught them how to raise the other half.

Joel always felt most comfortable speaking to the students directly. The greatest asset he brought to Hillel may have been his ability to understand the experience of Jewish college students and connect with them on a personal level. He put students at the center of strategic planning and also demonstrated his dedication through active participation with students on their campuses. He renewed a national assembly for student leaders in Hillel, placed 12 students on the Hillel board, and established several new programs designed to enhance the long-term influence of students.

With respect to external stakeholders, Hillel lacked any relationship with the philanthropic community before the 1990s. The first major gift, which came from one of Joel's contacts at Yeshiva University, was used to begin an endowment that provided grants to local Hillel foundations. This initiative spurred other one-time gifts from donors, which were used to pioneer new student-centered initiatives.

Hillel's Committee on the Fiscal Future later targeted Edgar Bronfman, President of the World Jewish Congress. By forging a long-term relationship with such an influential figure in the Jewish community, Hillel dramatically improved its reputation and attracted the support of other key philanthropists. Through Bronfman, Joel gained access to the Study Group, or "Mega Group," a collaboration of the most prominent Jewish philanthropists in the nation, and eventually secured $1.2 million from the group annually.

Joel recognized that the Jewish federation system (an important nationwide system) could provide the most stable and long-term funding for Hillel. He worked diligently to promote a partnership with the Council of Jewish Federations (CJF). A CJF Task Force on Jewish University Student Services report recognized the impact of Joel's leadership and recommended that the federations play a more active role in student services on college campuses. CJF agreed to provide 40 percent of the total budgets of local chapters (approximately $20 million in the first year)—"for the first time, Hillel and the federations would have a cooperative working partnership" (Rosen 2006, 55).

Organizational Capacity

As a large and long-established organization with many local foundations and an international office closely connected with B'nai B'rith, Hillel had a basic ability to design and implement major change initiatives. However, without skilled leadership, the organization might not have survived its financial crisis and inner turmoil. The separation from B'nai B'rith and transition to financial independence became the hallmark of Hillel's transformation, but Joel's first action as director was to sell his vision to internal stakeholders. Joel identified two distinct groups of Hillel participants: (1) those who were knowledgeable about Judaism and eager to become part of a Jewish community on their campus and needed empowerment and (2) those who felt uncomfortable or unfamiliar with their Jewish identity and needed engagement (which required more effort on the part of Hillel staff).

To restructure the Hillel system, Joel not only had to remove ineffective local Hillel directors, but he also wanted to make permanent changes in the composition of the national office and Hillel's governing structure (its board of directors and international board of governors). He began hiring individuals as Hillel directors based not on rabbinical experience but on skills for running a nonprofit. He named a new chairman of the board who could build credibility with the federations and appointed new "young, inspired, and intelligent" members, while adding women and students as representatives on the board of directors and other governing boards.

New fundraising campaigns that permitted freedom from fiscal reliance on B'nai B'rith, the hiring of the first director of development, and the new board of governors all empowered Hillel to develop self-sustaining programs and sparked a spirit of innovation in staff members. Original programs that propelled Hillel forward included the Steinhardt Fellows program and the Jewish Campus Service Corps. Jewish philanthropists appreciated the opportunity to sponsor particular programs that aligned with their own priorities. The national center ensured that local Hillel foundations maintained the capacity to adopt changes by providing professional development, training opportunities, and grants in recognition of good directors and good programming. Joel reconfigured Hillel's interface with its environment by maximizing timely opportunities (such as a population study that raised concerns about Jewish students marrying non-Jews) and reaching out to all the important groups of external stakeholders.

The business-like franchise model, which included centralized decision-making, performance measurement, and quality assurance, was and still is controversial, given the history of the organization and its reluctance to ascribe to a corporate framework.

Some Hillel insiders felt that the turnover in leadership from academically oriented rabbis to professional administrators weakened relationships between directors and university officials and detracted from Hillel's participation in the intellectual life on campus. Others believed that "Hillel had become too standardized, corporate, and impersonal" (Rosen 2006, 67). Seeking the students who needed engagement required the "mass marketing" of Judaism, and Hillel chapters began to measure success by the number of students reached through cultural and social programming. If outreach becomes "too religious," participation may drop, but if it is "too popular and secular" it may lead Hillel away from its central mission.

By 1995, Joel had clearly transformed Hillel into a new organization that was independent from B'nai B'rith with new, diverse revenue sources and fundraising systems. With the ability to generate 60 percent of its own funding, Hillel, under Joel's leadership, quadrupled its total annual budget from $14 million in 1988 to nearly $60 million in 1995. The accreditation program had improved quality at many local foundations, and some were even generating their own funding, conducting successful capital campaigns, and building new facilities.

New partnerships with CJF reconnected communities with Jewish college students, who were now viewed as an essential link in forging sustainable Jewish continuity. CJF secured Hillel's credibility when it identified Hillel, in a highly anticipated task force report, as the "central federation agency through which campus services are delivered" (Rosen 2006, 52).

▆▆ LESSONS LEARNED FROM THE CASE STUDIES

These six case studies do not presume to reflect the entire spectrum of challenges and change issues faced by public and nonprofit organizations in the 21st century. They are, however, strikingly similar in a number of important aspects that are likely to be common to most organizations facing the challenge of change. These cases highlight the role of leaders in analyzing the challenges involved and in devising strategies to support the change.

Complexity of the Change Initiative: Keeping the Focus on the Mission

Change efforts should always begin with a strong focus on the organization's mission. Revisiting the fundamental mission and goals of the organization is essential to ensure that nothing valuable is lost during the change. Keeping the mission foremost in mind helped the leaders in Fairfax County, VHA, the Coast Guard, NSV, and Hillel to cut through the complexity and challenges they faced and create a vision that clearly focused on what was most important to them, their organizations, and their stakeholders.

While incremental change may be the most successful in complex situations, such as Hillel and Fairfax County's Department of Systems Management for Human Services (DSMHS), sometimes organizations such as VHA or NSV face a "burning platform" that demands sweeping change for survival. At other times, the changing nature of the external environment (e.g., the Coast Guard's expanded mission brought about by the 9/11 attacks) requires immediate action.

Most public and nonprofit organizations have a clearly defined culture, often the product of the founders and other key leaders, that is likely to be resistant to change. Successful leaders of change do not underestimate the power of an organizational culture to hamper a change effort. In the Coast Guard Deepwater case, the use of a public-private partnership and the establishment of a separate Deepwater program unit added layers of complexity and conflicted with the underlying culture of the agency. As a result, many Coast Guard personnel felt marginalized; interviews revealed that internal communication was insufficient to bring personnel in line with the new vision of a "system of systems."

In the nonprofit sector, where most stakeholders exhibit a passionate dedication to the organization's mission, cultural change can be a formidable challenge. In the cases of NSV and Hillel, the challenge was to keep what was most important to the culture (their defined values and ethos) while working to modify the culture in a way that supported the change initiative. Leaders should frame their transformational vision as a compelling narrative that demonstrates an understanding of the organization's history, shared values, and ideals.

When a change registers high in complexity, it is even more important that effective change mechanisms be in place to minimize long-term risk. A recent study by Brandeis University found that local Hillel chapters have integrated the changes from Joel's tenure into their operations but have not developed the fluidity they need to react to changes in the environment on their campuses. Amy Sales notes, "The foundations learned to engage in the new behavior called for by a given innovation, but they did not learn how to become innovating organizations" (Rosen 2006, 77).

Furthermore, when Joel left Hillel, he had not facilitated any succession planning and thus left the organization vulnerable to the performance of future leaders. In contrast, at NSV, Mary Funke has already identified persons in the organization with the potential to assume leadership and is actively working to expand their leadership opportunities.

Sociopolitical Environment: Staying Aware of External Conditions

Scanning the sociopolitical environment is essential to lead public and nonprofit organizations through a change because their survival generally depends on external support—whether from a legislative body or from donors. Leaders have to be aware not only of the sources of that potential support, but also of their potential competitors for funds, and take advantage of opportunities (good reputations, important new studies, major crises, etc.) to attract additional support.

Our case studies demonstrate a number of successful efforts in this regard. At Hillel, the new director successfully understood the changing environment and issues for funders of Jewish causes and was able to position Hillel to take advantage of those changes. Similarly, at VHA, the director was able to exploit changes in healthcare technology and practices as part of the VHA transformation effort. In contrast, REAL ID is being implemented in a turbulent environment with significant state opposition; federal agency actors failed to understand likely state attitudes or to involve critical state actors in the implementation efforts, unnecessarily complicating their efforts.

Stakeholders: Building an Upward Spiral of Trust and Collaboration

Public and nonprofit organizations have to involve their multiple stakeholders in any change. Identifying and incorporating internal and external stakeholders at the front end of sweeping change is often critical to successful change and transformation. The key is building trust and confidence that the organization is capable of meeting the mission and objectives that motivate stakeholder involvement and collaboration. The new "vision" must capture what is important to stakeholders while moving the organization forward. Simply put, there is no such thing as too much communication!

In anticipation of the REAL ID implementation, the AAMVA REAL ID Steering Committee Chair Anne Witt initiated and consistently supported collaboration and transparency in her approach to her colleagues in state government. Collaborative processes are an important part of any change strategy. In this case, the failure of Congress to develop a transparent and negotiated rulemaking process will undoubtedly create problems in the 50 states and lead to more resistance than might have occurred with a more collaborative process.

Communicating with stakeholders, both internal and external, was a principal responsibility of the new leadership at VHA, NSV, and Hillel. In those cases, success depended on gaining the trust of a wide range of actors upon whom their organizations were financially dependent. Developing a compelling vision and common language that stakeholders could buy into was key to the success of those change initiatives.

Kizer had to convince a reluctant Congress that VHA was providing valuable healthcare to veterans. In the cases of NSV and Hillel, their leaders, Funke and Joel, really seemed to care about their donor stakeholders, creating deep, genuine relationships that went beyond the relationships typically found in public and private sector activities.

A leader's determination to achieve results can stimulate "upward spirals" from even the most deadlocked dilemmas. Both VHA and Hillel had fallen into poor repute, which repelled funders (in Congress and in the private sector) and in turn prevented the possibility of improving programming to rebuild reputation. Kizer focused on "domains of value" to energize the VHA system. Through the accreditation process, Joel brought movement to a stagnant situation and solicited financial support for new programs at Hillel. When others observed these great ideas in action, "the spiral was set in motion and success bred more success" (Rosen 2006, 77).

Organizational Capacity: Creating Change-Centric Organizations

These case studies and other reading in public and nonprofit management suggest that building organizational capacity is a key to long-term success and the ability of the organization to meet changing conditions and challenges. That capacity starts with— but goes beyond—"the leader" of the organization. Organizations like the Coast Guard, Fairfax County, VHA, NSV, and Hillel that are able to meet the challenges of change invest in leadership throughout the organization, often setting aside funds for individual growth and enrichment even in tight fiscal circumstances.

Successful public and nonprofit leaders are realistic about the present, but focus on the future. Just as important as presenting the grand picture, vision, or plan is the need to understand where the organization is and then to develop the incremental steps toward making improvements. It's important to find the right balance between "innovation" and sticking to the "fundamentals." Straying too far in one direction will result either in not changing enough or in spinning out of control.

Nonprofit organizations often get by with very loose and informal organizational and accountability structures. While this may work with small organizations, as the organizations grow and expand their mission, those structures are not able to support their needs. A key function of leadership is thinking about the nature of the challenge and the need for organizational structures to align with the change needs.

Performance measurement is an important strategic process in facilitating change. Even just the introduction of measurement can have an important symbolic effect, indicating that the organization is committed to a new model of operation. This was true with DSMHS's automated call center, VHA's domains of value, NSV's performance-based employee reviews, and Hillel's accreditation process. In the case of the Coast Guard's Deepwater program, the failure to identify key matrices prior to the public-private partnership may have contributed to the ultimate demise of the partnership. Good performance measurement helps everyone focus on the key elements necessary for the change and can be used to track the success of various change efforts.

In the nonprofit arena, fundraising is a key organizational capability—and it is everyone's job. An important leadership responsibility is instilling in the members of the organization the importance of fundraising, particularly of being attuned to potential donors and of nurturing current donors. For example, when leaders at all levels of Hillel began to work in concert to brainstorm new sources of revenue, the organization rapidly progressed. Nonprofits must be careful, however, not to just chase dollars and lose their central focus and mission.

Finally, leaders need to create change-centric organizations that can adapt to changing needs and challenges, that are open to new ideas, and that are entrepreneurial but still accountable. The best reforms can lead to unanticipated positive long-term outcomes. Amy Sales refers to these secondary effects as "ripples" (Rosen 2006).

In Fairfax County, it was the use of performance measures that encouraged greater coordination and productivity from the central call center workers. At VHA, it was the automation of patient records that allowed a better continuum of care. At Hillel, it was the accreditation process that enhanced quality, attracted funding, and heightened pride in the quality of performance. At N Street, Mary Funke's mantra of "do what has to be done," coupled with her investment in staff training, led to a more capable, performance-based organization that won the *Washington Post* award for nonprofit excellence.

IMPLICATIONS FOR CHANGE LEADERS

Our research in the six cases demonstrates that widespread change is possible, even under the pressure resulting from environmental forces and financially tight circumstances. The key is effective change-centric leadership: creating a vision that incorporates the organization's important values and engaging in effective communication and collaboration with key stakeholders. While recognizing the vast differences facing public and nonprofit organizations as they undertake major change or transformation, leaders of change can benefit by examining other successful (or unsuccessful) change initiatives and determining whether those lessons are relevant and can be applied to their own organizations.

PRACTICAL TIPS FOR THE CHANGE LEADER

- Maintain a focus on your organization's mission; incorporate it in your vision for change.
- Scan the external environment for leading practices and examples of successful change.
- Use performance measurements to focus and track the changes.
- Create mechanisms to involve your critical stakeholders—employees, volunteers, trustees, donors, and others.
- Build staff capabilities so members are better able to contribute to the change.
- Develop other change leaders who can take on additional responsibilities, now and in the future.
- Instill a sense of stewardship so that everyone in the organization understands that they are responsible for its financial success and performance, through fundraising and good management of resources.

SUGGESTED READINGS FOR CASE STUDIES

Allan A. Altshuler and Robert D. Behn, editors. *Innovation in American Government: Challenges, Opportunities, and Dilemmas,* Washington, DC: The Brookings Institution, 2007.

This book provides a number of case studies of innovation in American government at the local, state, and federal levels, including some that received the Innovations in American Government Award from Harvard's Ash Institute for Democratic Governance and Innovation. The authors argue for the importance of innovation within a framework of democratic accountability. They contend that innovation is necessary because current government programs are failing to meet the needs of 21st century challenges and citizens are demanding increased government performance.

Sandra J. Williams and Mary M. Hale, *Managing Change: A Guide to Producing Innovation from Within.* Lanham, MD: University Press of America, 1989 (paperback edition).

This book is based on Minnesota's "STEP" (Strive Towards Excellence in Performance) approach, developed in the mid-1980s to improve state government programs and services. STEP was developed by Minnesota's Department of Administration to spur and legitimize change efforts at the state and local levels. The key elements of the STEP approach are (1) closer contact with the customer/citizen; (2) increased employee participation; (3) increased discretionary authority for managers; (4) partnerships; (5) productivity improvement techniques; and (6) improved work measurement. The STEP program won the Harvard Kennedy School's Innovation Award.

Paul C. Light, *Sustaining Innovation: Creating Nonprofit and Government Organizations That Innovate Naturally.* San Francisco: Jossey-Bass, 1998 (paperback edition).

This book describes "preferred states of being" for organizations that seek to be innovative through removing barriers and debunking myths that discourage innovation; examining the preferred environment, internal structure, leadership, and internal management systems of an innovating organization; and encouraging organizations to "fit the list of preferred states to their realities." The conclusion looks toward the core values that help innovating organizations know what is right for them: trust, honesty, rigor, and faith.

PART II

Key Leadership Change Processes

CHAPTER FIVE

Communicating and Collaborating with Stakeholders

The new public service in the United States is a blended, multisector workforce comprising public and nonprofit servants who often work closely with the private sector to deliver public goods and services. The composition of the blended workforce means that stakeholders in change initiatives may have very different stakes in the outcomes, as well as diverse values and incentives affecting their behavior.

The challenge of forging the trust and cooperation among diverse stakeholders needed to implement complex change initiatives can be intimidating. Understanding who the key stakeholders are and where they are coming from, and then devising effective communication strategies to achieve productive collaboration, are fundamental challenges for transformational stewards.

THE SCOPE OF STAKEHOLDER INTERESTS

We define "stakeholders" as all the individuals and organizations involved in, or affected by, a change initiative. Internal stakeholders are managers and employees within the organization, which includes regular volunteers in nonprofit organizations. Private contractors to public sector organizations are identified as external stakeholders in that they are not direct employees of a public or nonprofit organization. In this age of networked government that is increasingly dependent on public-private partnerships and outsourcing of functions, contractors are often key stakeholders. Other critical external stakeholders may include Congress; executive branch agencies; private firms and interest groups; other governmental, nongovernmental, or international organizations; potential funders for nonprofit organizations; and individual citizens or residents. Leaders need to systematically identify all people and groups involved in the implementation of a change initiative.

Where does a change leader or manager begin in the effort to shape communication strategies that facilitate regular, open, and meaningful internal and external stakeholder collaboration? The change leader begins by looking inside, outside, and ahead of the immediate organization (Brinkerhoff, D. 1991a; Goldsmith 1995).

Looking inside, in the new public service environment, requires understanding and acceptance among internal stakeholders of each other's diverse work-related orientations and interests. Up-front investment in sound communication strategies to encourage collaboration can reap dividends.

Open deliberation, in settings considered by employees and other stakeholders to be safe and nonthreatening, helps foster a trusting culture. A trusting culture is conducive to securing buy-in to change initiatives. Both internal and external stakeholders are primary sources of ideas about how to strategize and implement change projects. Building trust among stakeholders through intentional communication processes can facilitate planning. "A 'mindset' or commitment to the whole" is a worthy yet hard-earned objective (Mandell 1994, qtd. in Mandell 1999, 46). When employees and other actors in networked public service delivery share similar values and ethics, they are more likely to develop workable approaches.

Along with implementing change effectively, ensuring accountability for contributions to performance is another key leadership responsibility. The larger the number of stakeholders, the more complex the accountability challenge. Agranoff and McGuire (2001) note that because multiple interests are involved in network transactions, everyone in the network is somewhat accountable, but no one individual is completely accountable, for outcomes or to various stakeholders (309–310). Strategies for ensuring accountability are even more problematic in nonhierarchical networks, and communication and collaboration structures are needed to clarify expectations about accountability for the achievement of change outcomes.

Looking outside at the external environment, leaders should engage stakeholders (such as citizens, labor unions, and consumers) and encourage open communications. Ongoing, routine monitoring of how external stakeholders view an organization and organizational performance certainly helps when innovation or external demands require change. Increasing the quantity, quality, and speed of feedback will engage stakeholders as changes are planned.

Looking ahead, leaders must anticipate new stakeholders who may become involved as a result of the change initiative. It is likely that organizations or interest groups may be drawn into the planning and implementation of change initiatives—by intention or not. Careful consideration of the requirements for successful change can help in preparing for the consequences of a larger and more diverse number of collaborators or interested parties. In either case, forecasting changes in implementation partners and stakeholders is helpful as a means of securing effective collaboration.

COLLABORATION

We view the term "collaboration" as multifaceted. For example, Agranoff suggests that collaborative networks may be informational or developmental, and they may involve outreach or action (2003). The need for interdependence in collaborative relationships may vary from cooperation, to coordination, to collaboration, to more intensive integration (Selden, Sowa, and Sandfort 2002). Collaboration is typically based on reciprocity, or two-way flows of information and expectations (Agranoff and McGuire 2003).

We believe that trust—in leadership and in other stakeholders—facilitates candid reciprocity in sharing views and ideas. However, collaboration may also be based on resource dependency, expertise dependency, or contracts that establish de facto hierarchical relationships. Regardless of the role of trust vis-à-vis other forces linking stakeholders who are responsible for implementing change, candid communication about tangible as well as intangible obstacles to change initiatives is a key foundation for effective collaboration.

We view authentic collaboration as candid, network-wide communication supported by a trusting, change-centric culture. Trust among stakeholders to share resources and ideas is more difficult to establish in networks than in the single public service organization. The process of engendering authentic collaboration is more labor-intensive than command-and-control management, but it is a more effective process for ensuring sustainable, improved performance overall.

Authentic collaboration among stakeholders in networked service delivery chains will likely lead to innovation and efficiency. Milward and Provan (2006) note five essential network management tasks: the management of accountability, legitimacy, conflict, design (i.e., governance structure), and commitment. We believe that authentic collaboration is essential to carrying out these tasks. Deliberations about accountability for accomplishments, the division of responsibilities, and personal commitments will clearly be more effective when based on authentic collaboration.

STAKEHOLDER ANALYSIS

Stakeholder analysis is a crucial first step toward understanding how stakeholders throughout an organization or network view a change initiative. Stakeholder analysis can be conducted in a variety of ways, from worldwide web-based surveys to focus groups consisting of representatives of the stakeholder interest groups. Leaders and managers should assess stakeholders by analyzing (1) the intensity of stakeholder perceptions, (2) the diversity of stakeholder beliefs and interests, and (3) the existence of collaboration networks to facilitate stakeholder relations.

Intensity of Perceptions

Perceptions matter. The more intensely beliefs are held or fears are felt, the more they matter. Fears and rumors about the effects of a change initiative can easily become exaggerated and blown out of proportion. It is the leader's job to work through overdrawn perceptions and adjust implementation steps to address reasonable but previously unknown or unaddressed concerns.

To reduce the friction produced by time-consuming rumors and to maximize stakeholder input, leaders should pay careful attention to assessing and addressing stakeholder perceptions on a continual basis. Understanding stakeholder perceptions should involve identifying the perceptions of gain and loss held by internal and external stakeholders; measuring the intensity of those perceptions; and gauging whether their perceptions will lead stakeholders to impede the implementation of change initiatives.

Diversity of Interests

The range of views about organizational mission, value preferences, and worldviews held by stakeholders is generally a function of the size and variety of the organizational units or groups involved in or affected by a change initiative. The need for effective communication processes and collaborative networks increases with the diversity of stakeholders.

Collaboration among diverse internal and external stakeholders is predicated on extensive communication processes and structures backed by steady commitment from leadership. Such collaboration should result in increased employee and external stakeholder buy-in. If relations among stakeholders prove difficult, conflict resolution may be in order, pointing to the need for conflict negotiation structures such as in-house negotiation experts.

Existence of Collaboration Networks

The third focus of stakeholder analysis is on the collaboration networks—both processes and structures—that are in place to facilitate the flow of communication among internal and external stakeholders. The more institutionalized and valued the collaboration networks are, the easier it will be to generate candid dialogue among stakeholders about their perceptions vis-à-vis the actual vision and goals for the change initiative. Sustainable improvement in performance is likely associated with communication and collaboration across multiple organizations. Consistent and frequent communication is all the more essential for grappling with the increasing complexity of change initiatives in the public sector.

FOSTERING COMMUNICATION AND COLLABORATION

Fostering communication and collaboration starts with visible leadership commitment. Once the leadership conveys its commitment, an effective communication strategy can be designed by establishing mechanisms to ensure that pertinent stakeholders are brought into the dialogue. Frequent opportunities for networked communication can help cultivate honest and open dialogue among internal and external stakeholders in the change initiative. Over time, a level of trust will be established, allowing differences in preferences, norms, and incentives to be mediated cooperatively rather than competitively.

Because organizational actors and goals differ, the processes and structures leaders employ will also vary. Table 5.1 provides a list of tasks involved in planning and implementing effective stakeholder communications.

TABLE 5.1:   Tasks Involved in Planning and Implementing Stakeholder Communications

PLANNING

1. Identify stakeholders (internal and external) affected by the change initiative.
2. Assess stakeholder perceptions.
3. Assess communication needs and gaps.
4. Practice "reflexive listening."
5. Negotiate roles, responsibilities, and strategies.
6. Use existing collaborative networks or develop new ones to ensure two-way communication.
7. Develop change performance metrics.
8. Identify media contacts and the organization's spokesperson.
9. Develop a common case for change.
10. Plan for unknowns, crises, and unexpected problems.

IMPLEMENTING

1. Institute a communication plan.
2. Develop and initiate feedback mechanisms.
3. Value and celebrate the contributions of stakeholders.
4. Monitor, evaluate, and report results.
5. Build communities of trust.
6. Encourage teaming and reward collaboration.
7. Partner with the community.
8. Keep public officials informed.
9. Take a long-term view.

SOURCES: Barge 2004; Darling, Parry, and Moore 2005; Elias and Cavana 2000; Harvard 2005; Klein 1999; Lazes and Savage 2000; U.S. GAO 2005b.

In the more traditional public service organization, cross-management teams are used to ensure communication and coordination among departments and other bureaucratic units. In networked public service, cross-management teams have the additional, critical function of instilling and normalizing creative brainstorming among managers at all levels throughout the network. Table 5.2 summarizes various communications and coordination structures.

TABLE 5.2: Structures to Facilitate Collaboration within Organizations and Network Service Delivery Systems

Structure	Process
Cross-Management Teams	Regular meetings of representatives of all relevant units are held to discuss management issues.
Ad hoc Collaboration Teams	
Collaboration Councils	Panels of experts meet with internal stakeholders to assess planning and implementation of change initiatives.
Virtuous Circles	Groups of citizens and external stakeholders meet to offer feedback on the consequences of change initiatives.
Collaboration Compacts	Formal agreements are established between stakeholders regarding resources.
After-action Reviews (AAR)	Internal and external stakeholders meet to evaluate specific changes.
Conflict Negotiation Experts	Conflict negotiation experts on teams can be secured internally (e.g., human resource officers) or by contract to meet with stakeholders involved in change initiatives.
All structures are supported by collaboration software, including podcasting, wikis, blogs, and listserves.	

Ad hoc collaboration teams are groups of people across the public service delivery systems who formally or informally organize as the need arises. For example, collaboration councils consist of stakeholders and other experts and advisors whose purpose is to guide and strengthen an organization's collaboration strategy, which is crucial to the effectiveness of public service networks. Virtuous circles refer to groups of citizens who voice their preferences and demands for improvements in public services to public officials on an ongoing basis, and might provide useful feedback from external stakeholders throughout the implementation of a change initiative (Brinkerhoff 1997 ref. in Mandell 1999, 51). Collaboration compacts, or formal agreements that anticipate the need for intergovernmental sharing of resources, are becoming more common in interagency emergency management. In after-action reviews (AARs), managers and staff assemble promptly after a program or project is implemented to evaluate program efforts. AARs are just as appropriate in the civil service as they are in the military, especially in public and nonprofit service environments where health and safety are paramount (Waugh 2006–07, 14).

Conflict negotiation experts are consulted when intractable issues arise during collaborative efforts. These experts can be located in program offices, human resource departments, or umbrella operations that work across a network of agencies and other cooperating organizations. In the long run, however, training permanent staff in negotiation techniques may be more efficient.

Principled negotiation is an approach to conflict resolution that emerges from dialogue about the merits of opposing stakeholder needs and desires, as opposed to (more commonplace) bargaining over positions (Fisher, Ury, and Patton 1991). Facilitated dialogue about various interests and needs can lead to recognition of mutual assets and purpose. Principled negotiation encourages thoughtful, respectful, appreciative communication. For implementing change involving more complex service delivery networks, principled negotiation has particular strategic value because the behaviors and expectations of various stakeholders will likely reflect different values and ethics.

A number of support mechanisms can be adapted to support cross-management and ad hoc team building. For example, various applications of information technology are helpful. Useful technological approaches to support collaboration include podcasting, wikis, blogs, and listserves (Leary 2006). These collaborative technologies can be used to complement (but not replace) face-to-face meetings and telephonic conferencing. Software should be simple to use, inclusive, and compatible with and adaptable to technology used by the multiple organizations in a network (Harvard 2005).

DEVELOPING TRUST AMONG STAKEHOLDERS

The development of a trusting relationship among stakeholders is clearly key to long-term communication and authentic collaboration. But how can this be accomplished? Hardin suggests that one type of trust is based on "encapsulated interests" and a second, deeper level of trust ("thick relationships") is based on constant interactions, mutual respect, and common purpose (2002).

Initially, most individual and organizational trust is based on mutual interests: We trust you to do a certain thing (e.g., to provide us with a certain service) because we believe that doing so is in your interest as well as ours. For the change leader, the challenge is to demonstrate to the various stakeholders that their individual or organizational interests are congruent with the proposed change—that both parties will "gain" from the relationship.

As individuals and organizations work together over a longer period of time, growing respect may lead them to trust each other without specific quid pro quos. During this phase of trust, individuals in public and nonprofit organizations (and the organizations themselves) work together for a common, public interest; their goals have become more aligned and there is less emphasis on what each party gains from the relationship. Thus, the long-term challenge for change leaders is to encourage individuals and organizations to work together to achieve a joint public purpose.

Leaders must craft and manage a governance structure that allows individual members to voice their interests and needs, yet minimizes the potential for outlying interests to obstruct improvement and change that will benefit the group as a whole. In other words, transformational stewards need to move forward by providing incentives to stakeholders to work together to protect the collective interest.

In essence, the public and nonprofit leader's responsibility for collaboration and change involves balancing individual and collective interests, while performing an integrating role that encapsulates the core values of public service and stewardship.

ILLUSTRATIONS FROM THE CASE STUDIES

Understanding stakeholder perceptions, recognizing the diversity of affected stakeholders, and involving key stakeholders, as well as understanding the availability of existing collaborative networks and working to create new networks, were critical aspects of change and transformation in all the cases we reviewed.

Involving Key Stakeholders

Many of the change leaders we interviewed felt that working more effectively with stakeholders could have helped them in planning and implementing their change initiatives. For example, the costs imposed on state motor vehicle agencies by the REAL ID Act have produced deeply held, intense perceptions among state-level stakeholders about the burden facing them. In fact, their anxiety and fears about costs have become tangible obstacles to implementation of the federal mandate as state politicians and associations have voiced opposition.

The act was passed in May 2005, but the rulemaking of proposed regulations was not issued until March 1, 2007, leaving only until May 2008 (later extended to December 31, 2009) for governors and their state motor vehicle administrators to implement the act's provisions. During the waiting period for the rulemaking, members of the American Association of Motor Vehicle Administrators (AAMVA) assumed a critical role in planning for REAL ID by assessing perceptions of key stakeholders in the change initiative. An AAMVA steering group conducted a national survey of members' perceptions of the potential impact as well as the estimated costs of the REAL ID Act. The survey allowed key stakeholders to "vent" and communicate their fears. Results from the AAMVA survey have informed the strategy for ongoing communication and collaboration processes among motor vehicle agencies.

In Fairfax County, the extensive engagement of external stakeholders, whose nonprofit organizations provide the majority of services and donations to clients, increased the need for coordination and networking among groups of professionals (such as social workers and communication technology specialists) with different worldviews and business orientations. Fairfax County leaders conveyed in interviews that they wished they had had more time to assess and address the perceptions of stakeholders. They realized that the change ultimately made was less extensive and effective than might have been possible had they learned about some key internal actors' perceptions at the beginning of the change effort.

Learning how key stakeholders view the impact of change can help change agents develop their "common case for change." For example, the leader of the VHA transformation authored *Journey of Change,* which became the reference manual for VHA staff (Kizer 1997). The VHA document was disseminated throughout the organization to address internal stakeholder perceptions about potential gains and losses. The involvement of key stakeholders in developing the change strategy and in formulating the "domains of value" that would drive the change initiative provided the opportunity for collaboration and involvement, and consequently reduced stakeholder fears about the proposed changes.

Diversity in group values and the professional training of key stakeholders can increase the challenges to leading change. This was true in the Coast Guard case, where a new public-private partnership required private sector engineers to communicate clearly with USCG officers. The differences in worldviews provided a particular challenge because the USCG officers and the engineers from the private sector literally did not share the same technical vocabularies.

At N Street Village, the director had to balance the needs of both internal and external stakeholders. Internal stakeholders included the clients being served, staff, regular volunteers, and the board of directors. External stakeholders included members of the Luther Place Memorial Church (NSV's founding organization) and current and potential donors and volunteers. Dealing with a "forced change" (brought on by the financial crisis), the directors initially focused on communicating to internal stakeholders the rationale for why changes were needed—and the consequences. As noted, the director reached out personally to staff and external stakeholders.

The Hillel transformation involved a complex group of actors, including the parent organization B'nai B'rith, the staff of the national organization, and the local Hillel foundations (including staff and students being served). The new national director had to develop extensive communication and collaboration strategies to achieve buy-in for the proposed changes and vision. In addition, the director believed that for long-term financial success it would be necessary to expand Hillel's support base by seeking support from Jewish philanthropists and entering into a partnership with the Council of Jewish Federations (CFC).

The challenge for the Hillel director (as for many nonprofit change leaders) was to demonstrate that Hillel's mission and goals were aligned with the priorities of the individuals and organizations that could provide financial support. To accomplish this, the Hillel director sought to position the organization as "one of the key forces for Jewish continuity and survival" (Rosen 2006).

In both the Hillel and NSV cases, new directors were hired to make changes and the fiscal problems they both inherited required an initial top-down approach to change. However, both directors exhibited a bottom-up leadership ethos through their detailed planning and implementation of the change, allowing stakeholders to play a major role in the design and implementation of the change strategy. For example, the NSV director saw the need to develop a stronger business model for the organization's operation, but was careful to incorporate the values of her stakeholders into the revised mission, vision, and community statements for the organization.

Creating Communication and Collaboration Networks

Although it is wise to use existing networks to communicate plans among stakeholders, the unexpected inevitably happens, so leaders and their organizations must be able to improvise. In the Fairfax County case, development of new collaborative networks and processes was critical to facilitate communication and to build trust as challenges arose during implementation of the change initiative. At Hillel, the director involved stakeholders through the extensive use of boards, task forces, commissions, and ad hoc groups that provided a platform for volunteer engagement, a bridge between lay leaders and rabbis, and advice and direction on implementation of the change initiative. For example, a National Committee on Quality Assurance (a diverse group of Hillel's internal stakeholders) developed an accreditation approach that addressed the need for greater quality and standardization of the services provided by local Hillel foundations.

New cross-functional teams can help create new networks for needed consultation about implementation of change initiatives. The teams should be interactive and nonhierarchical groups, with representatives from across lower levels or geographically dispersed units within the organization, and they should address change-related implementation issues pertinent to their organizational level.

For example, the AAMVA Steering Group was a team devised to strategize about implementation of the REAL ID Act. Motor vehicle administrations in the states have established "sub" change teams comprising other state-level stakeholders across the country. At N Street Village, at a full-day retreat, staff collaborated on a detailed fiscal stabilization plan and initiated a SWOT (strengths, weaknesses, opportunities, threats) analysis that allowed all staff to have input toward the new NSV vision.

Collaborative efforts should encourage an open, trusting organizational culture. Change leaders need to monitor morale and productivity consistently throughout the implementation of change initiatives. The REAL ID steering group chairperson's individual phone calls with each state MVA director and routine e-mails established a trusting relationship among AAMVA members. In Fairfax County, the DSMHS director established charrettes (planning meetings where all stakeholders are represented), "collaborameters" (for assessing the readiness of groups to collaborate on a project), and other feedback mechanisms to monitor the perceptions of critical stakeholders. At NSV, the director took a personal interest in her stakeholders, providing training funds for staff. At Hillel, the director discussed experiences with the Hillel association of rabbis. This allowed him not only to gauge the intensity of their perceptions, but also to find ways to incorporate their individual values into overall change values and direction—forging a common sense of shared interests.

Internal and external collaborative strategies, processes, and structures should reflect the type of change being implemented. For example, reorganization coupled with service integration, as in the Fairfax County and VHA cases, incorporated communication and collaborative structures and processes that addressed issues of cross-training and information system interoperability.

Direct contact and communication with all stakeholders involved in a change process are key to ensuring successful change efforts. In the analysis of the VHA transformation, a principal change leader observed that "there is no such thing as too much communication." VHA leaders recognized and communicated vulnerabilities and risks, and used many communication strategies to secure the buy-in of stakeholders by explaining the benefits of the changes for them.

Creating New Networks, Organizations, Teams, Systems, and Positions

In both VHA and Fairfax County, new organizations were created to manage the transformation. VHA leadership created 22 geographically defined Veterans Integrated

Service Networks (VISNs) to analyze potential structural shortcomings and recommend change. Effective management of these networks was key to the change design. Performance goals were developed for each VISN and each VISN director was accountable for his or her group's performance, thereby dispersing accountability throughout the organization. In Fairfax County, the DSMHS director formed a cross-management change team. Like the AAMVA steering group, Fairfax County's central change team sprouted "sub" change teams among various agencies and regional offices around the county.

In the REAL ID case, the AAMVA steering group was a nonhierarchical, geographically diverse team formed to strategize about implementation of the REAL ID Act across the national membership of AAMVA. Sub change teams have subsequently cropped up at the state level, involving motor vehicle administrations and other state-level stakeholders. As states opting to comply with the REAL ID law begin implementing it, their change teams are relying on the pre-implementation efforts of the AAMVA steering group to gather data and implementation cost estimates in anticipation of issuance of the actual regulations.

Fairfax County's deputy county executive wanted to create a "university system" for all the human services agencies. The system would develop a curriculum and deliver it to staff during the change, thereby increasing receptivity to the coordinated services approach, rather than just doing the traditional social work. While the university system project was scuttled (at least temporarily) because of budget constraints, the DSMHS leadership put all managers through the same training in "process analysis." At DSMHS, leadership used training to help shape common experience, a common language, and the same frame of reference in planning for and adjusting to the redesign.

Reinforcing that strategy, the Fairfax County's DSMHS director also created a "process manager" position to monitor and coordinate the telecommunication and data processes at the call center where client intake and referral occurs. The process manager has no supervisory responsibilities, but provides support to the social workers in the call center, which includes preparing regular reports on volume of client intake and response time, staff scheduling, and other data.

PROMOTING A SHARED VISION

When leaders communicate their vision of collaboration intentionally and consistently through various formal and informal channels of stakeholders, they promote a shared vision that generates common, public interests and a level of trust. New collaborative synergies that are critical to facilitating implementation of even massive changes in the ways of providing public services can be fostered.

Leaders cannot afford to overlook the views and motivations of their staffs—their internal stakeholders—or their contractors and other external stakeholders. In the increasingly complex networks of organizations that supply public services, leaders will pay a high price if they fail to secure stakeholder buy-in and collaboration from the outset when strategizing for change.

At the beginning of any change, leaders must diagnose the extent and nature of their stakeholders' perceptions about the change and the diversity of their viewpoints, and also assess the extent to which communication and collaboration processes already exist in the organization. The questions provided with our change model in Chapter 3 (Table 3.2) offer a starting place for that analysis. Second, change leaders must develop a strategy to address each of the internal and external stakeholders. In the short run, the goal is to develop trust based on shared interests; in the long run, it is to develop a shared perspective about the public interest so that all stakeholders are working toward a common purpose. Third, leaders must implement their strategy. This will generally require new approaches to communication and collaboration. Finally, change leaders must continually reinforce their directions, through their own actions and those of members of their organization as well as through incentives that encourage communication and collaboration.

PRACTICAL TIPS FOR THE CHANGE LEADER

- Devote adequate time up-front to listen to all relevant stakeholders to learn how they perceive the impact of a proposed change initiative on them and their responsibilities.

- Openly identify and address incentives (or disincentives) in the collaborating networks or organizations involved in the change initiative that may operate to reduce buy-in among stakeholders.

- Analyze and test the effectiveness of existing communication systems. Do horizontal and vertical communications flow quickly and without being garbled? If not, why not?

- Design new (or improved) communication mechanisms to ensure quick and clear communication with both internal and external stakeholders throughout change planning and implementation.

- Collectively develop new (or improved) mechanisms to facilitate collaboration with key stakeholders on issues throughout change planning and implementation. Take time to ensure that all stakeholders agree with the expectations about mode of input, timelines, and decision rules.

- Communicate consistently and openly with internal and external stakeholders to collectively identify and address potential obstacles as they arise and to encourage the development of shared perspectives on the public interest.

- Address what "shared accountability" means candidly and explicitly throughout the process so that expectations are clear from the beginning.

SUGGESTED READINGS ON STAKEHOLDERS

John M. Bryson, Barbara C. Crosby, and Melissa Middleton Stone, "The Design and Implementation of Cross-Sector Collaborations: Propositions from the Literature." *Public Administration Review* 66 (Special Issue): 44–55, 2006.

The authors explore how sectors in a democratic society interact, cooperate, and collaborate to deal with rapid change and important challenges. They contend that cross-sector collaboration is an important but achievable objective and can facilitate success in a complex world. This article provides a framework and propositions for cross-sector collaboration that will be useful and relevant for change leaders.

H. Brinton Milward and Keith Provan, *A Manager's Guide to Choosing and Using Collaborative Networks.* Washington, DC: IBM Center for the Business of Government, 2006.

This is a practitioner-oriented, succinct, and comprehensive report on the use and management of networks. The authors organize networks according to purpose and task, and discuss four types of public management networks: service implementation networks that actually deliver public goods and services; information diffusion networks that share data and best practices; problem-solving networks that attempt to resolve joint problems; and community capacity-building networks that build social capital. Management issues addressed include accountability, legitimacy, conflict, design, and commitment. The report also contains a good reference list.

Myrna Mandell, "Managing Interdependencies through Program Structures: A Revised Paradigm." *American Review of Public Administration* 24(1): 99–121, 1994.

Mandell provides a different perspective on networks, suggesting that they should be viewed as formal and organized structures. She terms these interdependencies "program structures" and emphasizes—through empirical examples—how better choices can be made for public programs as they seek to change.

Ann Marie Thomson and James L. Perry. "Collaboration Processes: Inside the Black Box." *Public Administration Review* 66 (Special Issue): 20–32, 2006.

Thomson and Perry discuss how to dissect the "black box" of collaboration processes. Their identification of key components of collaboration is interesting and relevant for both practitioners and academics. They also discuss the risks and benefits of collaboration in dynamic situations.

U.S. Government Accountability Office, *Results Oriented Government: Practices That Can Help Enhance and Sustain Collaboration among Federal Agencies.* Washington, DC, GAO Report 06-15, 2005.

In the face of new and growing challenges, U.S. federal agencies must find ways to collaborate to provide coordinated actions. This report evaluates three efforts that demonstrate how agencies have collaborated to achieve common objectives: Healthy People 2010, wildland fire management, and VA and DOD health resource sharing. In addition, GAO provides recommendations for the future, including specific ways to promote collaboration across agencies so they can respond better to the needs of the nation.

CHAPTER SIX

Creating a Change-Centric Culture

One of the most difficult organizational issues to address in introducing change is the culture of the organization. This chapter focuses on organizational culture and discusses some approaches to addressing problems that might arise if the culture is resistant to change.

UNDERSTANDING ORGANIZATIONAL CULTURE

Organizational culture consists of the norms and routines exhibited by people who work in organizations. Organizational norms signal to employees what they should do, how they should feel, and what they should think about organizational activities. As one of our interviewees noted, culture is "the way we do things around here." Culture often is deeply ingrained in an organization; behavioral, emotional, and psychological frameworks are adopted and perpetuated by an organization's members. Cultural considerations are critical in designing strategies and processes to mitigate risks and enhance organizational performance in the public interest.

By its nature, organizational culture perpetuates the existing way of behavior and is therefore often resistant to change. In many large public and nonprofit organizations, a bureaucratic culture, which is typically status quo-oriented, may dominate. Researchers have identified the following problems and attitudes of bureaucratic cultures:

- A tendency to avoid risk and blame
- Working to the letter of the rule, rather than for results
- Willingness to settle for less than high-quality results
- Believing that people are mere cogs in a machine, that the individual's work does not account for much
- A command-and-control philosophy where managers do the thinking
- Budgets, turf, and status viewed as more important than improving performance
- Poor customer service (e.g., citizens treated as supplicants of government services).

(Osborne and Plastrik 2000, 531)

Change efforts are most effective and easier to implement in organizations that already have a culture that welcomes change or that supports a continuous learning environment. Otherwise, a cultural shift may need to become an integral part of a long-term transformation strategy. It is the change leader's responsibility to diagnose the organization's culture to determine if it is "change-centric." If not, the leader must first work to understand the current culture and then develop a strategy to reduce resistance and increase support for change.

About the same time that Peters and Waterman identified strong corporate culture as one of the keys to excellent companies (1982), numerous books and articles began to advise leaders how to change organizational culture (e.g., Deal and Kennedy 1982). Consultants became available to assist leaders in shaping organizational culture—as if you could buy culture software "off the shelf" and simply load it into the organization. In fact, as most leaders know, organizational culture often is ingrained in an organization and is quite difficult to change.

Some aspects of organizational culture are more pertinent to change processes than others. O'Reilly and his colleagues (1991) developed a measurement instrument, the Organizational Culture Profile, that presents a set of statements regarding an organization's possible characteristics. While the profile is designed for the private sector, many of the concepts are valid for the public and nonprofit sectors. O'Reilly considers eight organizational attitudes and practices to be the most important in creating a culture supportive of change:

1. Attitude toward innovation and risk-taking
2. Attention to detail
3. Results focus or orientation
4. Aggressiveness toward the mission
5. Supportiveness of employees
6. Reward system
7. Use of collaboration and teamwork
8. Decisiveness.

(O'Reilly et al. 1991)

Most of these attributes are consistent with our concept of transformational stewardship. Thus, to the extent that leadership supports these values throughout the organization, the culture is likely to be more change-centric.

The reality is that culture change is slow, difficult work. If an organization's culture is already learning- or change-oriented, it likely has the organizational capacity necessary to support change initiatives.

DEVELOPING STRATEGIES FOR CHANGING THE CULTURE

Understanding the components of a change-centric culture may help a leader determine whether the organization has the characteristics of a change-centric organization. If you are dissatisfied with your organization's existing culture, the question is: What can you do about it? We believe that the key to culture change is changing the habits of employees in the organization by appealing to both their "hearts" and their "heads" (Kouzes and Posner 2003).

Changing Employee Habits

Implementing culture change involves changing the habits of your organization's employees; thus, once you have a strategy for culture change, you must implement mechanisms that expose employees to new ways of thinking and acting. This is not always easy. Perhaps the best possibility for individual change arises when an employee discovers a problem and experiences an "aha!" moment. Finding ways for employees to meet and interact with their "customers" or to go through the system as a customer can often have a big impact. Small group discussions about these experiences can reinforce lessons learned and create enthusiasm for new approaches to serving the customer.

During a training session for District of Columbia middle managers in their Certified Public Manager Program,[1] one assignment was for the managers to develop a program plan and budget for a D.C. agency other than their own. One group session was marked by grumbling about lack of information, failure to return phone calls, and a variety of other negative behaviors by the employees of the programs for which they were developing the information. After 10–20 minutes of discussion, one manager spoke up and said: "You know, this is how District residents must feel about all of our programs. We have met the enemy and it is us! What are we going to do about it?" That question prompted some enthusiastic dialogue about how D.C. agencies could get better at providing information and serving their customers, the people of the District of Columbia.

Strategies that have proven effective in facilitating organizational change by changing employee habits include the following:

- *Externships and Internships:* Find ways to allow your employees to work for your organization's customers to get a first-hand experience with being on the receiving end. This was very effective in the Utah Department of Administrative Services (see text box), where central finance and purchasing officers had the opportunity to work in the field and experience the demands on line officers. In the Coast Guard Deepwater case, the Coast Guard took its private sector partners to sea to show them exactly the kinds of conditions and challenges their new assets had to survive.

- *Large-scale, Real-time Strategic Planning:* Involve your employees in planning exercises that involve other stakeholders (such as a Future Search

---

[1] The Certified Public Manager (CPM) program is sponsored by universities for training managers of state and local governments throughout the nation. The George Washington University's program is designed for D.C. middle managers and others from the metropolitan D.C. area.

exercise, discussed in Chapter 7). Involving employees in strategic planning efforts was integral to the VHA and NSV transformations.

- *Redesigning Work:* Introduce new technologies, work redesigns, or process improvements that facilitate culture change, requiring employees to change their habits. Fairfax County's automated call center and VHA's computerized patient information system both required major changes in how employees acted, gradually altering the culture and facilitating the change.

- *Institutional Sponsorships:* Establish a formal process that attracts, supports, protects, and celebrates innovative behavior. Osborne and Plastrik (2000) cite a Michigan Department of Commerce "business incubator" program for civil servants to create new forms of customer service. Following the national Reinventing Government effort of the Clinton administration, many states undertook similar efforts. To succeed, such programs should have strong sponsorship from the department head (or chief elected official), allow everyone to participate, be straightforward (not bureaucratic), and reward successes (while not punishing failures).

Utah Department of Administrative Services: Making Culture Change Work
James Edwin Kee

My appointment and confirmation as the first executive director of the newly created Utah Department of Administrative Services (DAS) was the culmination of legislative action following a two-year study by the Governor's Committee on Executive Reorganization. The committee recommended combining a number of traditional state "control" agencies that had reported directly to the governor into a new, more service-oriented department. This was a major challenge, involving the integration of 10 separate divisions (formally departments) with a variety of missions and legal responsibilities.

One of my first actions was to commission a survey of Utah department and division directors to determine what they appreciated and what they disliked about how the DAS agencies were operating and interacting with their own agencies. The diagnosis, while not surprising to me, was shocking to the DAS division directors, who generally believed they were doing a good job. The other agencies, however, viewed DAS divisions more as roadblocks than aids to fulfilling their missions of service to the state's population. To begin to change the "mental models" of the division directors, my deputy, Roger Black, and I developed a strategy of looking at what made other service organizations successful and determining how those principles could be applied to the public sector.

At a directors' retreat, we discussed a new book by Peters and Waterman, *In Search of Excellence: Lessons from America's Best-Run Companies* (1982). While recognizing the obvious differences between the public and private sectors, we found a number of useful ideas, particularly the concept of being close to the customer. Who was the "customer" of DAS? Was it the other departments, the legislature, or perhaps the public in general? While a case could be made for each answer, the directors decided that DAS's customers were the other state agencies with which they interacted (Kee and Black 1985). If that was the case, they clearly were not satisfying their customers.

To try to capture a vision of better services, we initiated a department-wide contest to capture the mission of the new department in a short phrase or slogan. The winning entry (selected by a cross-section of department employees) was "partners in service." The phrase captured the department's new service orientation while stressing its partnership with line agencies. The message was that DAS was in the people service business and that DAS employees were partners in the broader missions of state departments and agencies.

Culture change is not easy and a good strategy and slogan are not sufficient. Implementation and continual reinforcement must follow. I believe that one of the most important new implementation policies was "never say no" to a request for service by another department. Even if the request seemed beyond possibility or not within legal bounds, the staff—including division directors—attempted to find a legitimate way to accommodate the other director's request. If ultimately they decided that it could not be done, it would be up to me or Black to deliver the bad news. The goal was for the DAS division directors always to be perceived as being on the side of the other department heads in serving their needs.

Other mechanisms to reinforce the culture change included the following:

- Job exchanges between DAS and line departments, to give each person a chance to walk in the other's shoes
- Decentralization of many control functions to the departments with ex post review rather than up-front approvals
- Establishment of a reengineering consulting function that would provide advice to other agencies on process improvements
- Ongoing measurement of client satisfaction and cost of service
- Creation of service awards to honor DAS personnel who had gone the extra mile to assist other agencies.

Within two years, surveys indicated that the new culture had taken hold, with a strong service orientation and increasing satisfaction among the agencies in the state.

Changing the culture of an organization requires a consistent message of leadership. First, leaders must provide a compelling vision of the new culture that captures the hearts of their employees and generates enthusiasm for change. Second, they must continually reinforce this new vision with their actions and provide a consistent rationale that makes sense to the employees—that they can understand in their heads. Table 6.1 provides some "heart" and "head" strategies for changing employee habits. While not all these suggestions will apply in every case, they can provide leaders with a foundation of approaches that have proven successful in other organizations.

Changing Employee Thinking and Attitudes

Over the long term, employee habits can be truly changed only by changing people's thinking, attitudes, values, and beliefs. Thus, while a slogan like "partners in service" (see the Utah DAS example in the text box) may capture what you want to occur, it eventually has to reflect a much deeper change.

Osborne and Plastrik (2000) cite the case of General Bill Creech of the Tactical Air Command (TAC), who wanted to create a culture based on quality, teamwork, and performance. He used an old chair of one of his field employees, which had casters missing and stuffing coming out, as a symbol of what was wrong. He took the chair to Washington, D.C., and put it in his conference room, continually pointing to it as an illustration of how TAC had neglected the people in the organization by not respecting them or giving them the quality tools they needed to become an excellent organization. The manner in which employees were treated led to their negative mindset about quality, which was reflected in poor performance and a lack of readiness of TAC assets (e.g., too many planes unable to fly). As Creech preached the value of quality, the chair became a symbol for the past and the need to change. People talked about the chair for years afterwards.

A symbol works only if there is follow-through that affects both the hearts and minds of those in the organization. Creech made investments in visible things that had an impact on individual employees as well as the organization's mission. To create ownership, for example, he tried to preserve some of the work (e.g., a new building) for the employees to finish. He even got involved in painting his own headquarters. He emphasized quality in everything—from uniforms to airplane maintenance—and rein-

TABLE 6.1:   Strategies for Changing Employee Habits

STRATEGIES FOR THE HEART	
• Inspire	• Create high expectations. • Develop a shared vision for change. • Model high ethical standards and work ethic. • Walk the talk—model the desired behavior.
• Involve	• Involve employees and other stakeholders in creating the shared vision and in planning for the change. • Create democratic structures to facilitate change.
• Empower	• Exercise power *with* (joint power) not power *over*. • Encourage individual initiative. • Make the necessary resources available. • Unleash—but harness—the change vanguard.
• Celebrate	• Share the victories. • Create small wins and momentum for change. • Recognize individual and team contributions.
• Serve	• Enable others to do their jobs. • Protect employees from outside interference. • Be patient—commit for the long haul.
STRATEGIES FOR THE HEAD	
• Provide Information	• Inform employees of the situation. • Be transparent in decision-making. • Bridge the "stovepipes," helping people reach across divisions and dividing lines.
• Clarify Purpose	• Simplify complex and ambiguous responsibilities. • Make goals and objectives clear.
• Encourage Risk-taking	• Reward innovation and risk-taking. • Drive out fear. • Celebrate success *and failures* (as good tries).
• Align Incentives	• Create a reward structure that supports the change.
• Require Accountability	• Determine what is important to measure for the change. • Measure results. • Provide timely feedback.

SOURCES: Kouzes and Posner (1995, 2003); Osborne and Plastrik (2000); Senge (1990); Senge et al. (1994).

forced the connectivity of everyone's jobs by colors. He had pilots with red scarves fly-ing airplanes with red tails that were maintained by mechanics in red caps. The result was that everyone felt empowered and connected to TAC's mission; safety and perform-ance increased dramatically.

ILLUSTRATIONS FROM THE CASE STUDIES

Our case studies demonstrate that culture change is difficult but possible. No one strat-egy is correct for each organization; rather, leaders must build the change while retain-ing those values that are important to the organization. Two common themes from our case studies are (1) breaking down "stovepipes" to create a common purpose and (2) developing mechanisms to reinforce the changes sought.

Creating Common Purpose from Multiple Stovepipes

The Fairfax County human services agencies, although previously recognized for qual-ity service, had a traditional stovepipe approach to client intake, referral, and delivery of services—each agency did its own thing, based on its own criteria and rules and reg-ulations. In seeking to implement a quicker and more coordinated approach to serving the growing population, county leaders knew they would face significant organization-al and cultural challenges. The redesign and implementation teams had to gain the sup-port of social workers within the new Department of Systems Management for Human Services (DSMHS), staff of other county agencies, and members of the community nonprofits. Not surprisingly, the organizational cultures of these entities varied widely. The cooperation of the nonprofit service providers was especially critical to creating a meaningful multiservice access point for citizens, but their organizational values, norms, and work routines were not uniform. The DSMHS change leaders understood that while the individual stovepipe values were important to each of the participants, the development of complementary, systemwide, integrated values was core to the change effort.

The DSMHS director established trust through constant and clear communica-tion and collaboration among all stakeholders, and signaled recognition that "everyone was doing the best they could" but that collectively we could do better. The director also created an environment of systems thinking and management based on continuous sharing of perspectives and deliberative, democratic decision-making. She demonstrated that it was possible to create a culture within her agency of expectations that all routines were open to rethinking. One member of the staff indicated that "there are very few sacred cows in this agency."

At the Veterans Health Administration, despite substantial agreement that things needed to change, there was widespread resistance to the change—and no overriding culture that could support the change. When the new Undersecretary of Health was hired, VHA conducted an exercise to identify core values. VHA hospitals were surveyed, and 130 of 180 responded. The results demonstrated no commonality, no central system of values; one staff member aptly noted, "If you have seen one VHA hospital, you have seen one VHA hospital." There also were very strong vested interests in the existing silo system of resource allocation, for example, to academic research and hospital laboratories. Thus, change proposals were met with great resistance and initial tension among the VHA staff.

Recognizing the lack of a consistent value system with respect to patient care, the VHA undersecretary began an inclusive process to establish core values for serving veterans. Establishing a shared mission with explicit core values was an important element in building a culture based on transparency and accountability and in shifting the focus of care from inpatient hospital care to patient-centered care.

The results of our interviews revealed a Coast Guard organizational culture committed to fulfilling its mission, regardless of the age of the assets or the difficulty of the task. Some referred to this as "a boy scout mentality," reflected in the Coast Guard motto, *semper paratus,* "always prepared." Ultimately, the Coast Guard's "can do" attitude makes personnel at all levels comfortable with taking risks, which was manifested in the notion that "we can pull off Deepwater," no matter how difficult or risky.

Some other aspects of the Coast Guard culture, however, proved to be a hindrance to the Deepwater system of systems initiative. As one person noted, "Everyone thinks in compartments—aviation, sea, and surface. Each community is great at what they do." But this silo thinking is the opposite of the system of systems concept. Many of the units are "still stuck in the old ways of the Coast Guard, especially the logistics side." In addition, many personnel may not see the full benefits of the system of systems approach, because of a narrower focus on search and rescue (SAR) missions. One interviewee called the Coast Guard culture "SAR optimized—it's what they do…at the end of the day, they save lives."

The Coast Guard culture appears to promote *individual* command initiative at the expense of more collective systems approaches to issues. That culture works well in a SAR environment, but perhaps not as well in planning for broader, systemic threats and challenges, such as those addressed by Deepwater. As Senge, a thought leader on organizational learning, notes, "'Systems thinking' is *the* key ingredient to change" (1990). A major change recognized by current Coast Guard Commandant Thad Allen is the need to relate the concept of system of systems to all phases of Coast Guard operations, not just the acquisition of new assets.

Developing Mechanisms to Reinforce Culture Change

When Mary Funke took over as director of N Street Village, she noted that the organization had a "God will provide" fiscal attitude. While understandable coming from an organization founded by a church, this attitude did not track with the necessities of planning for and implementing a complex set of services to clients. Funke realized that the organization and its staff had strong and important values, dealing with how services were provided, that needed to be preserved. At the same time, she needed to instill a new value—an expectation of excellence—that would put NSV on a sound fiscal footing while enhancing the services it provides.

Having diagnosed the problem with the help of outside auditors, the director immediately implemented a short-term fiscal stopgap and at the same time began involving the NSV staff and board in a strategic planning process. Her vision was to put in place a nonprofit "business model" and undertake a new, aggressive fundraising and grant-writing campaign. Funke's vision required that the organization rethink its most basic management and administrative processes. Execution of that vision affected all management, programmatic, and fundraising efforts, including performance; financial, administrative, and program accountability; client outcome measures; and staff, board, and volunteer communication systems.

Funke diagnosed weaknesses in the staff, but she made it clear from the start that staff members were expected to work hard, stay positive, and adopt a new results-oriented approach to their jobs. One of her key strategies was to gradually enhance the capability of NSV staff, board, and volunteers through specific development programs. For example, board members performed an extensive self-evaluation of their strengths and weaknesses in an effort to strengthen existing capabilities and determine what new skills were needed.

NSV's new culture revolves around the nonprofit business model but also encompasses a compassionate work ethic. A culture task force composed of staff and other stakeholders, led by a facilitator, produced a plan for maintaining a compassionate commitment to quality care for all clients—an important part of NSV's culture. For example, the task force formulated four diversity and four culture questions to be included in all job interviews.

Spirituality remains strong in N Street's core values, but staff now better understand their role in fundraising/external relations and truly want the organization as a whole to excel. Funke leads by example, in terms of her own spirituality and stewardship, her openness to staff suggestions and contributions, and her personal donations to NSV.

One of the keys to culture change in Fairfax County was the development of supporting change processes and measurement systems. Leadership worked with staff to test data-driven performance processes to better align service delivery with demographic changes in the county. While the traditional work environment and culture of social workers was based on face-to-face contact, leadership introduced the centralized, telephonic, automated call center idea for client intake and referral, as well as the use of performance metrics, to ensure successful change in the coordinated service planning (CSP) organization. A number of interviewees said that the metrics and data, which substantiated performance results for the call center, facilitated organizational change.

The most important process introduced in VHA, in support of the new culture, was the development of a performance measurement system. The undersecretary said that VHA had to demonstrate that it provides equal or better value (to both customers and taxpayers) than the private sector. VHA tried to benchmark its measures with comparable information collected by the private sector along a number of "domains of value," which are various measures of cost-effectiveness and customer satisfaction (see Chapter 8 for a detailed discussion of performance measurement).

All the leaders of the organizations in our case studies sought some change in the current culture of the organization. In general, their twofold strategy was to (1) engage the employees and create a new common vision to support the change, and (2) initiate processes, systems, measurements, or other mechanisms to reward and support the employees in the change effort.

IMPLICATIONS FOR CHANGE LEADERS

To begin to change their organization's culture, leaders must first *diagnose* the status of the current culture. The questions provided in the discussion of our change model in Chapter 3 provide a starting point for this evaluation. The more affirmative the responses to the questions, the higher the likelihood that the culture will serve as a strong foundation for change efforts. If there are more negative answers, efforts to make the culture more change-centric should be pursued during the change initiatives.

Second, the leader must develop a *strategy* for culture change. What is it about the current culture and its values that we want to preserve and what do we need to change? Third, leaders must *implement* the strategy for the culture change. This involves appealing to both the hearts and the heads of employees, altering their habits to support the change, and moving toward a permanent change in employees' values and beliefs.

Finally, leaders must continually *reinforce* what they want to accomplish. This means creating a reward structure and reinforcement mechanisms that support the desired behavior. In the long run, it means creating a learning organization that is comfortable with change (discussed in detail in Chapter 7). If this seems like a daunting task, it is. However, our case studies and the literature demonstrate that culture change is possible—with good leadership, employee involvement, and patience.

An old but timely story dating from the Middle Ages and the Monte Cassino monastery of St. Benedict perhaps says it best (Gordon 2006). A traveler came upon a group of three hard-at-work stonemasons and asked each in turn what he was doing.

The first said, "I am sanding down this block of marble."

The second said, "I am preparing a foundation."

The third said, "I am building a cathedral."

Culture change involves "building a cathedral." While organizations must pay attention to the details, the marble, and the foundation, leaders must inspire a shared vision of the cathedral they are building and thus appeal to both the hearts and heads of the people doing the building.

PRACTICAL TIPS FOR THE CHANGE LEADER

- Diagnose your current culture; what are its strengths and weaknesses?

- Provide employees practical illustrations of both strengths and weaknesses through data, personal testimony, anecdotes, etc.

- Involve employees in strategizing about which parts of the culture are central to the organization's mission and need to be kept, and which parts need to change.

- Involve both the hearts and heads of your employees in implementing culture change.

- Find ways for your employees to see other perspectives of their operation through internships or externships, or the redesign of work structures.

- Use your performance measurement system to reinforce the desired culture.

- Be patient; culture change is difficult and almost always takes longer than anticipated.

■ SUGGESTED READINGS ON ORGANIZATIONAL CULTURE

Edgar H. Schein, *Organizational Culture and Leadership*. San Francisco: Jossey-Bass, 2004.

Focusing on the complex realities of contemporary organizations, organizational development pioneer Edgar Schein lucidly demonstrates the crucial role leaders play in understanding and using culture to achieve their organizations' goals. Schein shows how to identify, nurture, and shape the cultures of organizations in any stage of development, and presents critical new concepts and practices in the field. Topics include team and organizational dynamics, cultural aspects of technology, and managing across diverse cultures.

Terrence E. Deal and Allan A. Kennedy, *Corporate Cultures: The Rites and Rituals of Corporate Life*. New York: Perseus Books, 1982.

This book argues for the importance of a strong corporate culture. Although the publication is a bit dated and deals predominantly with the private sector, it provides a good example of a local public organization that successfully implemented a change effort. It also gives a good explanation of a "strong" culture and provides general guidance for implementing change in an organization.

Gerald Sentell, *Creating Change-Capable Cultures*. Provo, UT: Executive Excellence Publishing, 1998.

Sentell argues that the process of evolution in an organization is much the same as evolution in organisms, except that in an organization leaders can affect the evolutionary process. Breaking through the observable behaviors and action patterns to the core of an organization's belief system is the essence of creating a change-capable culture. Sentell provides a ten-step "action plan" for creating and maintaining a change-capable culture. He begins with the organization's vision, analyzes the gaps between the vision and current reality, and examines the extent to which the current culture hinders or supports the new vision.

Timothy J. Galpin, *The Human Side of Change: A Practical Guide to Organization Redesign.* San Francisco: Jossey-Bass, 1996).

This book provides an excellent overview of the change process, including a model that outlines various phases of change, a number of useful "tool kits" for managers, and questions that need to be answered during each phase of change. Although Galpin presents only private sector illustrations, the section on culture change is valuable. He identifies ten "cultural components" that should be "screened" before changes take place: rules and policies; goals and measurement; customs and norms; training; ceremonies and events; management behaviors; rewards and recognition; communications; physical environment; and organizational structure.

Peter Senge, Art Kleiner, Charlotte Roberts, Richard Ross, George Roth, and Bryan Smith. *The Dance of Change: A Fifth Discipline Fieldbook for Mastering the Challenges of Learning Organizations.* New York: Doubleday, 1999.

This follow-up to Peter Senge's groundbreaking book, *The Fifth Discipline* (1990), identifies challenges that organizational leaders inevitably find themselves confronting, including a number of aspects of culture and an organization's "well developed immune systems, aimed at preserving the status quo." The book includes individual and team exercises, organizational learning illustrations from leaders (mostly private sector), and a great deal of practical advice on coaching and support (dealing primarily with fear and anxiety and diffusing change throughout the organization).

CHAPTER SEVEN

Building Change Implementation Mechanisms

Securing success in change initiatives—even if you have willing and cooperative stakeholders, a change-centric culture, external support, and committed leadership—requires effective use of strategies, processes, policies, structures, and appropriate organizational tools to implement and support the change efforts. Collectively, we refer to these elements as change implementation mechanisms. We have identified strategic planning and management, change structures, and organizational learning as three sets of implementation mechanisms that are critical for ensuring the success of major change and transformation initiatives.

STRATEGIC PLANNING AND MANAGEMENT

Strategic planning is designed to assist organizations in determining their future and how they will achieve it. Strategic planning processes usually involve the entire organization in an effort to define a strategy and align organizational resources to that strategy. A variety of perspectives, models, and approaches are used in strategic planning and each has its proponents (see, e.g., Banford, Duncan, and Tracy 1999; Bryson 2004; Jacobs 1994;

Weisbord and Janoff 2000). The specific process may depend on the nature of the organization and its leadership, the complexity of the organization's environment, and the nature of the change or transformation that is being considered. Strategic planning models include goals-based, issues-based, and organic (McNamara 2007).

Goals-based strategic planning, probably the most common approach, starts with a focus on the organization's vision or values and mission, goals to work toward the vision, strategies to achieve the goals, and action planning. Issues-based strategic planning often starts by examining issues facing the organization, strategies to address those issues, and action plans. Organic strategic planning might start by articulating the organization's vision and values and then developing action plans to achieve the vision while adhering to those values. According to McNamara, the "development of the strategic plan greatly helps to clarify the organization's plans and ensure that key leaders are all 'on the same script.' Far more important than the strategic plan document, is the strategic planning process itself" (2007).

Strategic management refers to processes for developing the vision, mission statement, goals and objectives, resource allocation planning, performance measurement systems, and alignment of people and resources to support a change effort.

Developing the vision is the process of achieving agreement on and commitment to the future of the organization. A good vision is an image of a "possible and desirable future state of the organization" (Bennis and Nanus 1985, 89). It is the "what"—what we hope to become or the picture of the future that we want to create. A vision statement captures that desired future.

> **Elements in a Strategic Management Process**
> - Vision
> - Mission Statement
> - Goals and Objectives
> - Resource Allocation Planning
> - Performance Measurement Systems
> - Alignment of People and Resources to the Change Effort

A mission statement affirms the direction an organization will move in toward the expressed vision. Mission statements serve as a basis for developing more detailed, measurable program goals and objectives. Keys to good mission statements are focusing on what is most important, keeping it brief, making it inspiring, and making sure it guides employees (Osborne and Plastrik 2000). Organizational mission or purpose is the "why"—why we exist. For nonprofit and public organizations, the mission is the public value we are creating.

Goals and objectives create specific targets for the organization and its employees. Goals are generally broader and longer term, whereas *objectives* are typically targets to be achieved within a specific time frame. Since the implementation of change initiatives is not always straightforward and linear, the strategic goals of change may need to be broadly stated. Instead of imposing an elaborate solution on the perceived problem, it may be better to disturb the equilibrium "in a manner that approximates the desired outcome," making midcourse corrections as necessary and allowing considerable flexibility for teams of employees to figure out the details (Pascale, Millemann, and Gioja 2000). Goals and objectives are the "how"—how the organization accomplishes its mission and vision. What specific things are we committed to do to change in the public interest?

Resource allocation planning includes budgeting, human capital planning, and the creation of flexible processes to allow resources to flow to the areas necessary to support the achievement of goals. While this planning provides the resources to the units responsible for developing and implementing change, it also may require decentralization of authority and power to those units so they can accomplish the change.

Performance measurement systems generate information about how well the organization is progressing (see Chapter 8 for an in-depth discussion).

Alignment of people and resources entails communicating clearly to all employees how their work contributes to the achievement of the organization's mission-based goals. Alignment, according to Kaplan and Norton (2005), entails a two-step process. First, leaders must communicate the strategic objectives of the change in ways that employees can readily understand. Second, leaders must ensure that individuals and teams have local objectives (with associated rewards) that contribute to the strategic objectives of the change. Alignment can be measured by whether employees are able to identify the strategic objectives of the change and whether their own objectives or performance plans are tied to those change objectives.

Many strategic planning and management processes are primarily internal. However, involving external stakeholders in the process of determining the organization's vision, mission, goals and objectives, and performance measurement systems can lead to a greater understanding of the organization in its environment and thus provide a basis for more effectively planning and implementing change.

One example of strategic involvement of stakeholders in the planning process (presented in the box below) is the successful transformation of the undergraduate business program at the George Washington University, which was led by Lois Graff, a newly appointed dean for undergraduate business programs. Keys to the success of the transformation were the heavy involvement and leadership of a wide group of stakeholders and a dean who demonstrated many of the qualities of a transformational steward, facilitating and empowering students, faculty, and alumni.

From Taps to Excellence : The GW Undergraduate Business Program
Lois Graff

At a spring retreat of department heads of the George Washington University School of Business and Public Management, I started my presentation by playing a recording of "taps." Indeed, the school's business programs, particularly the undergraduate program, faced a crisis of enrollments and quality. I had just been appointed associate dean for undergraduate programs. With a declining quality of new students and a low retention rate, I had to acknowledge that the program faced possible elimination.

The Process: A Future Search Conference

The "turning point" in transforming the undergraduate business program was a Future Search Conference, a group process for strategic planning that brought a large, diverse group of stakeholders together to share different perspectives on the challenge of transformation (Weisbord and Janoff 2000). The conference started on a Thursday afternoon and ended at noon on Saturday. Seventy administrators, faculty, staff, alumni, businesspeople, and students joined to study the GW undergraduate business program.

After a couple of exercises that focused on the past, the group created a "mind map" to explore the current trends, global and local, affecting the undergraduate business program at GW. Each participant was asked to identify those issues that seemed most critical. This process helped prioritize the trends, identifying which mattered to all stakeholders and which concerned only a particular group.

The second day ended with groups of diverse stakeholders imagining undergraduate business programs 5, 10, or 20 years in the future. Each group developed a skit in which it presented its chosen future and described the barriers that had to be overcome to get there. By the third day of the conference, the participants had learned a lot about undergraduate business programs and about each other. Now it was time to put this new learning to work.

Participants began the day by identifying the commonalities in the scenarios of the previous afternoon. Many skits portrayed experiential learning such as cases, simulations, projects, and internships, and even a student-run business. Technology and international business played critical parts in many settings. In every sketch students were guided throughout their sojourns at GW by more senior students, including graduate students, faculty, staff, alumni, and business executives—in other words, a community dedicated to helping each student develop his or her own future.

The final steps in the process were to create action plans, both short- and long-term, for the stakeholder groups and to ask individual participants to commit to actions that would further the future vision. The Future Search conference created a miracle. In its aftermath, my job changed from trying to make things happen to coordinating, facilitating, and participating in all the new activities that were inspired and led by committed stakeholders.

Many actions resulted from the conference, with impressive ideas being generated by the students themselves. These included a junior/senior retreat with outside alumni speakers from business and government; graduate student mentors; a "sophomore getaway" to discuss options for majors and careers; and an annual service day, involving more than 100 students, faculty, and staff. A core faculty committee for undergraduate programs was created to work with departments to include more experiential teaching, and faculty and alumni helped expand the internship opportunities and enhance the international programs available to students.

The Results—Achieving Excellence

In five years, we experienced a 70 percent increase in applications and a 130 point increase in the average SAT scores of admitted students. Our admit rate of 41 percent was the lowest of any undergraduate program in the university. Our first year retention rate of 94 percent and our four-year graduation rate of 75 percent were the highest rates at GW. Almost every student engaged in at least one internship during his or her sojourn at GW and many experienced two or three. The number of double majors grew, as did the number of students studying abroad. Our future was no longer in jeopardy and the sound of "taps" was no longer heard.

Throughout this effort of leading change I learned a number of lessons that served me in future educational positions:

- You have to find and inspire a committed group of stakeholders to make the change happen; you cannot do it yourself.
- A sound strategic planning exercise, such as Future Search, provides a good vehicle for energizing a wide group of stakeholders and achieving a consensus or common vision for the change.
- People in the organization (in this case students) will often perform above your expectations if you give them flexibility, freedom, and support.

CHANGE STRUCTURES

Change structures are developed to energize the people in an organization to become the "change vanguard" (Kelman 2005). For example, task forces or teams may be employed to facilitate collaboration across existing "stovepipe" or "silo" organizational structures. One current belief in management change is that change should be overseen by a "parallel organization." (Axelrod 2000)

Axelrod (2000) suggests that a change leadership team should be composed of a sponsor team, a steering team, and a design team, and should represent a large number of people from all levels and functions of the organization. Others argue that it is important to push change through existing structures (e.g., by decentralization of decision-making) and to engage all employees in change efforts as a way to foster accountability throughout the organization. There is not one perfect change structure; our cases illustrate a variety of successful approaches.

Change structures typically include the development of change teams, the creation of a change vanguard, or the appointment of other groups whose primary function is to assist in leading the change. Change structures also are supported by an institutional commitment to the training and development of change leaders, the inclusion of continuous improvement programs, and information technologies and management approaches that support a decentralized network of change agents.

ORGANIZATIONAL LEARNING

The importance of organizational learning is reflected in a comment by the former planning head for Royal Dutch Shell: "The ability to learn faster than your competitors may be the only sustainable competitive advantage" (De Geus 1988).

Why is organizational learning also important for public and nonprofit organizations? We believe that solutions to complex public problems will no longer come from hierarchical organizations and thinking in program "silos"; instead, solutions will emerge from more flexible networks of organizations that can learn from each other and pool their combined knowledge to attack a problem. Increasingly, public and nonprofit organizations also find themselves in competition for the support and trust of the public and the organization's funding sources (whether a legislative body, foundations, or private donors). Learning organizations will have a competitive edge in securing support for their missions and in finding creative solutions to today's problems.

Peter Senge, author of *The Fifth Discipline: The Art and Practice of the Learning Organization,* is considered the leading authority on organizational learning (1990). Senge suggests that the long-term goal of organizational leadership should be to create learning organizations that are comfortable with change and "where people are continually learning how to learn together" (1990, 3). To Senge, a learning organization is "an organization that is continually expanding its capacity to create its future." Leadership that adapts merely to survive will not be as successful as leadership that creates a climate of continuous, "generative learning" that enhances the organization's capacity to create. This generative learning is largely team learning "because teams, not individuals, are the fundamental learning unit in modern organizations" (10).

Senge is not too sanguine about the ability of public sector and nonprofit organizations to become learning organizations. Business, he claims, has a freedom to experiment that is lacking in the other two sectors. The private sector also has a clear "bottom line," so that experiments can be evaluated. While he undoubtedly is correct that public and nonprofit organizations pose additional challenges, his approach to creating a learning organization can certainly be applied to such organizations, which face the same kind of pressures to change and transform as business does.

Senge identifies the key elements of organizational learning as:

- Personal mastery
- Mental models
- Shared vision
- Team learning
- Systems thinking.

Personal Mastery

Organizational learning must start with individual learning. Leaders are responsible for creating an enriching, enabling environment for personal growth. Personal mastery, says Senge, goes beyond competence and skills; it means "approaching one's life as a creative work" (1990, 141). This involves continually clarifying what is important to us and seeing the gaps between the current reality and our quest for full personal development. Leaders have to be "truthful" to themselves and others, and to ask: To what extent are we currently deceiving ourselves and others? Leaders must create a personal vision, a specific destination, a picture of a desired future.

According to Senge, this is accomplished through self-reflection, integrating reason and intuition, continually seeing our connectedness to the world, compassion, and commitment to the whole (167). Many of these concepts reflect the attributes of transformational stewardship. If leaders are going to create organizations that are comfortable with change and are change-centric, they have to create organizations where it is safe for people to create their own visions, to explore the "truth," and to challenge the status quo. Leaders need to model that behavior and enable others to have the creative "space" to do so as well.

Mental Models

We carry in our minds certain images, assumptions, and views about the way the world and our organizations work. Our "mental models" determine how we make sense of the world and shape how we take action (Senge 1990). Leaders have to understand their current mental models and be open to other divergent models in exploring solutions to complex problems of change.

Multiple and divergent mental models can bring multiple perspectives to bear on issues. In contrast, entrenched mental models create powerful resistance to change initiatives. Ultimately, says Senge, leaders need to cleanse their "lens of perceptions" and shift "from mental models dominated by events to mental models that recognize longer-term patterns of change and the underlying structures producing those patterns" (204).

Shared Vision

The best shared visions lift people's aspirations; work becomes part of a larger purpose—"building the cathedral." Senge believes that "you cannot have a learning organization without a shared vision" (1990, 209). Strategic planning becomes reactive without a shared vision. But if a shared vision is imposed from above, the result is compliance (at best) or apathy, but never commitment. The only vision that motivates people is their own personal vision; thus, a shared vision must be one that encapsulates each individual's personal vision.

"Building shared vision must be seen as a central element of the daily work of leaders" (Senge 1990, 214). The best visions spread because of a reinforcing process of increasing "clarity, enthusiasm, communication and commitment. As people talk, the vision grows clearer. As it gets nearer, enthusiasm for its benefits builds" (227).

Team Learning

Team learning is "the process of aligning and developing the capacity of a team to create the results its members truly desire" (Senge 1990, 236). It is a crucial skill because almost all important decisions are now made in teams. Senge cites three critical dimensions of team learning: (1) thinking insightfully about complex issues, (2) innovative and coordinated action, and (3) networking with other teams.

Team learning requires mastery of the practices of dialogue and discussion and the avoidance of groupthink or unnecessary "trips to Abilene" (Harvey 1974)—when people go along with a seemingly prevailing view without questioning whether it really has the full support of the team. The purpose of dialogue is to go "beyond any one individual's understanding" and search for "common meaning" as the group explores complex issues from many different points of view (Senge 1990, 241).

Senge's view is very similar to Follet's concept of integration articulated nearly 100 years ago (Graham 2003). The goal of dialogue or integration is not to win or even to compromise, but rather to integrate various points of view into a common meaning that provides a new approach to the problem. In contrast, discussion is designed to reach a consensus or a solution, often requiring that someone's perspectives be sacrificed to the majority viewpoint.

Discussion is useful in explaining why an organization may need to change. Dialogue and integration go further and allow diverse voices to be involved in the change solution.

Systems Thinking

Tying the other four elements together is Senge's *fifth discipline,* systems thinking (1990; see also Ackoff 1999; Atwood, et al. 2003; Bellinger 2004; Richmond 2001). Systems thinking is a discipline for "seeing wholes," or the structures that underlie complex systems. It has its roots in feedback concepts of cybernetics and related engineering theories. By examining a problem's underlying structure, we are better able to identify the most appropriate leverage points to effect change within the system.

Before undertaking a major change or transformation, you must understand why the current system is behaving the way it is. The underlying structure provides a view of the interactions between the elements in the system that are responsible for producing the current behavior. Bellinger suggests a "Columbo," Socratic style of asking questions until you can see the "dynamic equilibrium" in existing systems (2004).

Multiple perspectives should be considered, and it may be necessary to create a simulation of the system in order to diagnose root causes of the problem and potential leverage points that can influence the system itself. Once you understand the system and the potential leverage points, it is necessary to develop/design/propose an alternative structure, ideally in conjunction with your leadership team and in consultation with important stakeholders.

Finally, the leader must develop a plan for transitioning from the current structure to the new structure and make sure that other organizational processes reinforce (rather then conflict with) the proposed new structure. Systems thinking is not easy; the value in its application is the ability of an organization's leaders to "see" in a way that can support ongoing change initiatives.

ILLUSTRATIONS FROM THE CASE STUDIES

The case studies illustrate various change implementation mechanisms. All the cases involved some efforts to undertake strategic planning and management, as well as to develop specific change implementation structures. Some went further, with leaders attempting to create a learning atmosphere for their organizations.

Strategic Planning and Management

The case studies highlight key aspects of strategic planning and management: developing a vision, crafting mission statements and setting goals, performing resource allocation planning, establishing performance measurement systems, and aligning people and resources.

Developing a Vision

In the Coast Guard's Deepwater program, the vision was a system of systems, and it conveyed the intention that the design of any single asset must take into account every other asset with which it will operate. The system of systems vision was intended to shape the acquisition strategy and to reflect the goal that Coast Guard forces be more strategically integrated to fulfill the expanding mission of the organization. Coast Guard Commandant Thad Allen articulated the need for more up-front strategic thinking: "We spend years training our workers to deal with the present; what we need is to teach them to think and act with strategic intent" (Allen 2006). While the system of systems vision has served as a good guide for the acquisition strategy, interviewees suggested that it does not yet fully resonate with all senior leadership or the rank-and-file—it has not yet become a shared vision of the USCG.

The leadership responsible for transforming VHA began by convincing agency personnel that the agency's very existence was in question. Kenneth Kizer is credited with involving a wide spectrum of VHA personnel in developing the agency's strategic direction. The articulated vision of moving from "inpatient, hospital-based to outpatient, patient-centered care" captured the need for VHA to move away from its aging hospital infrastructure toward a total networked system that provides a variety of patient care to veterans.

The widespread involvement of VHA personnel in establishing the strategy helped ensure support throughout the organization. As one interviewee noted, "If you dictate, no one will follow; with no vision, no one will follow. You need a shared vision. Listen to people; they know what is best for their community." Today, VHA employees seem to share that vision; on their website, they say: "Working together, we provide a continuum of high-quality healthcare in a convenient, responsive, caring manner—and at a reasonable cost" (VHA website 2007).

Similarly, Fairfax County leaders knew they needed to move away from an agency-centered, stovepipe approach to human services delivery. While its vision of a centralized intake and eligibility certification process was not fully realized, DSMHS was able to get buy-in for a more coordinated system that matched individuals with both public and nonprofit services. The agency's leadership persuaded nonprofit organizations to support the vision even before it was fully supported by other county agencies. By demonstrating that the new system is "helpful" to other agencies, the county vision is slowly becoming shared by important stakeholders in the change.

At N Street Village, the director needed to move from a "God will provide" funding approach to a nonprofit business model of sustained excellence, without losing the important values of compassion and concern and the vision of "serving and improving lives every day" (NSV website 2007). The NSV experience is a good illustration of balancing the broad vision with the current reality (a significant fiscal crisis) and maintaining core shared values while striving to create an organization that can sustain itself at a high level of performance.

Hillel's "bold and all-encompassing vision: for every Jewish Student to make an enduring commitment to Jewish life" is coupled with the strategic theme of "enriching lives, inspiring commitment, delivering the Jewish future" (Hillel 2006). The current vision continues the theme of Hillel's change and transformation during the late 1980s and 1990s. Richard Joel emphasized the importance of Hillel to "Jewish continuity and survival"; this key strategic vision tied the success of Hillel's services to Jewish college students with the long-term continuity of Jewish society. Thus, Joel was able to create a shared vision with philanthropists who were concerned about the broader social question, rather than the narrower mission of Hillel to serve Jewish college students.

Crafting Mission Statements and Setting Goals

Good mission statements typically bring clarity to the vision, helping everyone in an organization develop a shared understanding of the basic value they are helping create in the public interest. For example, Fairfax County DSMHS's vision/mission statement states:

> *Our system wide and regional efforts are dedicated to integrating and ensuring access to needed services, streamlining business processes, developing measurable outcomes and leveraging existing resources by engaging the community, at both County-wide and neighborhood levels, in the process to improve the quality of life for all residents.* (DSMHS 2007)

The DSMHS mission statement specifies five important values of DSHMS: integrating access, streamlining processes, measuring outcomes, engaging the community, and improving the quality of life for all residents. The mission statement easily serves as a basis for specifying more detailed goals and objectives.

Similarly, the VHA mission statement says, in part, that VHA "needs to be a comprehensive, integrated healthcare system that provides excellence in services as defined by its customers, and excellence in education and research, and needs to be an organization characterized by exceptional accountability and by being an employer of choice" (VHA 2007). Several important measurable goals are included in the statement. The last two goals speak to the importance of measuring VHA outputs and to improving the attitudes held by those working for VHA. They also go to the heart of the change: creating a value structure around the individual veteran that everyone in the organization can share.

The Deepwater program's mission statement is succinct, stressing the need for interoperability, but is not specific: "To acquire and deliver more capable, interoperable assets and systems that support Coast Guard's operational forces in executing missions effectively and efficiently." The Deepwater vision statement also specifies the goals of "increased operational readiness, enhanced mission performance and a safer working environment," which provide a basis for developing more specific goals and objectives.

Hillel's mission is to "enrich the lives of Jewish undergraduate and graduate students so that they may enrich the Jewish people and the world" (Hillel 2006). The organization's mission further articulates that Hillel professionals and lay leaders are dedicated to creating a pluralistic, welcoming, and inclusive environment for Jewish college students, where they are encouraged to grow intellectually, spiritually, and socially. Hillel strives to assist students to find a balance in being distinctively Jewish and universally human by encouraging them to pursue *tzedek* (social justice), *tikkun olam* (repairing the world), and Jewish learning, and to support Israel and the Jewish people globally. "Hillel is committed to excellence, innovation, accountability and results" (Hillel website 2007).

> N Street Village's mission statement makes it clear why the organization exists:
> *N Street Village empowers homeless and low-income women to claim their highest quality of life by offering a broad spectrum of services and advocacy in an atmosphere of dignity and respect. The Village also provides affordable rental housing for low and moderate-income individuals and families.*
> (NSV 2007)

NSV's mission statement provides a clear description of its programs and serves as a solid basis for the organization's more detailed goals and objectives, delineated in its strategic plan.

Both NSV and Hillel are good examples of successful nonprofit organizations whose strategic management processes support their change efforts. In contrast to many other public and nonprofit organizations, both provide extensive documentation on their websites on every aspect of their organization, including its mission, vision, and plans.

Resource Allocation Planning

Effective resource allocation planning enables an organization to shift resources in support of the mission. In Deepwater's case, the Coast Guard was requesting a massive infusion of new capital dollars, so a great deal of time was devoted to convincing the external stakeholders in the Office of Management and Budget and Congress of the value of the approach and the need for the additional dollars. Using a private sector partner (Integrated Coast Guard Systems, or ICGS, the Lockheed Martin/Northrop Grumman consortium) to assist in lobbying Congress, the Coast Guard was able to receive the funding needed to execute the strategy. In addition, the Coast Guard was able to expand its capability by taking advantage of the private companies' research and development and acquisition staff and resources. However, in doing so, the Coast Guard might have neglected building its own capability in the acquisition area, which was a contributing factor in the failure of the partnership and the eventual decision to take back the system integrator role.

In the VHA case, the need was to reallocate funds from a hospital-based system to a patient-centered system of care. Maintaining the status quo funding to the hospitals while building a new system of clinics would have been impossible. Part of the implementation strategy was to reduce the number of hospital beds from 53,000 to 19,000, while creating new outpatient clinics. This shift of resources created both winners and losers, and it was a necessary part of the strategy. With increased success and positive feedback, VHA was able to secure additional funding from Congress for program expansions. The number of patients served by VHA increased from 2.5 million in 1995 to more than 5.4 million in 2006.

Fairfax County was in a budget crunch at the same time that it was attempting to create a new agency to coordinate social services. As a result, part of its strategy was to pull resources from other agencies to fund DSMHS; the proposal generated expected initial opposition from other agencies. The DSMHS director's approach was to "stay out of the anxiety about the budget and worrying about what the Board [of Supervisors] would do next." Instead, she recruited people whose values she trusted and spent time building the organization's value structure. The director said, "You start with what you stand for in public service." The County Board of Supervisors couldn't have foreseen the budget crisis; there was a structural problem in the budget. In redirecting resources for the transformation, the board took some actions that greatly hindered the redesign efforts, such as targeted hiring freezes.

To support a change process, the DSMHS director pointed out, ideally you have a resource bubble—a human and funding capacity that is larger than usual. However, change initiatives are often undertaken despite budget constraints. Lacking any "excess" capacity, Fairfax County "agency directors went back to their silos." The DSMHS director basically had to take a lean, incremental approach—she could do only so much, so fast. The increased reliance on nonprofit agency involvement in the delivery of human services to county residents was an innovative way to implement a response to the demographic changes within budget constraints.

Funding has been a fundamental issue in the REAL ID implementation. The federal government's move to use states to develop identification cards that meet new requirements for interfacing with federal agencies has so far been accompanied by very little funding for state MVAs; thus, the federal requirement is being perceived as an unfunded mandate. Regulations were issued in 2008 and perhaps their issuance will be followed by additional appropriations. However, there is a short time frame for implementation given the December 2009 deadline specified in the law.

In several states where seasoned motor vehicle administrators have the political support to pre-plan and implement, they have secured initial funds to gear up for REAL ID implementation. Most state motor vehicle administrators, however, have not yet secured funding and will need to scramble to plan and implement REAL ID regulations.

In the cases of both N Street Village and Hillel, funding issues were at the heart of resource problems. Both leaders had to take immediate steps to bring the budget in

line with revenues and at the same time develop a strategy to provide for the long-term
fiscal health of the organization.

Establishing Performance Measurement Systems

Collaborative efforts to develop and use management systems as an integrated part of
the change can generate greater employee involvement during change processes.
Performance measurement systems were a big part of the implementation pictures in
five of our six case studies (see Chapter 8 for a detailed discussion).

In the Fairfax County case, for example, brainstorming teams were created to for-
mulate ideas on how to reduce call response time and increase the percentage of client
needs met. The call center social workers received training in the new performance
management system, which included such measurements as the number of minutes
clients were kept on hold and whether social workers were able to meet 80 percent of
a client's needs. After a three-month pilot test, social workers and managers were all sur-
prised that, despite their initial doubts about the measurement system's value, they were
satisfied with the new approach.

Aligning People and Resources

Organizational experts have stressed the importance of alignment to achieve broad-
based organizational change. This applies particularly to the human capital resources
necessary for the change process. "Alignment is the necessary condition…once aligned
the individual will empower the whole team" (Senge 1990).

Our case studies illustrate varying levels of success in securing alignment. In the
VHA and Coast Guard Deepwater cases, leaders laid out a strategic vision and aligned
people and resources to the mission. This was particularly successful in the VHA case,
where everyone has assumed some responsibility for the "domains of value." In the
Coast Guard, it is not clear whether leadership has yet been able to align everyone to
its system of systems vision—a major task for the new commandant.

In the Fairfax County transformation, budget cuts and initial hostility to a single
intake system required DSMHS leadership to back away from a specific, integrated
approach. Instead, the leadership worked toward a broader strategic vision that evolved
in an incremental fashion, allowing employees and partners to figure out the details. In

the case of REAL ID, the strategic direction is clear, but it remains unclear whether the federal government will take a prescriptive approach—detailing a specific technological solution—or whether it will take a performance-based approach that will give state MVAs the flexibility to devise their own solutions.

N Street Village director Funke seems to have had phenomenal success in getting her employees to "suck it up" and "do whatever had to be done." Even with initial staff layoffs, her inclusive approach to planning and staff training led to active engagement with the staff and wide participation in fundraising and other efforts, including the presentation that won NSV the *Washington Post* award for excellence.

Hillel's director also seems to have won over the organization to his basic strategy, even though the case study revealed some dissension within the organization over specific approaches. Although it has been more than a decade since Joel left for another position, Hillel's 2006 strategic plan very much reflects his imprint in terms of vision and strategy, suggesting a strong alignment with Joel's organizational direction.

Change Implementation Structures

The public organizations' transformation strategies studied here all involved creating change structures apart from the existing agency structures. In both the Coast Guard's Deepwater program and Fairfax County, new agencies were created to manage the transformation. VHA leadership created 22 geographically defined Veterans Integrated Service Networks (VISNs) to analyze potential structural shortcomings and recommend change. Effective management of these networks was key to the change design. Performance goals were developed for each VISN, with each VISN director accountable for his or her group's performance—dispersing accountability and change leadership throughout the organization.

One original idea of Verdia Haywood, Fairfax's deputy county executive, was to create a consolidated university system for all the human services agencies, which would focus on coordinated services rather than just doing the traditional social work. While this was not achieved, the DSMHS leadership put all managers through the same training in "process analysis" so they would have a common experience, common language, and the same frame of reference in planning for and adjusting to the redesign.

Another strategy employed by the Fairfax County DSMHS director was to create a "process manager" position to monitor and coordinate the telecommunication and data processes at the call center. The process manager has no supervisory responsibilities but provides support to the social workers in the call center, including preparing regular reports on the volume of client intake, response time, staff scheduling, and other data. Process management is an example of an innovative implementation structure that maximizes positive outcomes of a change initiative while providing reliable, accurate performance data to facilitate productivity and maintain an environment of continuous learning.

As states anticipate implementing the REAL ID law, a professional association, the AAMVA, has taken the lead in supporting its state motor vehicle agency constituents with data and implementation cost estimates in anticipation of the issuance of regulations. AAMVA created a steering group for dealing with the REAL ID law, and state motor vehicle administrators as well as governors' offices have formed change team structures in anticipation of actual implementation falling to each state's motor vehicle department.

For the two nonprofit organizations, directors Funke and Joel relied primarily on existing staff for the core of the change initiative, while also bringing some key persons into the organization (especially on the boards of directors) who could provide the needed skills the organization lacked for the transformation. For mid-sized organizations, which may not have the luxury of creating a separate "change organization," finding ways to use existing staff in the change effort can help with buy-in and alignment. To supplement existing staff efforts, both Funke and Joel created a variety of task forces and commissions that involved other stakeholders and expanded the base of those supporting the change initiative.

Organizational Learning

Organizational learning takes time and continuing effort. Within several of our case studies we found some evidence of organizational learning. For example, N Street Village's statement on its culture and community captures, in more visionary terms, what NSV hopes to become, both for its employees and for the individuals its programs support. This includes a commitment to respect, diversity, and personal growth—all central to organizational learning.

We also were impressed with the Fairfax County approach. County leaders and

Statement of Culture and Community

We are N Street Village.
We are a community of respect, recovery, and hope.
We create a safe and welcoming place with our words
and actions.
We expect kindness and we value honesty and diversity.

We honor and respect each other for the diversity
of our experiences
and the insight we bring to our work.
We commit ourselves to grow personally
and professionally.
We value spirituality and witness its many forms
in our daily work.

(NSV 2007)

DSMHS change leaders took a "whole systems approach" to their analysis of the problems and the changes they implemented. Further, the county seems to be placing real emphasis on personal staff development in support of the change.

IMPLICATIONS FOR CHANGE LEADERS

Successful change requires the development of structures and processes to support the change; in the long run, the leadership should strive to build change-centric organizations. This includes good strategic planning and management, the development of specific change mechanisms, and the development of organizational learning skills within the organization.

As leaders initiate major change, they must take a hard look at their existing strategies, processes, policies, and structures to see whether they support the change initiative. If agencies have continuous improvement programs or other change mechanisms in place, new changes will occur much more easily.

If the diagnosis reveals problems, the challenge is twofold. In the short run, leaders have to create a mechanism to initiate the change successfully. In the long run, leaders need to devise a strategy to make processes and structures more change-centric and to encourage their agencies to become "learning organizations."

Change leaders must find an implementation path that encompasses sound strategic management, change mechanisms, and organizational learning. While there is not one right way to approach this, the literature and case studies suggest that certain aspects are critical, including a shared vision, alignment of employees, and a specific change structure. In the long run, leaders build change capacity through creating change-centric, learning organizations.

Successful leaders know that change is seldom a one-night affair; rather, it is an ongoing relationship that seeks no less than the transformation of all parties. Achieving this requires a transformational stewardship approach, an aligning of individual visions with the organization's shared vision, and continual reinforcement through good human capital and performance management systems, appropriate training, and shared ownership of the change.

PRACTICAL TIPS FOR THE CHANGE LEADER

- Assist employees in creating their personal visions that could become part of a shared vision for change.

- Create a change vanguard, through use of existing teams or through a separate, parallel organization.

- Take time to understand the current structure and systems of your organization: What are the leverage points? What new structures are needed?

- Develop and articulate clear change goals, but be flexible about objectives and how you reach those goals.

- Ensure that change teams and structures have the resources necessary (including sufficient discretion and authority) to accomplish the change goals.

- Introduce the concept of organizational learning as part of the change strategy by developing and supporting learning teams within the organization.

- Engage and partner with other networks to fulfill your vision for the organization.

▄▄SUGGESTED READINGS ON CHANGE IMPLEMENTATION MECHANISMS

Peter Senge, *The Fifth Discipline.* New York: Doubleday, 1990.

Senge's seminal work on learning organizations includes five "disciplines": *systems thinking,* a conceptual framework that makes full patterns of organizational behavior clear; *personal mastery,* the discipline of continually clarifying and deepening our personal vision; *mental models,* "deeply ingrained assumptions, generalizations or images that influence how we understand the world and how we take action"; *building shared vision,* "when there is a genuine vision, people excel and learn because they want to"; and *team learning,* starting with "dialogue," the capacity of members of a team to suspend assumptions and enter into a genuine "thinking together."

Margaret Atwood, Mike Pedler, Sue Pritchard, and David Wilkinson, *Leading Change: A Guide to Whole Systems Working.* Bristol, UK: The Policy Press, 2003.

Arguing for a "whole systems" approach to leading change, the authors explore five "keys" to whole systems development: leadership, public learning, diversity, meeting differently, and follow-through. They contrast their approach with what they refer to as the "mad management disease" of top-down programmatic approaches to change that rely heavily on inspection and control. Their proposed alternative is a new form of organization that moves an organization away from traditional hierarchies toward communities of practice and managed networks for delivering public goods and services.

Peter Kline and Bernard Saunders, *Ten Steps to a Learning Organization,* 2nd edition. Salt Lake City: Great River Books (1993, paperback 1997).

The authors outline ten steps that an organization can take to become a learning organization: assess the learning culture; promote the positive; make the workplace safe for thinking; reward risk-taking; help people become resources for each other; put learning power to work; map out the vision; bring the vision to life; connect the systems; and get the show on the road. The book is highly theoretical, but offers some practical advice.

Steven Kelman, *Unleashing Change: A Study of Organizational Renewal in Government.* Washington, DC: Brookings Institution Press, 2005.

This is an interesting case study of major change in the public sector: the reform of the federal government's procurement function as part of the Clinton-Gore Reinventing Government movement. Kelman was director of the Office of Federal Procurement Policy at OMB from 1993 to 1997. He uses both theory and practice to relate his approach for garnering support for reform efforts. Key was identifying a "change vanguard" within the existing procurement system to lead the reform effort. Kelman's balancing of top-down and bottom-up reform initiatives led to sustained change.

CHAPTER EIGHT

Measuring Change Performance

One of the strong findings that has emerged from our case studies is the importance of using performance measurement strategically to facilitate change efforts. The use of performance data to inform management is not a new concept. The belief that concrete data on program performance, or performance metrics, should guide managers' decision-making has framed most discussions of management in public and nonprofit agencies in the United States since the early 1990s. With the increased emphasis on quantitative measurement of outcomes, "program performance" has become a higher priority. Measuring and reporting on program performance focuses the attention of public and nonprofit managers and oversight agents, as well as the general public, on what, where, and how much value programs provide to the public (see, for example, Newcomer 1997; Forsythe 2001; Hatry 1999, 2007; Newcomer et al. 2002; Poister 2003; and Newcomer 2008).

Managing performance in public and nonprofit programs has also received attention in the literature on public management reform across the globe (for example, see Kettl and Jones 2003; Hendricks 2002; and Newcomer 2008). Promoting the use of program data when making changes to improve program design and delivery or to reallocate resources is recognized as an extremely challenging but worthwhile goal (Ingraham, Joyce, and Donahue 2003). Performance management in the context of organizational change initiatives entails the coordination of program and employee performance management methods to minimize change risk and maximize change success.

USING PERFORMANCE MEASUREMENT TO FACILITATE CHANGE EFFORTS

The extent to which performance measures can be used to facilitate change efforts will reflect the extent to which performance or measurement has been institutionalized in an organization. The degree to which a performance orientation permeates the management culture is affected by many factors, including the tone set by leadership; the availability of valid, reliable, and credible performance data; and the relative freedom managers have to change things—in another words, authority to use performance data to inform managerial decision-making (Mihm 2002; Wholey 2002).

As Government Accountability Office (GAO) analysts and others have observed, there is great variability in the extent to which performance measures are used to support management decisions across federal agencies (for example, see U.S. GAO 2004a; Hatry 2006; and Newcomer 2006a). Federal agencies have complied with statutory requirements of the Government Performance and Results Act (GPRA) that they routinely measure progress toward performance goals. However, the extent to which managers use the data to make changes in processes or to reallocate resources varies widely.

Implementing change typically requires changes in both processes and resources; in addition, there must be a baseline of data on performance that are perceived to be valid and reliable and that managers can use to make more informed decisions. Deliberations about performance measures and targets, or the design of new measurement systems, are useful in increasing the frequency and the quality of collaboration among both internal and external stakeholders in change processes.

In organizations where performance measurement systems are already established and resources are already devoted to providing credible performance data in a timely fashion, performance data can be used effectively to support change efforts. Where performance measurement systems are not as institutionalized, efforts to develop useful performance measures can support change efforts in several ways. Performance data can be used to:

- *Inform* useful deliberations among key stakeholders about why and where change is needed—"to make the case for change"
- *Focus* on aspects of programmatic performance likely to be affected by change
- *Track* the effects of changes to reinforce and reward relevant stakeholders for the achievement of desired outcomes of change efforts.

Experience with performance measurement at all levels of government and in the nonprofit sector provides important lessons pertinent to change management. Specifically, for performance measurement efforts to add value in change efforts, change agents need to deliberate carefully about the *focus, process,* and *use* of performance measurement.

Focus

Concrete measures of performance can provide needed focus in change efforts. However, measurement of programmatic performance is imperfect and controversial, as it may unintentionally reduce managers' attention in areas where effort is needed but measurement is not made. For example, in an educational setting, teachers may "teach to the test" to meet measurement goals, diverting attention from other important educational objectives. Ideally, performance measures should be aligned with the missions, goals, and objectives of change projects. A focus on outcomes—the desired changes in behavior or conditions that are expected to result from the change project—is likely to direct stakeholder attention to the achievement of critical benchmarks. Stakeholders involved in change initiatives must believe that the performance measures used are credible, however.

The credibility of performance measures can be bolstered by ensuring that the measures are perceived as meaningful and useful. Table 8.1 provides a set of criteria helpful in assessing measures used in public and nonprofit organizations.

Process

Open collaboration regarding the selection and interpretation of measures is essential in performance measurement processes. All stakeholders who are affected by the use of

TABLE 8.1:   Criteria for Evaluating Performance Measures

- **Relevance**—measures are clearly linked to agency or program mission.

- **Timeliness**—measures are available when decisions must be made.

- **Vulnerability**—measures provide a fair assessment of the efforts of the organization and are not likely to be affected so much by external factors (beyond the control of the organization) that they are rendered useless.

- **Legitimacy**—internal and external stakeholders will find the measures reasonable.

- **Understandability**—internal and external stakeholders will understand exactly what is being measured.

- **Reliability**—consistent measurement procedures are used to collect data across time and across sites.

- **Comparability**—when feasible, measures are similar to measures used elsewhere.

the measures should have input. Identifying legitimate measures early to facilitate communication among key stakeholders can foster collaboration; conversely, the lack of open, transparent processes can engender extremely contentious relationships.

Collecting and reporting performance data may evoke uncertainty for internal stakeholders regarding a number of basic questions, such as:

- Why should we measure performance?

- What should we measure?

- How frequently should we measure?

- Who will collect and analyze the data?

- How should we measure performance?

Table 8.2 presents issues that leaders must address when they design, implement, and use performance measurement systems.

Controversy typically surrounds the use of data documenting programmatic accomplishments. From the perspective of social service providers, for example, when grant requirements specify that grantees must report on who they serve and how much improvement their services made, the message is that accountability is the objective of the measurement. Simply collecting data raises the risk that evidence of "effectiveness"

TABLE 8.2: Performance Measurement Issues

WHY

1. **What is the purpose of collecting the data?**

Make funding decisions ← → Improve performance

2. **Who will see the data?**

External funders ← → Internal staff

3. **How might the data be used?**

Empower program detractors ← → Empower program managers

WHAT

4. **What will be measured?**

Controllable outputs ← → Longer-term outcomes

5. **How many things will be measured?**

Insufficient/incomplete data ← → Information overload

6. **How clear and testable is the theory of change underlying the program?**

Complex system ← → Clear pathways

WHEN

7. **How frequently will performance be measured?**

Weekly ← → Annually

8. **What resources will be used for measurement?**

Operating program resources ← → Set-asides

WHO

9. **Who is responsible for data collection?**

External contractors ← → Program staff

10. **Who will bear the burden of data collection?**

External contractors ← → Frontline staff

11. **Who will participate in selecting measures?**

Only top-level leadership ← → Stakeholders throughout the organization

HOW

12. **How will participants' views on what to measure and what the measures mean be taken into account?**

Leaders decide ← → Democratic (all stakeholders' views deemed equal)

13. **How consistent are internal incentives supporting evaluation?**

Very little/inconsistent support ← → Consistent leadership support

14. **To what extent will the validity and reliability of the data be ensured?**

Not at all ← → On a regular basis

15. **How conducive is the organizational culture to evaluation?**

Clarity in internal communication

Low ← ——— Workforce Stability ——— → High

Level of comfort with quantitative analyses

Receptivity to organizational learning

Support for risk-taking

may not surface. Performance data provide the ammunition that can be used by program detractors as well as supporters—and this is not lost on program managers.

Even more important is the question: What are the most appropriate measures? In some arenas, quantitative evidence abounds. For example, in health services, data on immunization, morbidity, and mortality rates have been available and used for years. In other service arenas, such as shelters for homeless women and families and community revitalization initiatives, there are not always professionally recognized standard measures. When programs have clearly specified, understood, and validated theories of change, agreement on appropriate measures for outputs and outcomes is more likely than in the case of newer, less tested interventions.

Outputs are more likely to provide workload reporting (e.g., number of clients trained) than to capture the achievement of service goals. It is generally more feasible for providers to tabulate services delivered than to assess results. Workload is controllable; clients typically are not. Tracking the results of services also entails follow-up, which creates more work and requires more resources for providers.

Agencies collecting performance data face the common dilemma of determining how many things to measure. Again, it depends on the type of service provided and how far out on the outcome chain one goes, but there is rarely an obvious, "correct" set of measures. Experience with the U.S. federal and local governments has shown that service providers typically measure too many things, and the information overload can be distracting rather than enlightening.

Who bears the burden of data collection? Both the timing and frequency of data collection activities clearly contribute to the perceptions and real monetary burden imposed by measurement. Following up with clients is time-consuming, as noted. And the degree to which the feasible measurement of outcomes is in sync with reporting requirements can produce more headaches for providers. For example, when grant-reporting requirements specify submission of measures on an annual basis, and program theory indicates a longer trajectory for demonstrating effectiveness, providers face some tough choices.

The manner in which regular performance assessment processes are institutionalized in agencies can also pose dilemmas for program managers. Routine, virtually seamless systems for serving and tracking clients certainly make performance assessment less disruptive for program management. However, the design and maintenance of systems impose requirements and require staff investment of both time and commitment.

In the end, it is leadership support and organizational culture that will significantly affect stakeholders' receptivity to performance measurement. Consistent leadership support throughout organizations has been repeatedly identified as a critical ingredient for useful and smooth performance measurement (Newcomer et al. 2002; Poister 2003).

Aspects of organizational culture that are correlated with receptivity to organizational learning, such as clarity in communication and support for risk-taking, certainly are likely to increase the ease of measuring performance. Organizations in which the professional backgrounds of the staff make them comfortable with research and quantitative analyses are more receptive to performance assessment. Agencies with lower turnover also are likely to provide more stability for supporting assessment systems. Regardless, however, the tone set by agency leadership and reinforced in the culture will shape the way performance measurement plays out.

Linkages between performance measurement and other management processes, such as strategic planning and budgeting, can help managers see the importance of supporting measurement efforts. Nonetheless, selecting measures that will be used in holding stakeholders accountable for performance requires the candid and prolonged engagement of all affected.

Use

Collaborative development of relevant measures does not ensure that they will be used. Consistent leadership is needed to institutionalize the use of performance measures.

A climate supportive of performance measurement within the network of stakeholders involved in the change effort may be hard to cultivate but can reap benefits. Experience has shown that it is important to emphasize positive, not punitive, uses of the performance data to get buy-in, and to avoid setting targets until the organization has some experience with performance measurement and reporting. Using performance measures to "hold accountable" various stakeholders for change-related outcomes is likely to work only when adequate time is devoted to truly collaborative system-building efforts. Table 8.3 lists some of the many ways that performance measures can be used.

TABLE 8.3:   Potential Uses for Performance Measures

INTERNAL USES

1. Informing stakeholders about levels of performance
2. Identifying where improvement is needed
3. Seeking explanations for lagging progress
4. Identifying trends and making useful comparisons in performance across:
   - Time
   - Sites
   - Subgroups of program recipients (when appropriate)
5. Helping motivate stakeholders
6. Supporting resource allocation decision-making
7. Providing data available for use in in-depth studies and program evaluation

EXTERNAL USES

1. Sharing results with funders and citizens
2. Providing data for showcasing successes
3. Demonstrating successful practices

ILLUSTRATIONS FROM THE CASE STUDIES

Our six case studies offer important lessons about how performance measurement can support change management efforts, particularly in terms of focus, process, and use.

Focus

During the implementation phase of Deepwater, the Coast Guard program executive officer (PEO) prioritized development of a robust system of metrics to measure program success. In the VHA case, performance metrics were newly structured to encourage collaboration and innovation. In the Fairfax County case, a highly process-oriented leader and cadre of social workers and administrative professionals designed a use-oriented, numbers-driven performance system.

       One of the Coast Guard PEO's priorities during the implementation phase of Deepwater was to develop a system of metrics to focus efforts and monitor progress.

The resulting system for Deepwater, a "balanced-scorecard approach," was designed by contractor SAS to integrate various databases and focus on "real-time intelligence." The approach recently won the software industry's Enterprise Intelligence Award as a "best practice."

Some interviewees in our study felt that the information Deepwater's measurement system provides has been underutilized. In response, the current PEO has made better use of the information a priority. He wants to make the data more user-friendly and ensure the proper people are seeing the data they need to make better decisions.

To some, the measures used to monitor contracts with private sector partners (ICGS) were "soft and squishy," in part because the Coast Guard never developed "good technical performance measures for each asset; [nor was there] baseline documentation on cost estimates." The newer performance metrics for Deepwater may be useful but were not "written into the contract" with the private partner. The challenge was to get both the contractor and the Coast Guard to agree on the same rules and to use the same information. However, in 2007, the Coast Guard dissolved the partnership and took over the systems integrator function. This was in part because of pressure from Congress, but even more so because of cost overruns and failure of the new assets to meet performance targets. Perhaps this situation could have been avoided if better measures and benchmarks had been in place earlier.

To maintain a "shared environment" and collaboration of efforts, VHA launched a performance metrics program. This program measured six different "domains of value": quality of care, access to service, satisfaction (initially with patient care and later expanded to include employee satisfaction), cost-effectiveness, restoration of patient functional status, and community health. Each of the 22 directors in the Veterans Integrated Service Network (VISN) was accountable for his or her specific group's performance in each domain. This accountability was dispersed throughout the entire organization, from the top directors to the front-line workers. Members of the different VISNs had to work together to maintain success on these performance measures.

As a result of using performance metrics, employee motivation to perform good work improved. Meeting and exceeding the standard measures for performance became the norm. Directors and employees were held accountable for actions and work. Both positive and negative performance were exposed, both within the system and to the numerous stakeholders.

In the Hillel transformation, the new national leader introduced performance measurement and evaluation in the form of accreditation, a system he borrowed from his experience in college administration. The concept of accreditation helped the organization focus on the quality of the programming offered to college students. The entire process included local feedback and was implemented using a bottom-up approach (largely because the local Hillel directors felt the system threatened their job security). A retreat organized by a National Committee on Quality Assurance (composed of a diverse mixture of Hillel's internal stakeholders) resulted in the Everett Pilot Program for Excellence, which featured a phased accreditation process. Local Hillels engaged in their own self-study in the first stage and then worked with an outside Hillel team who led a site visit and delivered an action plan for the local organization in subsequent phases.

Process

The identification of credible and useful performance measures should be viewed as an inclusive and iterative process. Selection of outcome measures is an especially arduous task when multiple actors are involved in service delivery, as with the multiple agencies involved in social services in Fairfax County, or services are contracted out. Time and patience are needed to ensure that the diverse stakeholders accept and value measurement and reporting.

Performance metrics have been used in a collaborative process to support continuous and successful change in the coordinated service planning organization in Fairfax County. Measures were developed to assess the effectiveness and efficiency of different types of intake and phone processes. Weekly performance metrics reports are shared with the staff so they are aware of how they and the organization are performing, and they are directly, constantly engaged in improving service delivery.

Interviewees reported that it has been much easier to get buy-in from stakeholders when metrics and data substantiate the results and value of organizational change. While social services are sometimes thought to be nonquantifiable and social workers consider their people-focused work to be more qualitatively than quantitatively oriented, the call center staff took great pride in being "data driven" and believed that this approach led to better customer service. Transparency in both the development and sharing of metrics became an important means for reinforcing the change effort. In addition, to link employees across functions, the division employed a "common language" to avoid confusion on terminology.

At N Street Village, the director identified performance management as a core element of her goal to develop a successful "business" model for the nonprofit organization. The director assisted the staff through the learning and change processes. Specific objectives of performance management included updating job descriptions, staff members developing their own performance objectives to serve as the basis for their performance evaluations, and identifying staff training needs.

The NSV director's strategy involved setting a firm "expectation of excellence," and while staff members were initially wary of the new approach, they have since succeeded by "raising the bar on themselves." The director also used the organization's budget process to reinforce performance goals. For example, in the 2004/5 strategic plan, Objective 4 of Goal 2 (budget), states: "On a monthly basis, each unit manager will work with the Volunteer Coordinator to ensure the use of in-kind donations and *volunteers* to include a long list of items, including but not limited to: twenty-five percent of all food usage, seventy-five percent breakfast and lunch by volunteers, full evening and overnight coverage of residential programs by volunteers, and all clothing and bedding needs."

Use

Performance measures may make the implications of change personal, raising the stakes when managers see their own fortunes tied to the change. At VHA, the VISN structure mandated that all the parts of the whole be responsible for and to each other, share in the same risks and rewards, and use their resources in a collaborative effort to reach the same goals. One way VHA practices this type of "shared environment" is by holding medical professionals and administrators directly responsible for patient care. For example, the medical staff monitored how many heart attack patients received recommended beta-blockers and aspirin, and the patients' outcomes were then linked to the medical staff's and administrators' performance reviews.

Using programmatic performance measures to assess individuals or sets of stakeholders in a network requires credible and reliable data. When employee or stakeholder contributions to performance are clear, and performance is regularly assessed and discussed, organizational performance is strengthened. When leaders collaborate vertically with their managers and staff, and leaders and stakeholders work to create a performance-driven culture that is connected horizontally by common performance objectives, it is easier to implement the use of change-related metrics to inform decision-making.

Individual performance appraisals for employees involved in change initiatives and organizational performance management plans should include metrics that reflect the goals and implementation steps of change initiatives. As the vision or objectives in the change process evolve, the performance metrics should be adjusted.

IMPLICATIONS FOR CHANGE LEADERS

Performance measurement processes can be useful in facilitating the implementation of change initiatives. However, determining what to measure, how to measure, and how to interpret and use the measures to inform decision-making all require extensive and candid collaboration among stakeholders. The more diverse the stakeholders are in terms of their organizational values and objectives, the more challenging it will be to secure buy-in for the development and use of performance measures. Securing adequate resources to ensure that measurement systems collect and distribute the data in a timely and user-friendly fashion presents yet another challenge for leaders.

The first responsibility of a change leader is to *diagnose* the current state of the organization's performance management system. Is the current system adequate and can it help the organization focus on and track the important areas related to the change? The questions asked as part of our model for leading change in the public interest (in Chapter 3, Table 3.7) provide change leaders with a starting point for that diagnosis.

The second responsibility is to develop a *strategy* for designing the process to determine the best measures for the change. The involvement of key stakeholders will help ensure buy-in for the measures. *Implementation* requires the availability of sufficient technical expertise to transform the measurement strategy into data collection.

Finally, performance measurement systems are not effective unless they are used consistently throughout the change process. Change leaders must *reinforce* the measures through consistent usage and constant discussion of their importance.

The rhetoric about "results-based management" typically outpaces the reality.

Effective use of performance measures to guide decisions can become illusory for many reasons. Expectations that all stakeholders will want to systematically track performance in change initiatives, and use the performance data to ensure accountability on an individual, team, or organizational basis, may be unrealistic. Leaders should set politically and financially feasible objectives about the utility of performance measurement in a specific change scenario. Objectives should be tempered by the intra- and interorganizational context in which measures may be helpful.

Illustrations from our case studies, as well as other governmental success stories, suggest that performance measures are extremely helpful in focusing even diverse sets of stakeholders on the achievement of targets. Leaders should be careful not to underestimate the time and effort required to bring everyone on board, however (Hatry 2006; Metzenbaum 2006).

PRACTICAL TIPS FOR THE CHANGE LEADER

- Take stock of the status of performance measurement systems in use throughout the involved organizations: Do they exist? Do managers believe the data they provide are valid and credible? How are the data used (or misused)?

- Envision how performance measures might be useful to track the progress of proposed change initiatives.

- Involve all relevant stakeholders in identifying useful measures to track the progress of proposed change initiatives and in the design (or modification) of measurement systems.

- Communicate often with managers and staff about how and why performance measurement will be useful to accomplish effective change.

- Ensure that adequate resources and time are available to build or modify performance measurement systems

- Model the "use" of performance measures to inform decision-making frequently and visibly to other stakeholders.

- Be patient—identifying useful measures, building useful measurement systems, and getting managers accustomed to using performance measures take time!

◼ SUGGESTED READINGS ON PERFORMANCE MEASUREMENT

David G. Frederickson and H. George Frederickson, *Measuring the Performance of the Hollow State.* Washington DC: Georgetown University Press, 2006.

The authors review the influence of performance measurement in the federal government. They undertake a clear analysis of five U.S. agencies, including the Food and Drug Administration and the Department of Health and Human Services, to demonstrate how performance measurement works when applied to third-party government.

Harry Hatry, *Performance Measurement: Getting Results.* Washington, DC: The Urban Institute, 2006.

This book is appropriate for beginners as well as practitioners in performance measurement. Hatry clearly explains performance indicators and benchmarks, and evaluates different uses for performance measurement. He also thoroughly considers new relevant issues, such as the increased availability of technology, as well as issues of quality.

Theodore H. Poister, *Measuring Performance in Public and Nonprofit Organizations.* San Francisco: Jossey-Bass, 2003.

This academic book on performance management design and implementation is an intermediate text on how to create a performance management system. Poister provides both public and nonprofit leaders with tools for devising accurate benchmarks and indicators that can be used to enhance program performance.

CHAPTER NINE

Leadership in Emergency Management Networks

Ron Carlee

9/11. Katrina. Virginia Tech. These few words evoke indelible images and emotions. When we catch our breath, we ask: What could have prevented these tragedies? What could have improved the response? What have we learned to make us safer in the future?

The "what" quickly becomes "who" because, ultimately, in all matters of human endeavor, someone or some group of people has to take responsibility. In events involving multiple actors, finger-pointing is easier because no single person is in charge, but this merely circumvents the issue. Leaders—especially transformational leaders—have to be willing to accept responsibility even when they lack hierarchical power. This chapter explores why and how leaders can facilitate change in multi-organizational networks, using emergency management as an illustration of the complexity of leading such networks.

Ron Carlee is county manager of Arlington County, Virginia, and adjunct faculty at George Washington University.

RESPONSE IN A MULTI-ORGANIZATIONAL ENVIRONMENT

It should not be surprising that no single person or organization is in charge in a major emergency or disaster. In the U.S. system of government, power is diffused among the federal government, the 50 states, the three branches of government within the federal and state structures, elected state department directors, and appointed boards, authorities, and commissions—and across a dizzying array of over 80,000 overlapping local governments that include counties, cities, towns, special districts, and more boards, more authorities, and more commissions.

No one is in charge because we, with great intent, do not want anyone to be in charge. In the United States, we have historically been afraid that a strong central government with consolidated power will threaten our core value of personal liberty. Our resistance to consolidated power was incorporated into the Constitution and expounded upon by our Founders in *The Federalist*. Debates over the Patriot Act during the post-9/11 environment illustrate the enduring nature of the concern.

In a time of catastrophe, however, we expect this complex network of multiple organizations, within and among the different layers of U.S. governments and private interests, to suddenly come together in a seamless network to protect and rescue us. If all falls apart, as in the case of New Orleans, we expect "the government" to put it back together again (see, e.g., Keifer and Montjoy 2006). In such a network, "with no single authority, everyone is somewhat in charge, and thus everyone is somewhat responsible; all collaborative players appear to be accountable, but none is absolutely accountable" (Agranoff and McGuire 2003, 189).

As we move toward the end of the first decade in the 21st century, significant events challenge us to initiate changes to improve this system of interrelationships:

- 9/11 revealed a failure among federal intelligence agencies (Federal Bureau of Investigation and Central Intelligence Agency) to identify and act on information that might have prevented the attacks and should have been communicated to other agencies: federal (Federal Aviation Administration), state (Department of Motor Vehicles), and local (police). In the New York City response, lack of information integration between the police and fire departments contributed to devastation of the latter.

- New Orleans demonstrated that there is no effective back-up plan to the total decimation of a local government.

- Virginia Tech poignantly illuminated the complex network on which we rely daily to connect law enforcement, courts, mental health agencies, schools, employers, and families to identify and treat people with serious mental illness.

When things go bad, we want change and better coordination among governments—without trampling on our liberties. Despite a dispersed system of government with diffused power, the effective use of networks can accomplish transformational change.

NETWORKS AND ORGANIZATIONAL CHANGE

Other chapters in this book have addressed the difficulty of organizational change. The authors provide a diagnostic model in Chapter 3 that suggests that major organizational change is a function of four issues that must be addressed through diagnosis, strategy, implementation, and reinforcement: change complexity, stakeholders, sociopolitical environment, and organizational capacity. When change involves more than one organization, the effort can be daunting. So how do we create effective multi-agency networks to tackle society's greatest challenges, especially in the field of emergency management?

Change Complexity

The challenges of emergency management illustrate well the complex and dispersed system of government networks. Within the federal government, players include *at least* the Department of Homeland Security, Justice Department (especially the FBI), CIA, Department of Health and Human Services, Environmental Protection Agency, and Department of Defense. State agencies include emergency management offices, police, and health departments. At the local level, first responder agencies include 911 call centers, police, fire, emergency medical services, public health, transportation, mental health, and public works. Together all these agencies form a vertical structure of networks among the levels of government.

An additional layer of horizontal relationships occurs nationally through the state-to-state Emergency Management Assistance Compact (EMAC) and through local government-to-government mutual aid arrangements. Further complicating the network are additional horizontal relationships at the local level with the for-profit sector (hospitals, physicians, pharmacies, hotels, suppliers, and contractors), the nonprofit sector (the Red Cross, Salvation Army, and numerous others), faith-based organizations, and civic groups.

Consider the array of governments in the Washington, D.C., National Capital Region (NCR):

- Federal government
- District of Columbia
- Two states: Maryland and Virginia
- Two Maryland counties: Montgomery (with three overlapping cities) and Prince George's (with three overlapping cities)
- Four Virginia counties: Arlington, Fairfax (which overlaps with two towns), Loudoun (with two towns), and Prince William (with one town)
- Five independent Virginia cities: Alexandria, Falls Church, Fairfax City, Manassas, and Manassas Park.

Two Guys with a Gun
The Police Response to the 2002 Sniper Attacks

The most severe test of police coordination came in the sniper incident in 2002 when two deranged men with a rifle and a beat-up car terrorized the entire National Capital Region. Schools began playing their outside sports on military bases and individuals were gripped with fear whenever they went shopping or bought gas. The multi-jurisdictional attacks involved at least nine primary local police agencies, two state police agencies, and four federal police agencies. The investigation was a classic ad hoc network that coordinated intelligence and ultimately prosecution of the perpetrators while preserving the independence of the network members (see Horwitz and Ruane 2003).

The region also has multiple water, sewer, highway, park, and airport authorities. Some of the chief executives are elected, others appointed. Likewise, in law enforcement there are appointed police chiefs and elected sheriffs; fire departments are professional, volunteer, or some combination. The Non-Profit Roundtable of Greater Washington has over 150 members. The Greater Washington Board of Trade has 1,100 members. Across the sectors, more than 30 different law enforcement agencies operate in the National Capital Region.

Effective response to a regional emergency would require the collaboration of most if not all of these entities. Yet, the complexity of public and private agencies with responsibilities for emergency management in the Washington, D.C., area is hardly extraordinary. While Washington is unique as the seat of the federal government, equal or greater complexity can be found in all metropolitan areas, especially New York, Los Angeles, and Chicago. Medium and smaller areas can be similarly complex (note New Orleans), but with fewer overall assets from which to draw.

Bringing all these diverse entities together into an effective network was the purpose of the federal government's National Response Plan. The preface of the initial version of the plan explained its purpose:

> ...the President directed the development of a new National Response Plan (NRP) to align Federal coordination structures, capabilities, and resources into a unified, all discipline, and all-hazards approach to domestic incident management. This approach is unique and far reaching in that it, for the first time, eliminates critical seams and ties together a complete spectrum of incident management activities....The end result is vastly improved coordination among Federal, State, local, and tribal organizations to help save lives and protect America's communities by increasing the speed, effectiveness, and efficiency of incident management.

(U.S. Department of Homeland Security 2004)

Whether idealistic or naive, the preface suggests that the very existence of such a plan will eliminate "critical seams" and "vastly improve coordination." Katrina demonstrated that more than a plan is necessary. The task of dealing with a major catastrophe is far more complicated.

Apart from the complexity of integrating governments and governmental agencies both horizontally and vertically, the work of emergency management itself is dauntingly complex. The best illustration comes from the Department of Homeland Security's 2006 efforts to create a Target Capabilities List (TCL) to describe and set targets for all the capabilities required to achieve homeland security. One version of the TCL was a 600+ page tome, which was later reduced to *only* 481 pages. The work identified 15 national planning scenarios and defined 36 "capabilities" necessary to prevent, protect, respond to, and recover from incidents of "national significance." To achieve these capabilities, DHS developed 1,600 tasks (its Universal Task List—UTL) across all levels of government and disciplines (see Figure 9.1).

The UTLs are aligned with performance measures and performance objectives. The mere compilation of the document was a major feat, but it was ultimately so detailed as to be incomprehensible or impractical, even to emergency management practitioners.[1]

FIGURE 9.1: DHS Universal Task List

SCENARIOS	TASKS	CAPABILITIES
The National Planning Scenarios highlight the scope, magnitude, and complexity of plausible catastrophic terrorist attacks, major disasters, and other emergencies.	The Universal Task List (UTL) provides a menu of tasks from all sources that may be performed in major events such as those illustrated by the National Planning Scenarios.	The Target Capabilities List (TCL) provides guidance on specific capabilities and levels of capability that federal, state, local, and tribal entities will be expected to develop and maintain.

- 15 scenarios
- Chemical, biological, radiological, nuclear, explosive, food and agricultural, and cyber terrorism
- Natural disasters
- Pandemic/influenza

- Prevention
- Protection
- Response
- Recovery

- 36 capability summaries
- Includes capability description, outcome, relationship to national response plan ESF/annex, groups of tasks performed with the capability, associated critical tasks, performance measures and objectives, capability elements, linked capabilities, and references
- Tailored to geographic regions, performance measures and objectives, and capability classes

SOURCE: Department of Homeland Security website: http://www.ojp.usdoj.gov/odp/assessments/hspd8.htm (accessed March 13, 2008).

---

[1] At the time that this chapter was written, a hot debate was raging between the Department of Homeland Security and state and local governments over the replacement of the National Response Plan with a newly conceived "National Framework" that would be supplemented by an extensive web-based resource guide. There was general consensus that the original NRP was too complex, but no consensus on what should replace it.

Stakeholders

In addition to the large number of public agencies involved with emergency management (essentially, internal stakeholders in a networked environment), numerous external stakeholders are involved in responding to emergencies; these include government contractors and the array of nonprofit and for-profit organizations. The ultimate stakeholders are the people who live, work, or visit in a community—the people the networks are supposed to serve and protect.

Sociopolitical Environment

The overall sociopolitical environment has a profound influence in a multi-organizational network. Most often it is the external environment that motivates leaders across organizations to come together to effect change—unfortunately, often only after something bad has happened. The motivation may be a purely political desire to give an appearance of action to get past the memory of public opinion. When elected officials are members of a network's leadership, media relations and election impacts will never be far from the surface. If elected leaders in the network are from opposing parties or political positions, the environment will be even more fertile for posturing than for meaningful change.

The vertical nature of the governmental system also creates an important environmental dynamic as both the federal and state governments impose a variety of mandates on local governments, usually in the form of requirements linked to funding. In the post-9/11 environment, these mandates have been marked by rules that change annually and are imposed with tight deadlines and evolving evaluation criteria. A good illustration was the intense criticism of DHS regarding its 2006 grant awards for the Urban Area Security Initiative (Lipton 2006; U.S. GAO 2007).

Organizational Capacity

Organizational capacity is crucial for making changes, and here's the rub: In a network, change is not dependent on the capability of one organization, but on the capability of multiple organizations, each with the potential of being *incapable,* of becoming the weakest link in the system. Creating further instability is the dynamic nature of organizations. People come and go, especially political leadership. From 2001 to 2007, D.C.,

Maryland, Virginia, Montgomery County, Prince George's County, and Alexandria all changed executive administrations once. The Office for the National Capital Region within the U.S. Department of Homeland Security was on its third leader and its third different reporting structure within DHS.

Managing diversity of capability in a change effort is especially problematic. Assessing the ready state of a single organization is simple by comparison—a leader can defer the change effort and focus on developing the organization's readiness. In a network, a simultaneous state of readiness of all the members may never be achieved.

WHAT DOESN'T WORK

Is change possible given the complexity of the homeland security environment, the large number of stakeholders, and the disparate and changing capabilities of the different organizations in a network? The short answer is yes. Change is possible, but there is no single formula to make it happen. Research on interorganizational relations and networks reveals a host of contingent variables that help guide efforts. Two panacea strategies that we know do not work are mandates and reorganization.

Cries for change of a significant nature are typical when something goes really badly—usually involving a lot of people dying, as occurred on 9/11, with Katrina, and at Virginia Tech. Rather than admitting the complexity and fragility of life and the cumulative consequences of many actions and policies over time, elected leaders frequently seem compelled to act immediately, usually with an expert study and some kind of dramatic action to convince constituents that the specific tragedy will never happen again. Often that dramatic action is some type of legislative mandate.

REAL ID is a major, mandated change effort to ensure that terrorists will never again get a driver's license in the United States. The assumption, stated in the extreme, is that if REAL ID had been in place prior to 9/11, the terrorist attack surely would have been thwarted. In reality, no real assessment of the potential benefits and unintended consequences of this mandate—in an area not previously subject to federal oversight—has been performed.

Another popular panacea is reorganization, the poster child of which is the creation of the U.S. Department of Homeland Security. The crucial failure of the federal government in the terrorist attacks of 9/11 was in not connecting the dots from intelligence agencies prior to the attack. However, the massive reorganization had very little to do with intelligence gathering since the CIA, FBI, and Defense Department all remain independent of DHS.

So what was the purpose of the DHS reorganization? Outside of acting on pre-attack intelligence, the federal government has few direct roles (other than financial support) in response and recovery to emergencies such as terrorist attacks. The coordination problem in New York City was not a federal issue, but was rooted in deep historical schisms between the fire and police departments. Ironically, at the Pentagon, where the federal government was directly involved in responding to the terrorist attack, coordination among local and federal responders was successful (National Commission on Terrorist Attacks upon the United States 2004; Kettl 2007).

Only history will determine if the magnitude of change mandated by the creation of DHS will ultimately make the nation better prepared to deal with emergencies. The massive tragedy of Hurricane Katrina showed conclusively, however, that mandated reorganization is not an immediate solution.

COMPLEX SOLUTIONS FOR COMPLEX PROBLEMS

Complex problems sometimes require complex solutions. In emergency management, the work itself is complex. Numerous organizations—public and private—must work cooperatively both horizontally and vertically. At the same time, most of these organizations have routine functions that they perform daily—activities that compete for time and resources. Collaboration in homeland security and emergency management requires building a networked capacity that goes beyond the day-to-day tragedies to deal with something that we hope will never happen—and, in most communities, in fact will never happen.

Fundamental to achieving successful network relations are leaders in the network (1) making a voluntary commitment to work together, (2) defining a clear purpose of the work, (3) creating a multi-agency structure for implementation, and (4) building trust with one another.

Making a Voluntary Commitment

Engaging in interorganizational activities is fundamentally a human endeavor, and its initiation and success depend on leadership. Networks do not just happen: Leaders at multiple levels of the relevant organizations must make personal and institutional commitments to work together. For leaders to make such a commitment, they must believe that something of value can be achieved through working with another organization—and that the value outweighs the cost. However, leaders can come to this conclusion only if they have explicit awareness of other organizations and the ways in which cooperation with them can contribute to the success of their own organization. Thus, one of a leader's most important tasks is conducting a stakeholder analysis to explore the range of networked interactions with the external environment that may be beneficial. From such an analysis, a leader can begin to assess interdependencies that are necessary for his or her own organization to achieve its mission.

Interdependencies, however, are not always symmetrical. One organization may be extremely dependent on another to fully perform its mission, but the other organization may not need the first one. In emergency management, asymmetrical interdependence is easily illustrated by mutual aid relationships between a large city/county and a small locality.

A case in point is Fairfax County, Virginia, and the adjacent, independent City of Falls Church. Fairfax has a population of over one million, stretches over 400 square miles, and has a fire department of over 1,300 sworn personnel. The City of Falls Church is barely two square miles, has a population of less than 12,000, and contracts with another adjacent jurisdiction (Arlington County) for its fire services. Fairfax is large enough to be self-sufficient for most of its incidents and Falls Church is so small that an event of almost any significance would overwhelm its resources. Nonetheless, both jurisdictions are part of a Northern Virginia fire and emergency services network that routinely responds to calls based on the nearest responder, irrespective of jurisdiction. Both are also part of a larger National Capital Region mutual aid network that responds across state boundaries in significant events, such as presidential inaugurations, July 4th celebrations, and major demonstrations.

These relationships are extremely asymmetrical, so why have they been established? The simple answer is that leaders, mostly fire chiefs, determined that everyone would be better off if they had a pact to always work together.

Axelrod offers five suggestions for leaders who want to promote cooperation (1984, 124–141), which have particular salience for emergency management leaders:

1. "Enlarge the shadow of the future" by helping other leaders in the network understand the long-term importance of working together. In the Northern Virginia case, clearly the fire chiefs see a larger future through cooperation. Axelrod also recommends making the interactions more durable and more frequent toward this objective. In the case of the fire network, the interactions are incorporated into formal agreements and literally happen on a daily basis.

2. "Change the payoffs." In the fire example, the consequences are literally life and death. Even a jurisdiction as large as Fairfax is not willing to risk the loss of life because it is too proud to accept the response of an adjacent locality that could get to an incident faster.

3. "Teach people to care about each other." Axelrod notes that "giving to charity (altruism) is often done less out of regard for the unfortunate than for the sake of the social approval it is expected to bring." The fire chiefs tout their network as a model of professionalism above parochialism and an example of their efficiency and effectiveness.

4. "Teach reciprocity." This strategy suggests the importance of being explicit about the rewards and punishments of cooperating in the network so that behavior will be self-policing. In the fire example, peer pressure is intense since the impacts are so immediate.

5. "Improve recognition abilities." The idea is that one needs to know whether the members of the network are performing or not (i.e., verification of cooperation). In the fire example, the knowledge is immediate: Either resources were dispatched and received from the partner or they were not. Actions in other networks may be more subtle and less visible.

In developing and managing networks, Goldsmith and Eggers express a need for leaders to have aptitudes in "negotiation, mediation, risk analysis, trust building, collaboration, and project management" (2004, 157). A leader within a network lacks the "powers" that exist within a single bureaucracy, including the power to impose one's will below or the power to summon support from above. Thus, collaborative management systems must be developed to ensure the effectiveness of the network.

Milward and Provan (2006, 18–24) identify five such essential management tasks related to accountability, legitimacy, conflict, governance, and commitment. As with other organizations, in emergency management organizations, "managers have split missions and, sometimes, split loyalties" (18). Leaders have a responsibility to the network only to the extent that the interests of the network are not in conflict with the interests of their own organizations and the ability of their organizations to handle an emergency. This is why "enlarging the shadow of the future" is so important. A leader must consider not only the immediate needs of his or her organization, but the larger public interest and the leader's stewardship responsibilities in the context of an interdependent world.

EMS Network at Virginia Tech

In August 2007, the Virginia Tech Review Panel released its report on the April 16 tragic massacre of students on campus. The report included 21 findings and 70 recommendations for improvement. Overall, the report was highly critical of most elements of the university's response. Among the positive findings was the existence of a network across multiple governmental and private emergency medical services agencies that had trained and drilled on how to handle a mass casualty event. The panel reported the following:

> Although there is always opportunity for improvement, the overall EMS response was excellent and the lives of many were saved. The challenges of systematic response, scene and provider safety, and on-scene and hospital patient care were effectively met. Responders are to be commended. The results in terms of patient care are a testimony to their medical education and training for mass casualty events, dedication, and ability to perform at a high level in the face of the disaster that struck so many people. (Virginia Tech Review Panel, 2007)

A total of 14 different agencies assisted in the medical emergency, led by the Virginia Tech Rescue Squad (VTRS), which is a student-led, volunteer organization. The panel concluded that EMS agencies worked effectively behind the scenes procuring the necessary resources and supporting the response of their EMS crews. The panel found that the agencies "demonstrated an exceptional working relationship, likely an outcome of interagency training and drills."

Defining a Clear Purpose

From a public policy perspective, collaboration would seem to be a good thing to do. The model for change presented in Chapter 3 emphasizes the importance of the public interest. In a multi-organizational network, the overall complexity mitigates against change for the sake of change. Working together requires a well-articulated public interest to overcome barriers to creating a network from which immediate tangible organizational benefits may not be derived. This means that organizations must first determine why they are networking. What are they going to achieve? Of what value is the effort to the individual organizations and their broader missions of service to the public?

The asymmetrical network of fire departments in Northern Virginia illustrates the concrete nature of work that a network may conduct: enhanced day-to-day fire and emergency medical response capability combined with significant surge capacity. Networks with less compelling immediate outcomes face substantial barriers to their creation. Minimally, network participation requires a commitment of time, the opportunity costs of which are significant, especially for executives. Organizations cannot afford to waste their time working with others for little or no potential return on the investment.

Milward and Provan identify four types of networks based on their underlying purpose (2006, 10–17): service implementation, information diffusion, problem solving, and community capacity building. These different types are not mutually exclusive. An emergency management network may share information on an ongoing basis, especially about threats, which is the role of an increasing number of "fusion centers." The network can identify and solve problems through various responses, such as creating a medical surge capacity, as in the case of Virginia Tech. The network can build community capacity by creating volunteer groups such as Citizen Emergency Response Teams (CERTs) and Medical Reserve Corps. In an actual emergency, members of the same network may have on-the-street response implementation, as in the cases of Virginia Tech and the Northern Virginia fire departments.

Moe (2006) notes that intergovernmental homeland security networks at the regional level operate in two dimensions of performance: performance in an actual emergency and performance in planning, coordination, investment, and training.

Ultimately the ends are the same, but the activities and the structures within which they are conducted are very different.

The purpose, or mission, becomes the touchstone against which the effectiveness, and indeed the very existence, of the network is measured. Interestingly, in the early stages of a network, the purpose may be ambiguous and vague. Leaders may come together for the simple reason that they feel they should know one another. In the Coast Guard, which prides itself on a collaborative approach to problems, this is sometimes referred to as "pre-need networking" (Whitehead 2005).

At the other end of the continuum, networks can have formal decision-making authority that significantly impacts all members. In the National Capital Region, the Chief Administrative Officers (CAOs) from each jurisdiction meet monthly, mostly to share information. When their subcommittee on homeland security meets, it has the explicit purpose of reaching joint decisions on regional priorities for emergency activities, including how to spend millions of federal grant dollars. In an actual emergency event, the CAOs move into a command-and-control structure to manage the disaster response.

Creating a Multi-agency Structure

A variety of governance structures for organizing a network are possible, depending on what the network is seeking to accomplish. Provan and Kenis (2007) identify three types of network governance:

- *Participant-governed networks* are highly decentralized and require the initiative of individual members to perform administrative tasks. Such networks operate with organizing principles ranging from unwritten and very loose structures to formal rules and regulations. The administrative work of the network (which may be minimal) is divided among the different members and requires their voluntary willingness to share the effort.

- A network with a *lead organization* relies on one of its members to perform the administrative functions. The effectiveness of the network depends on the competency and commitment of the lead organization.

- Networks with an *administrative manager* tend to be more formal because of the need to fund the third party that performs the administrative functions.

Additional basic elements of governance that network members should consider include the following:

- *Officers:* What officers does the network need? How are they chosen? How long may they serve? Is there an executive committee? If so, what is its authority?
- *Membership:* Who can be a member of the network? What are the expectations of members?
- *Network status:* Is the network an entity with a name, under which actions or positions can be taken, or is the network more a mechanism for sharing information with all actions taken by individual members in their own names?
- *Decision-making:* Are actions or positions taken by the network decided by unanimous agreement, general consensus, or voting? What are the responsibilities of dissenting members?
- *Resources:* Are the administrative costs borne by members on a voluntary basis or are there formal expectations of either in-kind or cash contributions by members? How are contribution levels determined for members of varying financial capacity?

In structuring the network, Goldsmith and Eggers outline the challenge as "creating a model malleable enough to accommodate each partner, dynamic enough to adjust to changing circumstances, but fixed enough in mission to serve the common goal" (2004, 55). This notion is an echo of earlier work by Lipnack and Stamps (1994), who also emphasize the importance of flexibility. They maintain that the planning process that engages the network members is a vital part of building the network's capabilities. They describe the network as an "organic" form of organization that is nourished by both structure and process (19).

Among the most important structures in emergency management is the Incident Command System (ICS). ICS has received extensive national attention since 9/11, but it is actually the product of more than 30 years of use in the field by all levels of government. First used in fighting forest fires, ICS was voluntarily adopted as a best practice by many organizations prior to 9/11 and was the system that was used explicitly to manage the response to the attack on the Pentagon. ICS helps clarify the objectives of an emergency response and is inherently logical and flexible.

As a change initiative, ICS is nonthreatening. Rather than posing risk to an organization, it is seen as a means of mitigating risk, and thus has wide acceptance among stakeholders. People experienced in emergency response understand that in a major event no one person or organization can be in charge and in control of everything. The question is not, "who is in charge?" but "who is in charge of what?" The complex web of interdependency in an emergency requires organizations to work together; ICS provides a common pathway to structure such a network in a crisis.

Building Trust

As noted in Chapter 5, trust is a critical factor in stakeholder relations. "Underneath all is trust, the soil in which networks grow connections and relationships" (Lipnack and Stamps 1994, 24). Networks both need and generate trust (177). As trust accumulates, it creates social capital. Trust is especially important in light of the voluntary, nonhierarchical nature of networks. Leaders within a network, lacking bureaucratic power, each become one of many in a system of shared power. Doyle and Smith discuss the need for leaders to take shared ownership of problems and issues, to have the capacity to learn, and to share in "open, respectful, and informed conversation" (2001, 4).

The first step in developing trust in networks involves leaders simply getting to know each other—having a conversation. We do not want key leaders exchanging business cards for the first time on the scene of a disaster. Some members will come into the network with established relationships; others will be meeting for the first time. Members of the network will change over time, requiring that new relationships be developed and new members be assimilated into the network.

The challenge of assimilation is especially critical where key actors change based on election cycles. A year and a half before the 2008 presidential election cycle, approximately one-quarter of executive jobs in the Department of Homeland Security were vacant (Hsu 2007). How much effort should be allocated to developing relationships with people in lame duck status?

One of the foundations of trust is the expectation that there will be reciprocal support among members of the network. Lipnack and Stamps (1994) use the metaphors of bartering and banking. In the former, reciprocity results in an immediate exchange. In the latter—which they also refer to as the "barn-raising principle"—members of a network help one another in expectation of some benefit in the future. If individuals are not expected to be members of a network for very long, they are not likely to be in a position to reciprocate, and therefore not in a position to build much trust unless they have something immediate to offer the network.[2]

The other side of the trust coin is mistrust. Communication goes down and formality increases in an effort to check "political games and backstabbing" (Lipnack and Stamps 1994, 186). Mistrust breeds a "vicious cycle" that depletes social capital. Members, in turn, look for ways to avoid the network and achieve as much stability as they can within their own organizations.

Central to all these trust-building efforts is communication. This is why just being together can be important. Extended meetings provide enough time to have meaningful communication (Agranoff 2003).

There is no shortcut to creating trust. As succinctly put by Kenneth Arrow (quoted in Chisholm 1989, 112):

> *Trust is an important lubricant of a social system. It is extremely efficient; it saves a lot of trouble to have a fair degree of reliance on other peoples' work. Unfortunately, this is not a commodity which can be bought very easily.... Trust and similar values, loyalty or truth telling, are examples of what the economist would call "externalities".... They are not commodities for which trade on the open market is technically possible or even meaningful.*

Not only is there no shortcut to trust, but Alter and Hage (1993) suggest that a culture of trust is in conflict with traditional values in the United States, where a climate of distrust has been fostered by the "myth of Horatio Alger, the self-made man, and the supremacy of the competitive model...." (265). These values carry over into organizations where there is a natural bureaucratic tendency to act independently. What permits collaboration is the "long shadow of the future," taking a longer term view of costs and benefits in the public interest. If the collaboration is to be effective and sustained, however, people within the network must act in a trustworthy manner.

---

[2] Reciprocity is discussed intensively in the network/interorganizational literature. For a more detailed discussion of the "tit for tat" concept, see Axelrod (1984). Also, see *Bowling Alone* by Robert D. Putman (2000), Chapter 8, "Reciprocity, Honesty, and Trust."

IMPLICATIONS FOR CHANGE LEADERS

In the end, leading emergency management organizations in a multi-organizational environment is difficult. A complex web of interdependency requires organizations to work together to protect communities. The efforts involve stakeholders across all sectors of society and require working around participants that lack basic organizational capacity. Forming and managing effective networks requires leaders who will identify and convene the network participants, define clearly the purpose of the network, implement structures that support the purpose, and build trust that enables members to accept the challenge of transformational change on behalf of the public interest. Numerous examples of highly functioning networks exist, supported by vast literature on networks spanning over 50 years. We know what to do and how to do it. The critical variable is leadership to make it happen.

Events such as the 9/11 terrorist attacks, Hurricane Katrina, and the Virginia Tech shootings will happen again. Learning from the past and building stronger networks, however, offer the promise of a greater likelihood of preventing that which is preventable and responding more capably to that which is not.

PRACTICAL TIPS FOR THE CHANGE LEADER

- Conduct a stakeholder analysis based on an assessment of organizational interdependencies and map those relationships. On what other emergency management organizations does your organization depend to achieve its mission?

- Establish direct professional relationships with peers in the organizations on which your organization depends. Have lunch, invite them to special events your organization hosts, and share newsletters and annual reports. Ask for advice. Learn about each other and your respective organizations. Introduce key staff to one another.

- Create a new network if needed; find an inner circle of three to six peers who will champion the effort with you. Work as an informal executive committee to develop a draft purpose and structural alternatives. Explore governance and finance options for the network.

- Be active in the networks in which you are a member. Regularly attend meetings and actively participate, but don't dominate. Integrate the network relationships into the operation of your agency.

- As a network member, maintain one-on-one relationships with members outside of network activities. Reach out to new members who may be critical to your organization's emergency response and facilitate their assimilation into the network.

- As a member of an emergency management network, jointly conduct a threat analysis: What are the most likely scenarios under which the network will be needed? Plan, train, and test to those scenarios.

- Build social capital in the network by always being trustworthy yourself.

▬▬ SUGGESTED READINGS ON EMERGENCY MANAGEMENT NETWORKS

Claire B. Rubin, editor, *Emergency Management: The American Experience, 1900–2005.* Fairfax, VA: Public Entity Risk Institute, 2007.

The authors provide an excellent and comprehensive look at the field of emergency management over the last century, including earthquakes, hurricanes, droughts, floods, pandemics, and terrorist attacks. This book includes solid summaries of the 9/11 attacks and Hurricane Katrina, and it examines the federal responses to those disasters. The book also reviews how the federal government got involved in emergency management and how local, state, and federal roles have changed over the years.

Stephen Goldsmith and William D. Eggers, *Governing by Network: The New Shape of the Public Sector.* Washington, DC: Brookings Institution Press, 2004.

Authors Goldsmith (former Mayor of Indianapolis) and Eggers describe networks as the next major wave of change for government managers—a shift away from managing divisions of employees. They recommend a combination of contracting out, public-private partnerships, and networks (of commercial and nongovernmental organizations) as a replacement for the current bureaucratic structure of the public sector. This book is practitioner-oriented and is considered a must-read on the subject. It won the public administration 2005 Louis Brownlow Book Award.

Robert Agranoff and Michael McGuire. *Collaborative Public Management: New Strategies for Local Government.* Washington, DC: Georgetown University Press, 2003.

Agranoff has been writing about interorganizational relations since the 1970s, when he focused on the integration of human services. The book is academic, but is based on a number of interesting case studies. The authors examine network processes, the promotion of networks, the importance of trust, authority structures, the use of technology, and how decisions are brokered. Managers interviewed for the book offer numerous useful suggestions. See also, Agranoff, *Leveraging Networks: A Guide for Public Managers Working across Organizations* (Washington, DC: IBM Endowment for the Business of Government, 2003).

Jessica Lipnack and Jeffrey Stamps, *The Age of the Network: Organizing Principles for the 21st Century.* Hoboken, NJ: John Wiley & Sons, 1996.

This is a private-sector-oriented and at times somewhat esoteric book; however, it provides a different lens than the public administration orthodoxy and is intellectually stimulating.

PART III

A Vision for the Future

CHAPTER TEN

Developing Transformational Stewards

Looking ahead, public and nonprofit service is likely to continue to be characterized by challenges that require leaders to be agents of change in the public interest—what we have been calling *transformational stewards*. Leaders will be operating in turbulent conditions, including the following:

- Rapid communications that penetrate traditional barriers to information-sharing
- Increasing transparency and public scrutiny regarding ethics, results, and opportunities for improvement
- Evolving information technology, which will break down organizational silos and connect and integrate organizational functions in ways not previously possible
- Changing strategic influences and mission requirements, exacerbated by the

This chapter is adapted from James Edwin Kee, Kathryn Newcomer, and Mike Davis, "A New Vision for Public Leadership: The Case for Developing Transformational Stewards." In *Innovations in Public Leadership Development,* Ricardo Morse and Terry Buss, editors. Armonk, New York: M.E. Sharpe, 2008.

nature of cross-jurisdiction, cross-sector, and cross-function interdependencies

- Expectations for more agile and performance-oriented work and organizations
- Increasing top-down guidance and coordination of operational standards and improvement priorities, with some trends toward decentralized operations
- A workforce characterized by shifting demographics and blended public/ private/nonprofit partnerships.

We believe that responding to these changing conditions requires a new way of thinking about public and nonprofit leadership development.

LEADERSHIP DEVELOPMENT FOR TRANSFORMATIONAL STEWARDS

Over the last several decades, traditional leader and manager roles, development approaches, and competency profiles have been assumed to be sufficient to support change leadership in the public and nonprofit sectors. However, recent events have exposed many organizations' (e.g., FEMA, NASA, Red Cross, Smithsonian Institution) weaknesses and apparent leadership failures to implement changes needed in the public interest. Given the changing nature of the required tasks and the available workforce, a reconsideration of approaches for public and nonprofit sector leadership development is in order.

Many training and development programs have begun to incorporate competency models and instructional designs that address change leadership. Yet government and nonprofit leaders and managers often report that such instruction fails to provide the necessary skills and experiences (see, e.g., NAPA 2002, 2003). While collaboration and interorganizational information sharing are taught, the *ideal* of open, articulate, trusting stakeholders often conflicts with the *real* operational environments of complex issues and sometimes hostile stakeholders.

Change leaders are often left feeling that survival requires them to vastly scale back or even abandon these collaborative approaches. However, to fulfill their role in protecting the public interest, public and nonprofit leaders have the responsibility to implement change effectively while simultaneously working collaboratively with affected populations to address their interests in a constructive manner. Unfortunately, many current training and development options available to public and nonprofit leaders focus on collections of specific leadership "competencies" that, when developed individually, fail to adequately equip individuals to meet the complex tradeoffs involved in the real world.

Developing transformational stewards requires a holistic approach. Rather than using traditional competency models that represent a collection of more or less separate yet complementary abilities, transformational stewardship begins with a set of attributes that represent the general characteristics of change leadership. These attributes serve as a foundation from which to address specific change requirements. The requirements are summarized in our leadership model's four processes: diagnosing, strategizing, implementing, and reinforcing change. In each process, the leader must find a practical balance between moving the transformation or change initiative forward and stewarding the stakeholders and organizational interests involved in the issue.

Transformational stewardship development is an approach for public and nonprofit leaders to understand and develop the necessary skills and abilities with regard to the tradeoffs they must make as they endeavor to lead change in the public interest. In this way, stewardship development reframes traditional competencies, validates the core requirements and related skills, and provides the opportunity to apply these tools in the context of real-world challenges. The development aspect stresses the need to balance interests, recognizing the importance of achieving a dynamic equilibrium that reconciles the need for change with the competing needs of stakeholders and the organization.

So how can public and nonprofit organizations develop transformational stewards? We have written this chapter as a practical guide for those in leadership and management positions faced with change-related challenges that require transformational acumen, and also for directors of training and development organizations seeking to create and improve programs aimed at enabling change leadership in their organizations.

THE TRANSFORMATIONAL STEWARDSHIP DEVELOPMENT PATH

As we examine the attributes of a transformational steward and contrast them to current approaches for developing leaders of change, we find three significant shortcomings in the current approaches:

1. Insufficient linkages are drawn between the work of organizational change and the required knowledge, skills, abilities, and developmental efforts necessary to accomplish that work.

2. Explanations of what is and is not involved in organizational change are incomplete.

3. Training and development approaches fail to convey the necessary real-world skills for effective change leadership or to explore the change-related interdependencies and practical challenges involved.

In this section, we outline the components of a transformational stewardship development path (TSDP) as a step toward addressing these deficiencies. Drawing on the transformational stewardship responsibilities as a foundation, the TSDP is a framework that clarifies the nature of transformational leaders' roles and practices, as well as the fundamental components of leadership development related to leading change and transformation.

The TSDP organizing framework, depicted in Figure 10.1, includes four inter-related elements: (1) attributes; (2) responsibilities; (3) knowledge, skills, and abilities; and (4) developmental experiences. The elements of the framework articulate the ingredients of transformational stewardship, as well as the "nuts and bolts" necessary for translating this vision into an operational reality in public and nonprofit sector organizations.

The competencies of effective stewardship include the attributes and responsibilities of transformational stewards as well as the required knowledge, skills, and abilities.

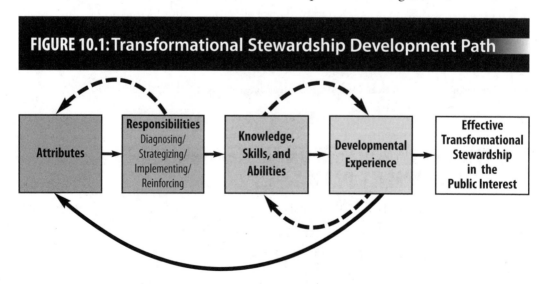

FIGURE 10.1: Transformational Stewardship Development Path

Attributes → Responsibilities Diagnosing/ Strategizing/ Implementing/ Reinforcing → Knowledge, Skills, and Abilities → Developmental Experience → Effective Transformational Stewardship in the Public Interest

The path from the attributes to the responsibilities to knowledge, skills, and abilities represents a progression of increasing detail and tactical specificity. Developmental experiences are the experiential aspects required to put transformational stewardship skills into practice.

In our leadership responsibilities model (presented in detail in Chapter 3) we conceptualize the change process in four general phases: (1) diagnosing change risk and organizational capacity; (2) strategizing and making the case for change; (3) implementing and sustaining change; and (4) reinforcing change by creating a change-centric organization. The TSDP addresses leadership development in each phase of organizational change.

Phase 1: Diagnosing Change Risk and Organizational Capacity

The initiating phase of organizational change includes the tasks and related competencies of determining *why* to change and *what* to change. This stage begins with an assessment of strategic influences and trends that drive the need for change. Change risks and the organization's capacity to make the needed changes are then carefully analyzed.

We believe that the four most important tasks of change leaders during this phase are to:

1. Determine the change drivers for the organization within the context of the sociopolitical environment
2. Examine the perceptions of the organization's stakeholders, both internal and external, likely to be affected by a change
3. Assess the complexity and risks of change and determine how to limit any unanticipated impacts of change
4. Assess the organization's capacity to undertake change and mitigate change risk.

These four tasks require change leaders to be good at diagnosing and assessing various organizational aspects of the change, and require an integrated, systems thinking approach to the analysis. Our model (presented in Chapter 3) and the list of questions presented in our diagnostic instrument (see Appendix A) provide a starting point for this phase of leading change.

Table 10.1 outlines how attributes contribute to these responsibilities and tasks translate into specific knowledge, skills, and abilities for a change leader. The table also displays how these aspects translate into specific development activities.

TABLE 10.1: Diagnosing Change Risk and Organizational Capacity

PHASE 1: DIAGNOSING CHANGE RISK AND ORGANIZATIONAL CAPACITY			
Attributes	**Responsibilities**	**Knowledge, Skills, and Abilities**	**Developmental Experiences**
Visionary/ foresight; integrative/ systems thinking; mission-driven	Determine change drivers and sociopolitical environment for change.	Understand current strategic public sector influences and trends and the broader environment; understand the relationship of strategic trends to mission requirements, vision, and the implied requirements for change. Ability to diagnose internal and external strategic and environmental influences, define organizational change implications, and translate strategic drivers into mission requirements.	Conduct an environmental scan and trend identification exercise; conduct a strategic organizational assessment and define organizational change requirements.
Empathy; power-sharing; coalition-building; trust-building; democratic	Facilitate identification/ realization of common interests and objects among diverse stakeholders.	Understand stakeholder interests, perceptions, and expectations; understand approaches to designing and managing stakeholder collaboration. Ability to design and steward stakeholder collaboration forums and processes, synthesizing common interests and recognizing stakeholder perceptions of gain or loss.	Conduct a stakeholder audit to identify stakeholders and stakes for a change issue; facilitate a stakeholder forum; meet and engage stakeholders to understand needs and expectations.
Integrative/ systems thinking; attention to detail; foresight	Ability to assess change-related complexity and identify potential high-risk areas.	Identify change-related risk factors and dynamics across project complexity, stakeholder relations, and organizational change capacity areas. Ability to assess the risks of the proposed change and limit unintended effects.	Conduct a change complexity assessment and identify change risk areas.
	Ability to assess current organizational capacity; ability to deal with change and change risk.	Understand elements of organizational capacity especially as related to change and change-related risk; develop change leadership skills within organizations. Ability to assess the capacity and readiness of the organization for change.	Conduct an organizational capacity audit.

The Balancing Challenge

Transformational stewardship in the public interest almost always involves balancing interests and priorities. During this first phase, the balance involves determining how much analysis and preliminary work should be completed before the leader initiates the effort of articulating a change strategy. We have all been afflicted, at one time or another, by the problem of "paralysis by analysis," where a problem (in this case a proposed change) is so complex and involves so many stakeholders that it is hard for a leader to know where to begin. At the other extreme is the leader who blindly goes forward without a good understanding of the change complexity and risk or a sufficient awareness of the organization's capacity to accommodate the change.

Effective stewards recognize that a certain level of knowledge is necessary before proceeding, but that they will never understand everything. There is a need to move forward based on a diagnosis of risks, but this must continue as new information becomes available.

The Developmental Agenda

Desired leadership attributes during all phases, including change initiation, are interdependent and integrative in nature. As depicted in Table 10.1, three key attribute clusters are especially important for diagnosing change needs and risk, as well as for assessing organizational capacity for change: (1) visionary perspective and foresight; (2) empathetic ways of relating to others, coalition-building abilities, and a participative democratic approach; and (3) integrative, systems awareness and thinking. While these clusters of attributes are of critical importance across all phases of organizational change, they are essential in helping transformational stewards diagnose the need and nature of change and understand and appreciate the needs of others involved in the process.

The knowledge, skills, and abilities necessary for the diagnosis phase include the following:

- Diagnosing internal and external strategic influences on the change agenda
- Facilitating stakeholder meetings to diagnose stakeholders' perceptions of gain or loss with various change options
- Assessing the complexity of proposed changes and the likely risks to the organization

- Assessing training needs to strengthen change-leadership skills throughout the organization.

To accomplish these objectives, transformational stewards require an understanding of change-related risks associated with change complexity, stakeholders, and organizational change capacity, as well as an understanding of the interdependencies that link impacts across strategies, organizing structures, work processes, reporting relationships, job/role requirements, and developmental needs.

While it is possible to learn how to assimilate these abilities and skills through reading and taking courses, they are greatly reinforced through experiences, such as conducting an environmental scan or a SWOT (strengths, weaknesses, opportunities, and threats) exercise, conducting a stakeholder audit to determine stakeholder perceptions, and conducting a risk assessment of various action options. Individuals striving to become transformational stewards should take advantage of opportunities to become involved in these types of activities in their organization.

Phase 2: Strategizing and Making the Case for Change

Strategizing is probably the most commonly recognized part of the change process. Almost everyone is familiar with the process of "strategic planning," building "business cases," and "scoping" a project. Yet, while some of the tasks in this stage are a part of many management vocabularies, the actual nature of transformation-specific activities during this stage is much more detailed than most leadership training. Making the case for change is not easy in any organization, and this challenge can be particularly complicated in government and nonprofit organizations, where rules and procedures may dictate the collaborative process among stakeholder groups. Development of an integrative, collectively supported strategy is important at this stage.

Specific leadership tasks related to strategizing include the following:

1. Creating a vision for change and making the case for change
2. Understanding the total system and how proposed changes may affect various parts of the organization and its stakeholders
3. Designing realistic, comprehensive change strategies and risk-mitigation plans
4. Preparing a business case that stays within capacity limitations and offers maximum return on resources.

These four tasks require the change leader to have the foresight and ability to create and make the case for change, to have a total systems perspective on how the change will affect various stakeholders, and to be detail-oriented in designing the change strategy.

Table 10.2 outlines how attributes contribute to these responsibilities and tasks translate into specific attributes, knowledge, abilities, and skills. The table also displays how these aspects translate into specific development activities that provide the change leader with the necessary background to become more effective in his or her work.

TABLE 10.2: Strategizing and Making the Case for Change

PHASE 2: STRATEGIZING AND MAKING THE CASE FOR CHANGE			
Attributes	Responsibilities	Knowledge, Skills, and Abilities	Developmental Experiences
Foresight/ visionary, accountable	Create a vision for change; make the case for change.	Ability to articulate a vision for the organization that includes the agenda for change. Ability to make a case to internal and external stakeholders of the need for change.	Create an organizational vision statement; develop a case for a change initiative.
Integrative/ systems thinking; attention to detail; foresight; ethical; empathy	Anticipate the scope required for integrated total-systems change and how that may affect various parts of the organization and its stakeholders.	Understand systems dynamics of organizations, interdependencies across organizational systems and strategy, structure, process, skills, and culture/ climate. Ability to anticipate potential scope of impacts resulting from planned changes and determine a baseline.	Complete an impact/ complexity analysis exercise related to a particular change event to determine potential impact.
	Develop a change implementation and risk mitigation plan.	Identify change-related risk factors and dynamics across project complexity, stakeholder relations, and organizational change capacity areas. Assess the complexity and the risks of the proposed change; limit unintended effects.	Develop a change implementation and risk management plan.
Attention to detail; trust; accountable	Accomplish change within capacity limitations and with maximum return on resources.	Understand types and limitations of organizational capacity; understand methods for assessing/balancing capacity through priority-based resource allocation. Ability to assess dimensions of organizational capacity and cost against requirements; determine change priorities, allocate resources, and manage available capacity to achieve objectives; determine return on investment (ROI).	Complete a capacity assessment and cost-benefit/ROI analysis.

The Balancing Challenge

To successfully initiate change in the public interest, transformational stewards must balance a number of factors: working within structural bureaucratic limitations; satisfying (to the extent possible) the diverse, complex interests of stakeholders; attending to fairness and equity concerns; maintaining appropriate political/trustee accountability; and yet consistently moving forward with a practical change agenda that enhances agency effectiveness. By understanding the nature of making the case for change more completely, transformational stewards can develop a much broader array of practical tools and approaches for creating a balanced process that moves the organization forward yet recognizes and appreciates the complexity of the issues involved.

The limited tenure and frequent turnover of top government leadership also mean that the public sector norm often is a completely new change agenda with each new leadership team. The short-term mindsets of political bosses may create a pervasive anxiety among civil servants regarding organizational change. In many instances, new leadership paves over and even contradicts efforts that civil servants are attempting to implement from previous change efforts. By including an appreciative, empathetic focus throughout the strategic assessment and stakeholder collaboration processes, transformational stewards can more effectively balance various interests and thereby effect positive change.

The Developmental Agenda

During this phase, five key attribute clusters are most important for supporting the actions of initiating change: (1) visionary perspective and foresight, (2) empathetic ways of relating to others and coalition-building abilities, (3) integrative, systems awareness, (4) attention to detail, and (5) adherence to strong ethical standards. These attributes help the transformational steward articulate the need for change and understand and appreciate the needs of others involved in the process, while crafting a realistic change strategy.

The transformational steward must have the ability to identify and assess various strategic influences on the change landscape. Regardless of whether the change is at the organizational, interorganizational, or team level, strategic influences must be translated into change requirements. Developmentally, leaders and managers must understand strategic management principles and the process of determining operational requirements from strategic factors. Even at the most tactical levels, having the ability to translate strategy into the case for change is critical when interacting with stakeholders. The following abilities are especially pertinent:

- Facilitating and creating a common change vision among competing stakeholder interests and perspectives
- Devising and communicating a convincing case for change
- Communicating and collaborating effectively with stakeholders in developing the change strategy
- Accomplishing change initiatives within the capacity limits of the organization and with a maximum return on resources used
- Developing and including effective risk mitigation measures in the strategic plan.

In practice, the strategic process requires transformational stewards to be proficient at conducting stakeholder assessments/audits, planning and facilitating stakeholder forums, and developing a resulting "common" case for change. These tasks require the foundational knowledge of stakeholder relations and the dynamics of collaborative processes, with an understanding of methods for analyzing stakeholder perceptions of their gain or loss with the proposed change. Experientially, the tasks of conducting a strategic assessment, facilitating stakeholder dialogues, determining requirements, and making the case for change all provide practical venues for the initiating competencies to be developed.

While learning and development can come from "book knowledge," we would argue that the most valuable development is experiential learning—whether in the classroom or on the job. Developing a vision statement, for example, is something you can learn about, study samples, and understand. However, unless you actually participate in the effort to find a common set of values and norms among competing interests, full development is unlikely to occur.

Transformational stewardship requires practice. Understanding "how" to define an organizational vision is no substitute for participating in a vision-setting exercise that incorporates change and transformation.

Similarly, transformational stewards have a responsibility to facilitate identification of the common values, interests, and objectives of the organization's stakeholders.

You can learn how to conduct a stakeholder audit, how to facilitate collaborative processes, and how to develop a "common case for change." However, unless you have actually attempted to do this, you will have inadequate skills to adapt to the many and various conditions and issues that are likely to arise.

Again, while case studies can provide one method of "gaining experience," there is no substitute for actually conducting a stakeholder audit and facilitating a stakeholder meeting to develop common interests. Individuals seeking to become transformational stewards should complement their book knowledge by volunteering to participate in these activities, and thereby gain the experience and confidence to fulfill their leadership responsibilities.

Phase 3: Implementing and Sustaining Change

The third set of transformational stewardship responsiblities involves aligning the processes, structures, policies and procedures, roles, and jobs of the organization or team to the change effort. Implementation begins, ideally, when the initial dialogue of why and what to change has led to a collective focus on a particular priority for action. Complete consensus is frequently a luxury for change leaders; nevertheless, general agreement is critical to keep the risks of unanticipated, undesirable consequences to a minimum.

The need to monitor and address change-related risk, in conjunction with the requirement to navigate the interdependencies and systems impacts of changing work and workforce roles, emerges as a challenging task during implementation. As with strategizing and making the case for change, these tasks are supported by the principal attribute clusters of (1) maintaining constant awareness of the "bigger picture" or long-term vision, (2) translating feedback, challenges, and decisions empathetically to maintain a commitment to democratic participation and mutual ownership, and (3) applying an integrative, systems awareness and attention to detail. In this stage, leaders need to communicate effectively, act with transparency and ethical standards, and understand and engage evolving interests and sources of resistance.

Change is inherently unsettling to some degree, regardless of how well it's led and managed. During implementation, the transformational steward must address the upheaval and uncertainty of change with a consistent and unwavering commitment to maintain focus and clarity, recognize and understand capacity limitations and the needs behind resistance, and facilitate forums for dialogue where everyone owns a part of the process. Specific leadership tasks include the following:

- Establishing transparency, engagement, and collective ownership of the change effort
- Identifying potential obstacles and resistance to change and developing approaches to mitigate those obstacles and resistance
- Setting and stewarding specific change objectives
- Aligning organizational processes, policies, and incentive structures to support the change initiative
- Developing, where necessary, partnerships with other organizations in the change effort
- Managing change-related risk.

Table 10.3 provides a summary of implementation responsibilities and tasks, relating them to specific transformational stewardship attributes, knowledge, skills, abilities, and developmental experiences.

The Balancing Challenge

Over the last 15 years of emerging interest in technology implementation and project management, the prescriptions for change leadership have tended to focus on "managing" the change process in a limited, tactical way. While this focus has pushed leaders and managers to consider the mechanics necessary to manage project-based transformations, it also has somewhat concealed the more holistic aspects of successfully leading and managing in the public interest. In one sense, this technical concentration has been a backlash of sorts to the more "touchy-feely" practices that were proposed by organizational psychologists in the late 1970s and early 1980s. In our view, change leadership during implementation (as in other phases) is neither purely tactical and technical nor exclusively facilitative and subjective.

Rather, as the knowledge, abilities, and skills depicted in Table 10.3 suggest, transformational stewardship requires fluency in the technical and tactical as well as the strategic and traditional aspects of organizational management. We suggest that the dynamic equilibrium proposed by the transformational stewardship concept provides a

TABLE 10.3: Implementing and Sustaining Change

PHASE 3: IMPLEMENTING AND SUSTAINING CHANGE			
Attributes	**Responsibilities**	**Knowledge, Skills, and Abilities**	**Developmental Experiences**
Empathy; coalition-building; trust-building; democratic	Establish transparency, engagement, and collective ownership.	Understand decision-making and issue resolution methods and approaches; understand dynamics of trust and methods for establishing transparency and resolving disputes. Ability to identify communications needs; design, deploy, and manage change-related communications; and manage communications across multiple channels and audiences. Ability to establish mechanisms for ownership and collective engagement in the implementation process.	Conduct a communications needs assessment and develop a change communications plan. Complete role-play and scenario analysis exercises related to issue resolution and determining balance of execution and participative deliberation.
	Appreciate, understand, and address obstacles and resistance to the proposed change.	Ability to recognize, understand, and address obstacles to change, including overt and covert stakeholder resistance, culture and climate variables, and organizational defensive routines.	Conduct role-play resistance exercises; conduct a brainstorming session to address potential obstacles to a proposed change.
Trustee, accountable	Set and manage specific change objectives and measures.	Understand nature and types of change-related performance measures. Ability to define, implement, and manage clear, credible objectives; ability to employ measures and performance information to identify impediments and successes.	Develop change strategy, objectives, and measures for a change project or initiative.
Integrative/ systems thinking; attention to detail	Align organizational capabilities.	Understand process, role, and skill interdependencies and business process improvement approaches. Ability to assess and understand workforce impacts and to plan and manage workforce transition activities; plan and manage job/role restructuring and requisite training and development efforts.	Complete a work/workforce impact analysis, business process improvement plan, and workforce transition plan.
Creative/ innovative; coalition-building	Partner to implement transformation successfully.	Understand partnership agreement methods and approaches, including interagency and intergovernmental partnerships, as well as procurement vehicles for addressing change needs. Ability to design and manage blended workforce as part of change-related procurement actions or interagency/intersector partnerships.	Complete blended implementation scenario exercises and/or role-plays involving procurement partnerships and interorganizational change partnerships.
Comfortable with ambiguity; integrative/ systems thinking	Managing change-related risk.	Ability to perceive operational and strategic challenges in terms of systems-originating opportunities and risks; ability to identify high-risk areas and develop risk mitigation plans.	Complete simulation exercises that extend awareness to risk obstacles and opportunity variables.

practical framework for specific, concrete developmental actions.

The Developmental Agenda

The competency requirements for implementing transformation are relevant for all leaders and managers involved in the implementation process, not just the transformation team. During the initial span of the implementation process, it is critical that the organization's business process owners and program managers involved in the change actively participate in shaping and guiding the action of transformation. In addition, contractors or other extra-organizational partners should be involved in this step. This "blended-workforce" reality of most change situations involves a core and extended team working together to jointly design and implement the transformational initiative.

Specific abilities change leaders need during this phase include the following:

- Identifying communications needs and designing and carrying out an effective communication strategy
- Establishing mechanisms to create collective ownership of the change effort
- Recognizing and addressing obstacles to the change initiative
- Defining, implementing, and managing clear, credible measures and objectives for the change initiative
- Aligning personnel and organizational resources with the change effort
- Designing and managing partnerships with other organizations necessary for a successful change effort.

Transformational skills are everyone's responsibility, and widespread transformational competency is a necessity to ensure successful change initiatives. When such capability is absent in the larger community of involved stakeholders and responsibility for change success is restricted to more central officials "at the top," the tendency to focus on official accountability may overshadow the need for collective ownership. In the federal government, for example, change efforts that involve significant procurement aspects, such as contracting out, can fall into the trap of focusing accountability and risk-mitigation activities on the contract vehicle and the requirement for the vendor to deliver. While contracting relationships and public-private partnerships present their own unique risks, failed implementation is easy to pin on irresponsible contracting, when it is frequently a result of ineffective collaboration among implementation partners.

Two important, complementary transformation skills are worth consideration: (1) the ability to anticipate change impacts and (2) the ability to understand and mitigate transformational risk. Both of these aspects are grounded in the attributes of integrative, systems thinking and attention to detail. Transformational stewards must have the ability to draw on the explicit, objective-driven definition of the project and then deduce the needs for process, policy, procedure, structure, and competency changes. This ability requires that the transformational steward be proficient in employing a systems approach to identifying the primary and secondary impacts of the change initiative.

In addition to the transformational stewardship competencies related to change scope and risk identification, successful transformational stewardship during implementation requires an empathetic connection with the stakeholders participating in the initiative. Through consistent communications, democratic, participative decision-making, issues resolution, and obstacle/resistance awareness, the transformational steward can strike a balance that builds and sustains trust and commitment while still moving forward with change.

Effective implementation and sustaining change require a combination of foundational knowledge and practical experience. The complementary and reciprocally reinforcing nature of these two components is necessary to provide the transformational steward with a solid base for applying competencies.

For example, one key responsibility of transformational stewardship is creating a transparent environment in the organization with informed and involved stakeholders. From books, we can learn about various approaches to communications, how to develop channels of information flowing both down and up throughout the organization, and how important it is to involve others in the implementation of change and transformation. But for a transformational steward, there is no substitute for actually facilitating specific transformational planning, decision-making, and risk management efforts. Training and development programs can lay the groundwork, but as in many endeavors, there is simply no substitute for hands-on experience.

Phase 4: Reinforcing Change and Stewarding Growth and Renewal

The final phase of transformational stewardship is reinforcing the change effort and stewarding the growth and renewal of both the organization and its individual leaders. In this phase, all the transformational stewardship attributes are in play; however, some are more important to the organization while others are more important in the growth and renewal of individuals. This phase is slightly different from the other phases, as leaders focus on building transformational capability both individually and organizationally in addition to focusing on the successful completion of the change initiative that is underway. The role of the transformational steward includes responsibility for accomplishing specific change initiatives and for moving the organizational culture to be more change-friendly.

Specific responsibilities of transformational stewards include the following:

- Facilitating organizational learning, improvement, and innovation
- Establishing an environment of ethical collaboration, information-sharing, and collective ownership
- Establishing change implementation practices, measures, structures, and policies to reinforce change efforts
- Developing change-centric leaders within the organization
- Developing a transformational ethic in approaching their responsibilities
- Nurturing their own development and growth as transformational stewards.

Table 10.4 provides a breakdown of the competencies and development dimensions for the growth and renewal of leaders and their organizations.

The Balance Challenge

The key challenge during this phase for both the organization and the individual is balancing the need for continuity with the need to improve and evolve. Constant change that occurs without meeting the need for closure, recognition of success, and establishment of process maturity is unhealthy and disruptive. Yet, neither the organization nor the individual can remain complacent, with an imbalance toward security and comfort at the expense of evolving to better meet stakeholder and customer needs. Growth and renewal in the public interest ultimately involve balancing tradition and consistency

TABLE 10.4: Reinforcing Change and Stewarding Growth and Renewal

PHASE 4: REINFORCING CHANGE AND STEWARDING GROWTH AND RENEWAL			
Attributes	**Responsibilities**	**Knowledge, Skills, and Abilities**	**Developmental Experiences**
Systems thinking; creative/ innovative	Facilitate organizational learning, improvement, and innovation.	Understand organizational learning and innovation dynamics. Ability to scrutinize and question current practices and develop new ideas and approaches; ability to design and implement organizational learning mechanisms such as feedback channels and after-action reviews. Ability to identify lessons learned and align practices accordingly.	Review a historical change project and develop a case/after-action profile of lessons and recommendations; establish feedback channels and forums for reflective practice; facilitate creative problem-solving and innovation.
Empathy; ethical; democratic	Establish an environment of collaboration, information-sharing, and relational responsibility.	Understand group dynamics and team development and accountability approaches, social capital, and information-sharing and problem-solving networks. Ability to develop approaches to collaboration over competition, create a sense of team unity, and structure rewards for collaborative behavior.	Complete coaching and leadership self-assessment exercises; conduct team-building activities; lead and manage task-organized multidisciplinary teaming arrangements and work structures; establish mentoring practices.
Empowerment; power-sharing; coalition-building; trust-building; attention to detail	Establish change implementation management practices, structures, and strategies.	Ability to understand, implement, and manage processes for assessing change and change risk; ability to create roles for individuals and units that encourage transformational practices.	Seek new areas of responsibility and/or share existing areas with others in the organization; suggest new structures or processes that will be change-oriented.
	Develop change-centric leaders and managers.	Ability to institutionalize practices to develop transformational stewardship competencies and awareness in other employees, managers, and leaders.	Initiate a 360-degree evaluation that includes attributes of transformational stewardship; establish change-oriented rotational assignments.
Ethical; empathy; foresight; reflective/ learning-oriented; trustee	Develop a transformational ethic in approaching responsibilities.	Recognize and appreciate own transformational responsibilities as a steward to the larger purpose of public service, and the requirement to work toward synthesizing the collective interests of stakeholders. Ability to be acutely aware of both the strategic and evolving nature of the mission/ agency, as well as to demonstrate commitment and responsibility to the stakeholder needs and interests involved in pursuing change.	Complete role simulation exercises that extend awareness of multiple perspectives and roles; speak, write, and act in a transformationally aware, accountable, and responsible manner.
	Develop a personal growth and development plan.	Understand the Constitution and applications of fairness, equity, and due process of law in all operations. Ability to assess own strengths and weaknesses; ability to devise a personal development plan and the courage to implement it.	Complete a 360-degree evaluation and develop a personal plan for growth and renewal.

while steadily scanning for improvement opportunities and creative solutions.

The Developmental Agenda

We have listed six broad areas of responsibility for transformational stewardship for renewal and growth. For the organization, transformational stewardship responsibilities include creating a learning organization; enhancing ethical collaboration; creating change-centric practices, systems, and strategies; and developing other change leaders. The responsibility to nurture transformational capacity requires change-centric ways of perceiving and relating (e.g., creativity, comfort with ambiguity, integrative/systems thinking) as well as interpersonal attributes that emphasize extending the concept of transformational stewardship throughout the organization (especially building trust, empowering, and power sharing). These attributes help transformational stewards create organizations that are open and adaptive to change, with people throughout the organization willing to assume leadership roles in the constant renewal of the organization.

Transformational stewards also are responsible for their own nurturing—which in the crush of work often gets less attention than it should. In this case, the continued development of a person's "inner-personal beliefs and values" is vital. These traits include ethical reasoning, self-reflection, empathy, vision or foresight, and creativity. In addition, attributes related to developing a change-centric operational mindset also are important (especially attention to detail, comfort with ambiguity, and integrative/systems thinking). The development of these attributes often comes only when a person is willing to take the time to step back and assess where he or she is, what is going well, and what could be improved. This reinvigoration should be something that continues throughout a person's life and career.

Personal retreats, conferences, sabbaticals, university courses, journal writing, and ongoing dialogue with a mentor are all methods of self-improvement that have their advocates. Similarly, assessment instruments (such as 360-degree evaluations) that assess an individual's or team's transformational skills are often useful to help leaders become more aware of their transformational proficiency. (Appendix B provides an illustration of one such 360-degree evaluation.) These methods can be applied formally through organizational training and development programs, or informally by individual leaders and managers seeking to become more confident and effective. Ideally, a combination of formal and informal means can be employed to facilitate skill development.

Each of these responsibilities is associated with particular knowledge, skills, and abilities. Just as with the attributes, there is some overlap in this area; however, we believe there is enough differentiation to provide guidance to a person wanting to exercise transformational stewardship. For example, the responsibility of creating a learning organization is associated with the ability (and willingness) to scrutinize and question current practices and to be open to new ideas and concepts. It means creating feedback mechanisms within the organization to encourage learning. It means not punishing mistakes, but learning from them. Reflective practice requires developing specific skills and implementing realistic approaches for assessing experience, recognizing lessons, and taking action to address deficiencies.

Other abilities include the following:

- Becoming more risk-aware, perceiving strategic and operational change initiatives in terms of both opportunity and risk
- Assessing and creatively managing risk to minimize its potential negative consequences
- Enhancing ethical communication and authentic collaboration within the organization or network
- Engaging in personal learning and growth.

Transformational stewards are responsible for enhancing ethical communication and authentic collaboration within their organizations. To accomplish this, stewards must understand workplace standards, good ethical practices, and approaches to mentoring and individual development, as well as how to structure team and work collaborative incentives. However, this knowledge serves as just the frame for actually providing the mentoring, coaching, and individual and team development—practices that all managers and leaders should follow, particularly those seeking to practice transformational stewardship.

When transformational competencies and experiences are recognized explicitly as requirements for promotion, leaders and managers are much more likely to consistently seek out and commit to investing time and effort in pursuit of such skills. As an example, in the early days of the "Six Sigma" process improvement initiative at General Electric, Chief Executive Jack Welch established the requirement that, in order to be promoted into a management position, an individual had to complete process improvement and reengineering training and had to accomplish a successful transformation project (Cavanagh, Neuman, and Pande 2002). The result was not surprising: Would-be managers got the training and went out in search of opportunities to lead change.

IMPLICATIONS FOR CHANGE LEADERS

We believe that the traditional approaches to leadership development in the areas of change and transformation are insufficient in today's challenging public service environment. Transformational stewardship is a way of understanding change leadership in the public and nonprofit sectors. We have identified specific attributes that we think are closely aligned with this concept and have indicated how they relate to the various phases of change and transformation: diagnosing, strategizing and making the case for change, implementing and sustaining, and growth and renewal. Finally, we have presented a developmental framework relating attributes and the knowledge, skills, and abilities to the responsibilities and tasks required of effective transformational stewards.

Transformation in the public interest is difficult, even with the necessary skills and abilities. However, the ability to lead change successfully is such an important task that we cannot continue to merely "wing it" and rely on traditional training for public and nonprofit leadership and management. The basic responsibilities, abilities, and skills that we have identified are necessary ingredients to the success of all organizations, and particularly those entrusted to serve the public interest. Approaching this challenge in an informed, comprehensive manner is critical, and a combination of enhancing transformation knowledge and learning from developmental experiences is needed to make talented leaders.

PRACTICAL TIPS FOR THE CHANGE LEADER

- Ask your employee training officer whether your organization is providing training in leading change or transformational stewardship concepts.

- Find ways to reward/celebrate evidence of creativity, innovation, and systems thinking in your organization.

- Volunteer to be part of a team conducting an analysis of one of the elements of change (e.g., environmental scan, organizational capacity, risk assessment).

- Initiate a major strategic planning exercise and involve both internal and external stakeholders that might be affected by possible changes.

- Commit to a mentoring program, both for your own growth and to assist others in the organization. Become a mentor yourself.

- Conduct a 360-degree evaluation of your transformational stewardship skills to assess areas of strength and weakness.

- Take the time for personal reflection and growth—retreats, meditation, courses, etc.

◼ SUGGESTED READINGS ON DEVELOPING TRANSFORMATIONAL STEWARDS

C. Michael Thompson, *The Congruent Life: Following the Inward Path to Fulfilling Work and Inspired Leadership*. San Francisco: Jossey-Bass Publishers, 2000.

Thompson argues that we should not separate our personal and professional selves; both have to be guided by our inner spiritual values. Development of the individual spirit, he contends, can lead to both personal and organizational fulfillment. The author's research and illustrations provide a compelling case for the "fruits of the spirit." Questions and exercises for further reflection are included to enable readers to apply the author's concepts to their personal lives.

Daniel Goleman, Annie McKee, and Richard Boyatkzis. *Primal Leadership: Realizing the Power of Emotional Intelligence*. Boston: Harvard Business School Press, 2002.

Goleman, author of the groundbreaking *Working with Emotional Intelligence* (New York: Bantam, 1998), which advanced the concept of a leader's emotional intelligence (EI), teams with McKee and Boyatkzis to further explore the concept and provide readers with an approach to leadership development. Their approach includes assessing, developing, and sustaining personal EI over time, cultivating "resonant" leadership throughout teams and organizations, and building emotionally intelligent organizations. Included is Boyatkzis' "theory of self-directed learning," which provides a feedback process for leadership development.

Peter B. Vaill, *Learning as a Way of Being: Strategies for Survival in a World of Permanent White Water*. San Francisco: Jossey-Bass Publishers, 1996.

In his 1989 book, *Managing as a Performing Art* (San Francisco: Jossey-Bass), Vaill coined the term "permanent white water" to characterize the turbulent environment of modern organizations. In this book, Vaill argues that traditional management programs have not equipped managers to be leaders in a changing environment. If managers are to navigate this environment, they must make continuous learning part of their personal being. Such learning encapsulates risk-taking, self-direction, and the integration of life's lessons from both our personal and professional lives.

Warren Bennis and Joan Goldsmith, *Learning to Lead: A Workbook on Becoming a Leader.* New York: Perseus (Basic) Books, 2003.

Bennis, who with Burt Nanus wrote an important book on leadership, *Leaders: The Strategies for Taking Change* (2nd ed., New York: Harper-Business, 1997), teams up with Joan Goldsmith to fashion a workbook for those who want to become more effective leaders. The authors take the reader through a set of practical exercises for understanding their concepts of leadership and learning modes and becoming more effective leaders in three broad areas: creating and communicating a vision, maintaining trust though integrity, and realizing intention through action. The workbook also contains an excellent bibliography of resources on leadership development.

CHAPTER ELEVEN

Final Thoughts: An Invitation to Change

As an old Arabic saying goes, the only thing certain in this world is change. It is inevitable that the workforce, the economy, the nature of public problems, and the complexity of public service will continue to evolve in unexpected ways in the coming years. The challenges, or change imperative, that public service leaders will face are not predictable in subject matter, timing, or magnitude (as we discuss in Chapter 1). While we cannot know what the future holds, we can nevertheless prepare for the "certainty of uncertainty."

Part of this uncertainty stems from the reality that public service today involves networks of public, nonprofit, and private organizations. We expect private sector leaders' values to arise from the self-interest of their own organizations; public and nonprofit leaders, in contrast, must focus on the broader public interest as articulated in their country's constitution, laws, and other governing documents. Increasingly, nonprofit and private organizations are serving as important supplementary or complementary actors to public agencies in delivering public goods and services (Young 2007); their business *is* public service.

Serving the public interest in an increasingly uncertain and diverse world requires new and different skills. Increasingly, change-centric leadership is needed to anticipate and act proactively, whether a change is voluntary or is imposed on the organization. The public needs caring, empathetic leaders who steward people and organizational resources with vision and integrity through changing circumstances. We have defined the nature of that leadership as *transformational stewardship* (defined and explored in Chapter 2). Attributes of that leadership include personal values, an operational mindset, and interpersonal abilities and skills that are essential for all public service leaders (see Table 11.1).

TABLE 11.1: Attributes of Transformational Stewards

Inner-personal Beliefs or Values
- Ethical, personally and organizationally
- Reflective, learning-oriented
- Empathetic, an active listener
- Visionary, acts with foresight
- Creative, innovative

Operational Mindset
- Trustee, caretaker for the public interest
- Mission-driven
- Integrative, a systems thinker
- Accountable, transparent
- Attentive to details
- Comfortable with ambiguity

Interpersonal Abilities/Interactions with Others
- Trust-builder
- Empowers others
- Democratic, participatory
- Power-sharer
- Coalition-builder

Anticipating and planning for change in public and nonprofit organizations also requires leaders to be proficient in assessing the risks associated with change, considering the consequences for stakeholders, assessing relevant organizational capacities, and developing appropriate strategies for change. Effective stewardship in the public service is likely to be more challenging—and yet more rewarding—than in the private sector. The risks of failure rise with the number and diversity of the stakeholders involved in networked governance, and because of the multiple objectives and values that guide governmental action.

WHERE TO START?

The key is to embrace change as the new reality and develop more change-centric leadership and more change-centric organizational cultures in our public and nonprofit organizations. Our leadership responsibilities model provides a foundation for the duties of public and nonprofit leaders in this regard (see Figure 11.1 and Chapter 3 for details). Perhaps most important for leaders is a clear analysis of their organization's capacity to facilitate change in an often turbulent environment. We offer a personal assessment tool (Appendix B) to help change leaders assess their own abilities to lead public and nonprofit organizations.

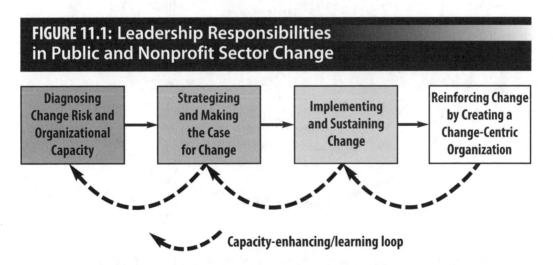

FIGURE 11.1: Leadership Responsibilities in Public and Nonprofit Sector Change

Our model for leading change in the public interest (see Figure 11.2 and Chapter 3 for details) provides an approach to assist leaders in assessing how change-centric their organizations are and how much risk they will face in implementing specific change initiatives. Our model is an analytical tool to help public and nonprofit leaders identify key predictors of organizational challenges associated with change initiatives. Our diagnostic instrument (Appendix A) can be used by leaders and managers to evaluate the types of risks imposed by specific change initiatives.

FIGURE 11.2: A Model for Leading Change in the Public Interest

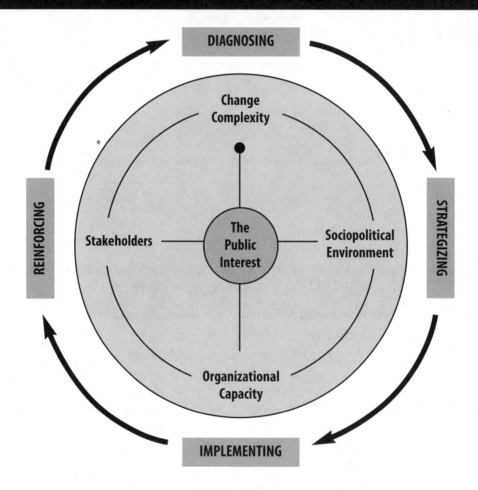

EFFECTIVE STEWARDSHIP IN THE PUBLIC INTEREST

Existing knowledge on organizational leadership, enhanced by our own case research (presented in Chapter 4) and our model, leads us to offer some insights on the effective leadership of change.

First, organizational cultures that support innovative and risk-taking leadership are more likely to facilitate change successfully. Creating and enhancing such cultures, while not an easy task, are principal responsibilities of good public and nonprofit leadership (see Chapter 6). The multisector workforce involved in 21st century public service presents the reality that people from multiple individual and organizational cultures must work together. Recognizing and appreciating the diverse values and norms that shape different work cultures, which are part of public service, are the first steps toward enhancing the values and rewards of innovation and learning.

Ultimately, the goal of good stewardship is to forge common goals and values that multisector partners can all support, enhancing trust and mutual respect. This approach proved particularly effective in both the Fairfax County Department of Systems Management for Human Services (DSMHS) and the Veterans Health Administration change initiatives.

Second, the enormous complexity of change initiatives imposed on public agencies, such as pay-for-performance, competitive sourcing, enhanced accountability standards, and public-private partnerships, require public and nonprofit leaders to work effectively with their diverse stakeholders. Together they must develop new work processes and ensure that incentives reward decisions that benefit public rather than private interests.

Evaluating change complexity is extremely important, both in formulating the initial strategy for the change and in developing change capacity in organizations. In our case studies, the leadership often underestimated the complexity of a change initiative, resulting in delays and subpar performance.

Third, unanticipated changes in the external environment, particularly in resources or political support, can exacerbate the risk of change, increasing the likelihood that the initiatives will fail. The more nimble leaders are in navigating a fluid change environment, the greater the potential to address and overcome that risk. Proactive intelligence gathering about the relevant environment is essential; collecting that intelligence requires consistent communication with internal and external stakeholders.

Strategies to gain the support of the public or potential allies in the change process are integral parts of most change initiatives. Such strategies have been particularly important for the U.S. Coast Guard, which faces a turbulent post-9/11 environment. The resulting changes in structure and mission have greatly influenced the scope and process of the Coast Guard's change initiative.

Fourth, thorough communication and collaboration with stakeholders are time-consuming and sometimes costly up-front; however, they add great value to organizational capacity and are essential for operating in an environment of multisector governance. Establishing trust and authentic collaboration with stakeholders facilitates decision-making that protects the public interest. Active listening is a critical component of effective stewardship; it often takes more skill and energy than speaking, but can yield important information that is key to successful collaboration.

All our change cases contain valuable lessons about the importance of developing an authentic dialogue among diverse internal and external stakeholders. The most successful initiatives were those where leadership spent the time to build trust and collaboration for the long-term change objectives (see Chapter 5).

Fifth, leaders cannot rely on their existing organizational structures to facilitate change. There is no one approach that is applicable in all cases; however, the development of an independent change organization, restructuring of the existing organization, institution of new processes, or reliance on a "change vanguard" may be important to support the change initiative.

Our cases demonstrate the success of a variety of approaches, including ad hoc and formal task forces, strategic planning efforts, new accreditation processes, empowered regional structures, and integrated service networks (described in Chapter 7). Our one example of a public-private partnership, the U.S. Coast Guard Deepwater program, proved more problematic, as conflicting cultures hindered the change effort. However, as Ron Carlee points out in Chapter 9, networked approaches will be increasingly important in an era of globalization and multisector actors in change initiatives.

Sixth, relevant performance data allow leaders to initiate, measure, and communicate about the progress of change initiatives. However, as with stakeholder collaboration, building trusting relationships among those impacted is a prerequisite for both the collection and use of performance data. Our cases demonstrate that when stakeholders develop ownership in the measures of performance, they are more likely to buy into the objectives of the change (as shown in Chapter 8).

Finally, change-centric leadership can be learned and developed, but only practice ensures prowess. Organizations should work to develop change-centric leadership—

throughout the organization—by providing the knowledge, skills, and developmental experiences that individuals need to become effective agents of change (as proposed in Chapter 10). Effective stewards need to transmit their values through their behavior and their commitment to providing resources that support employees' learning and growth.

CHANGE IS POSSIBLE—IF LEADERS AND ORGANIZATIONS ARE PREPARED

Our research indicates that successful public sector change is possible. Success stories include the transformation of the Veterans Health Administration from a frail, beleaguered institution to a dynamic and value-driven system of patient care. Similarly, the Fairfax County DSMHS transformed the manner in which the county and nonprofit organizations coordinate human service delivery programs. While the U.S. Coast Guard's Deepwater program faces difficulties in an exceedingly complex environment, strong change-centric leaders are determined to transform the performance and effectiveness of service assets and personnel. REAL ID is in its preliminary implementation phase, but good leadership has assisted the state motor vehicle administrations in planning for the major change. The two very effective nonprofit leaders at N Street Village and Hillel took risks when they reengineered their organizations' ways of doing business through extensive outreach to relevant stakeholders.

We are optimistic that public and nonprofit organizations can meet the evolving challenges of 21st century public service. We believe that the analyses, models, and instruments we provide here can assist leaders of those organizations in becoming successful stewards of people, resources, and processes in the public interest.

APPENDIX A

Leadership Change-Risk Diagnostic Instrument

This Leadership Change-Risk Diagnostic Instrument is designed to assist public and nonprofit sector leaders/managers as they plan a major change or transformation effort. The instrument considers aspects of change risk and organizational capacity, examining how "pertinent" a particular risk or capacity is to the change effort versus "organizational change preparedness or performance." Measuring pertinence assists a change leader in identifying the extent to which different aspects of the organization and its environment are important to the change effort (i.e., the aspects that may influence the success of the change or transformation effort). Measuring preparedness/performance indicates the extent to which the organization is addressing those aspects as it prepares for and implements major change.

The difference between the pertinence of an aspect of change and an organization's preparedness/performance highlights potential areas of risk for the organization regarding the proposed change. The greater the identified risk, the more compelling the case for either scaling down the change or addressing areas of weakness.

ASSESSING CHANGE RISK

This diagnostic instrument is based on our transformational stewardship risk model (presented in Chapter 3) and research we conducted on change and transformation in the public and nonprofit sectors. The model suggests that "change risk" is a function of change complexity, stakeholders, organizational capacity, the sociopolitical environment, and their interactions (see Figure A.1).

Change Complexity

The more complex the change, the greater the change risk. Complexity is a function of the scope, magnitude, and fluidity of the change effort. Complexity affects and is affected by stakeholders in the change (both those internal and those external to the organization). Increased scope adds to the number of stakeholders that are impacted. Stakeholders' perceptions about their potential loss or gain from the change increase the "magnitude" of the change.

Change complexity must be assessed and planned for in advance of a major change and periodically addressed during the change itself. A change that is too complex, without the corresponding organizational capacity, will likely fail. The Leadership

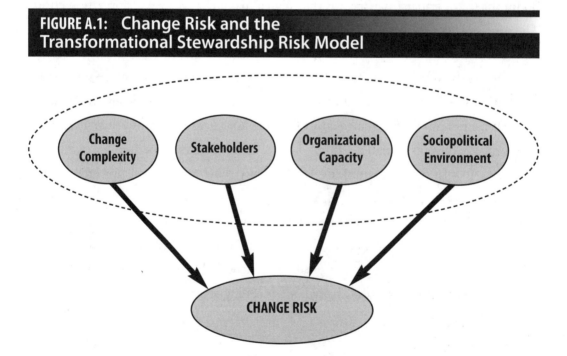

FIGURE A.1: Change Risk and the Transformational Stewardship Risk Model

Change-Risk Diagnostic Instrument enables change leaders/managers to assess various aspects of complexity in terms of (1) how pertinent or significant they are to the change effort, and (2) how well the organization is prepared to deal with the complexity.

Stakeholders

The greater the number and diversity of stakeholders, the greater their concerns about gain or loss resulting from the change effort; the level (or lack) of networks among stakeholders also affects the risk of change. Change managers should assess the role of stakeholders in change initiatives by analyzing the intensity of stakeholder perceptions, the diversity of the stakeholders, and the existence of collaborative networks to facilitate stakeholder relations. If this is done well, it reduces complexity and change risk. If it is not done well, both complexity and risk increase.

The Leadership Change-Risk Diagnostic Instrument enables change leaders/ managers to examine the pertinence or significance of stakeholder perceptions and the existence of communication and collaboration strategies that might ameliorate the concerns of stakeholders.

Sociopolitical Environment

Any change effort takes places in a larger context. This context will include legal and policy constraints, economic conditions, and the influence of actors outside the organization as well as the public. To identify how the sociopolitical environment affects change risk, change leaders must examine whether the organization (1) has a process for monitoring the external environment to identify problems and opportunities, and (2) has structures in place to influence the sociopolitical environment. The Leadership Change-Risk Diagnostic Instrument enables change leaders to assess their relationship with the sociopolitical environment.

Organizational Capacity

For any major change effort, organizations must have the internal capacity to initiate and sustain a major change effort. While there are many aspects of organizational capacity, we believe that the most important for successful change are effective organizational leadership, organizational culture, change mechanisms, and performance measurement. Like change complexity, stakeholders, and the sociopolitical environment, the various aspects of an organization's capacity can be measured to determine the extent to which they are pertinent or important to the change effort and the extent to which they are already being performed by the organization. The Leadership Change-Risk Diagnostic Instrument enables change leaders/managers to assess both the pertinence and the performance of a number of key organizational capacity variables.

■ USING THE LEADERSHIP CHANGE-RISK DIAGNOSTIC INSTRUMENT

The Leadership Change-Risk Diagnostic Instrument consists of a set of questions designed to assist change leaders/managers in measuring both the pertinence and the organizational preparedness/performance of various aspects related to the proposed change. A wide set of an organization's leadership and staff should complete the instrument to gain a variety of perspectives on the importance of various aspects of the change (i.e., its pertinence) and the organization's preparedness/performance with respect to each aspect. The questions are general enough to have wide applicability to a number of types of change efforts, and the instrument can be used by various levels of organizational management.

Administering the Instrument

The diagnostic instrument is designed to be logical, user-friendly, and as useful as possible. Below is a guide to answering the first set of questions as an example of how to use the instrument.

The first set of questions involves change complexity: the magnitude, scope, and fluidity of a change effort. The first question examines "to what extent are many organizational units and employees impacted by the change?" Those filling out the instrument are asked to rate (in the left column) the question's pertinence to the successful change using the following ratings:

1. Not pertinent or relevant to the change effort (that is, it either does not impact many employees or organizational units, or its impact is virtually nil).
10. Extremely important.

Next, those filling out the instrument are asked to rate (in the right column) how well the organization is prepared to deal with this aspect of complexity (i.e., the number of people and units impacted), using the following ratings:

1. Not analyzed at all (that is, the organization makes no attempt to consider the number of employees or units impacted by the change)
10. Systematically analyzed (that is, the organization systematically analyzes the number of employees and units affected by the change and how they might be impacted).

Gaps between pertinence and performance heighten change risk and identify potential problem areas that organizational leaders and managers need to address. The Leadership Change-Risk Diagnostic Instrument is flexible; the questions under each element address a range of change characteristics that are not necessarily relevant for every change or intended to be used by every "change team." Team members can modify the questions to address their specific change. While the questions are designed to be self-explanatory, they are supported by appropriate literature and case studies in this book.

To capture the perceptions of all stakeholder categories within an organization, the survey instrument should be administered to leaders, managers, first-line supervisors, nonsupervisory staff, and technical staff. If external stakeholders or consultants are involved in this assessment process, their perceptions should be compared, but not commingled, with internal stakeholder perceptions. The survey instrument should be administered before and during implementation of the change.

Breakdowns and composite scoring provide the differences for each area and each question, highlighting areas of "high pertinence" and "low performance." Significant deficiencies are areas that leaders should target for organizational improvement prior to or during a change initiative.

Leadership Change-Risk Diagnostic Instrument

Complexity: the magnitude, scope, and fluidity of a change effort

PERTINENCE How pertinent is the identified aspect of complexity to the change effort? Scale 1–10 1 = Not at All Pertinent 10 = Extremely Pertinent	COMPLEXITY ASPECT OF THE CHANGE To what extent:	PREPAREDNESS To what extent is the identified aspect of complexity analyzed and considered in planning for the change? Scale 1–10 1 = Not at All 10 = Systematically Analyzed and Considered
1 2 3 4 5 6 7 8 9 10	1. Are many organizational units and employees affected by the change?	1 2 3 4 5 6 7 8 9 10
1 2 3 4 5 6 7 8 9 10	2. Are the organizational units affected by the change widely dispersed geographically?	1 2 3 4 5 6 7 8 9 10
1 2 3 4 5 6 7 8 9 10	3. Are partnerships with external stakeholders and organizations required to implement the change?	1 2 3 4 5 6 7 8 9 10
1 2 3 4 5 6 7 8 9 10	4. Are the organization's policies and procedures affected?	1 2 3 4 5 6 7 8 9 10
1 2 3 4 5 6 7 8 9 10	5. Will employees be required to acquire new skills?	1 2 3 4 5 6 7 8 9 10
1 2 3 4 5 6 7 8 9 10	6. Does the change initiative intrude on or alter the current routines of employees?	1 2 3 4 5 6 7 8 9 10
1 2 3 4 5 6 7 8 9 10	7. Is revision (or replacement) of information systems technology required to support the change initiative?	1 2 3 4 5 6 7 8 9 10
1 2 3 4 5 6 7 8 9 10	8. Is the organization undergoing significant changes in mission or responsibilities as a result of changes in the external environment that will require the change initiative itself to adapt?	1 2 3 4 5 6 7 8 9 10
1 2 3 4 5 6 7 8 9 10	9. Is the change initiative prescribed in a rigid manner (without discretionary flexibility)?	1 2 3 4 5 6 7 8 9 10
1 2 3 4 5 6 7 8 9 10	10. Is the external environment likely to change in ways that may affect implementation of the change initiative?	1 2 3 4 5 6 7 8 9 10

Stakeholders: The intensity of stakeholder perceptions, the diversity of stakeholders involved, and collaborative networks that are in place to facilitate the flow of communication among internal and external stakeholders

PERTINENCE How pertinent is the identified aspect of stakeholders to the change effort? Scale 1–10 1 = Not at All Pertinent 10 = Extremely Pertinent	ROLE OF STAKEHOLDER PERCEPTIONS, DIVERSITY, AND COLLABORATIVE NETWORKS To what extent:	PREPAREDNESS To what extent is the identified aspect of stakeholders analyzed or performed in the organization? Scale 1–10 1 = Not at All 10 = Systematically Analyzed or Performed
1 2 3 4 5 6 7 8 9 10	11. Are the key stakeholders diverse in terms of their professions or worldviews?	1 2 3 4 5 6 7 8 9 10
1 2 3 4 5 6 7 8 9 10	12. Have leaders adopted a common language for implementing the change that is familiar to most or all stakeholders?	1 2 3 4 5 6 7 8 9 10
1 2 3 4 5 6 7 8 9 10	13. Are efforts being made toward building trust regarding the change initiative?	1 2 3 4 5 6 7 8 9 10
1 2 3 4 5 6 7 8 9 10	14. Do stakeholders feel intensely that the proposed change will adversely affect them?	1 2 3 4 5 6 7 8 9 10
1 2 3 4 5 6 7 8 9 10	15. Are resistant stakeholders likely to negatively affect timelines or the overall success of the change?	1 2 3 4 5 6 7 8 9 10
1 2 3 4 5 6 7 8 9 10	16. Is the change initiative likely to gain the support of stakeholders who perceive they will gain from the change?	1 2 3 4 5 6 7 8 9 10
1 2 3 4 5 6 7 8 9 10	17. Are explicit, multidirectional, regular communication and collaboration structures and processes in place to facilitate the sharing of accurate information and feedback?	1 2 3 4 5 6 7 8 9 10
1 2 3 4 5 6 7 8 9 10	18. Are organizational performance plans and individual performance appraisals used as tools for communicating about and collaborating on planning and implementing changes in operations?	1 2 3 4 5 6 7 8 9 10
1 2 3 4 5 6 7 8 9 10	19. Are conflict resolution techniques available to address disagreements or misgivings about the change initiative?	1 2 3 4 5 6 7 8 9 10
1 2 3 4 5 6 7 8 9 10	20. Are stakeholder interests managed through a network of key stakeholders and program managers, rather than through a separate function (e.g., public affairs)?	1 2 3 4 5 6 7 8 9 10

Interface with Sociopolitical Environment: the organization's relationship to the outside world in terms of general support or hostility

PERTINENCE How pertinent is the identified aspect of the sociopolitical environment to the change effort? Scale 1–10 1 = Not at All Pertinent 10 = Extremely Pertinent	ORGANIZATION'S INTERFACE WITH THE SOCIOPOLITICAL ENVIRONMENT To what extent:	PREPAREDNESS To what extent is the identified aspect of the sociopolitical environment analyzed or addressed? Scale 1–10 1 = Not at All 10 = Systematically Analyzed or Addressed
1 2 3 4 5 6 7 8 9 10	21. Does the organization enjoy a positive image among policymakers, the general public, and the media?	1 2 3 4 5 6 7 8 9 10
1 2 3 4 5 6 7 8 9 10	22. Do government policies and procedures support the proposed change?	1 2 3 4 5 6 7 8 9 10
1 2 3 4 5 6 7 8 9 10	23. Is the organization likely to receive any additional resources needed to accomplish the change?	1 2 3 4 5 6 7 8 9 10
1 2 3 4 5 6 7 8 9 10	24. Have changes in legislation that are necessary for the change initiative been identified?	1 2 3 4 5 6 7 8 9 10
1 2 3 4 5 6 7 8 9 10	25. Do policymakers and citizens support the proposed change?	1 2 3 4 5 6 7 8 9 10
1 2 3 4 5 6 7 8 9 10	26. Does the organization have mechanisms in place to scan the external environment for potential threats or opportunities?	1 2 3 4 5 6 7 8 9 10
1 2 3 4 5 6 7 8 9 10	27. Are conflict resolution procedures available for the organization to use when facing opposition from key external stakeholders?	1 2 3 4 5 6 7 8 9 10
1 2 3 4 5 6 7 8 9 10	28. Has the organization prepared options if the resources needed to implement the change are not forthcoming?	1 2 3 4 5 6 7 8 9 10
1 2 3 4 5 6 7 8 9 10	29. Does the organization have an effective liaison with the legislature?	1 2 3 4 5 6 7 8 9 10
1 2 3 4 5 6 7 8 9 10	30. Does the organization have structures in place to generate support from the public?	1 2 3 4 5 6 7 8 9 10

Organizational Capacity
- Organizational Leadership
- Organizational Culture
- Change Implementation Mechanisms
- Performance Measurement

Organizational Leadership: change-centric leadership that uses a "whole systems" approach, finding the proper balance of top-down and bottom-up direction to facilitate a successful change effort, and adjusting the leadership approach depending on the nature of the change risk

PERTINENCE How pertinent is the identified aspect of organizational leadership to the change effort? Scale 1–10 1 = Not at All Pertinent 10 = Extremely Pertinent	ORGANIZATION'S LEADERSHIP CAPACITY To what extent:	PREPAREDNESS How prevalent is the identified aspect of organizational leadership in the organization? Scale 1–10 1 = Not at All 10 = Throughout
1 2 3 4 5 6 7 8 9 10	31. Do leaders provide a compelling vision and case for the proposed change?	1 2 3 4 5 6 7 8 9 10
1 2 3 4 5 6 7 8 9 10	32. Have leaders identified gaps between the vision for change and implementation realities, and developed strategies to close the gaps and strengthen the case for change?	1 2 3 4 5 6 7 8 9 10
1 2 3 4 5 6 7 8 9 10	33. Have leaders provided a common vocabulary to guide change?	1 2 3 4 5 6 7 8 9 10
1 2 3 4 5 6 7 8 9 10	34. Have leaders ensured that employees see the connection between their own work and the organizational vision for the change?	1 2 3 4 5 6 7 8 9 10
1 2 3 4 5 6 7 8 9 10	35. Have leaders negotiated a change plan or strategy in a democratic, inclusive manner?	1 2 3 4 5 6 7 8 9 10
1 2 3 4 5 6 7 8 9 10	36. Have leaders identified potential sources of change resistance and developed strategies to manage them?	1 2 3 4 5 6 7 8 9 10
1 2 3 4 5 6 7 8 9 10	37. Is the organization's senior leadership unified in support of the change vision?	1 2 3 4 5 6 7 8 9 10
1 2 3 4 5 6 7 8 9 10	38. Do mid-level managers act as change champions to help with staff buy-in and maintain a good pace for the change process?	1 2 3 4 5 6 7 8 9 10
1 2 3 4 5 6 7 8 9 10	39. Do leaders encourage collaborative decision-making and joint ownership throughout the organization?	1 2 3 4 5 6 7 8 9 10
1 2 3 4 5 6 7 8 9 10	40. Is leadership development, particularly the development of skills in change leadership, promoted throughout the organization?	1 2 3 4 5 6 7 8 9 10

Organizational Culture: the organization's internal culture and how compatible it is to change in general and to the specific change proposed

PERTINENCE How pertinent is the identified aspect of organizational culture to the change effort? Scale 1–10 1 = Not at All Pertinent 10 = Extremely Pertinent	ORGANIZATION'S CULTURE To what extent:	PREPAREDNESS How prevalent is the identified aspect of organizational culture in the organization? Scale 1–10 1 = Not at All 10 = Throughout
1 2 3 4 5 6 7 8 9 10	41. Does the culture support a systems view of issues and problems that is open to different worldviews or mental models?	1 2 3 4 5 6 7 8 9 10
1 2 3 4 5 6 7 8 9 10	42. Does the culture reinforce team learning and cross-team collaboration?	1 2 3 4 5 6 7 8 9 10
1 2 3 4 5 6 7 8 9 10	43. Is the culture supportive of innovation and risk-taking?	1 2 3 4 5 6 7 8 9 10
1 2 3 4 5 6 7 8 9 10	44. Does the culture promote creativity and change through supportive feedback, recognition, and rewards?	1 2 3 4 5 6 7 8 9 10
1 2 3 4 5 6 7 8 9 10	45. Are power and influence in the organization determined by personal attributes and skills rather than position?	1 2 3 4 5 6 7 8 9 10
1 2 3 4 5 6 7 8 9 10	46. Are employees personally committed to the organization's mission?	1 2 3 4 5 6 7 8 9 10
1 2 3 4 5 6 7 8 9 10	47. Are employees comfortable challenging organizational traditions, norms, and values?	1 2 3 4 5 6 7 8 9 10
1 2 3 4 5 6 7 8 9 10	48. Do employees share ideas for improving the quality of their work?	1 2 3 4 5 6 7 8 9 10
1 2 3 4 5 6 7 8 9 10	49. Do organizational norms and processes support a learning culture?	1 2 3 4 5 6 7 8 9 10
1 2 3 4 5 6 7 8 9 10	50. Does the culture support a democratic approach to decision-making?	1 2 3 4 5 6 7 8 9 10

Change Implementation Mechanisms: the organization's structures, processes, and policies that might be pertinent to the change efforts

PERTINENCE How pertinent are change implementation mechanisms to the specific change initiative? Scale 1–10 1 = Not at All Pertinent 10 = Extremely Pertinent	ORGANIZATION'S CHANGE IMPLEMENTATION MECHANISMS To what extent:	PREPAREDNESS To what extent are change implementation mechanisms in place in the organization? Scale 1–10 1 = Not at All 10 = Throughout
1 2 3 4 5 6 7 8 9 10	51. Are vision and mission statements pertinent to the change and clear to the members of the organization?	1 2 3 4 5 6 7 8 9 10
1 2 3 4 5 6 7 8 9 10	52. Is there flexibility to move human and financial resources to support the change effort?	1 2 3 4 5 6 7 8 9 10
1 2 3 4 5 6 7 8 9 10	53. Are performance measures in place to track outcomes of the change initiative?	1 2 3 4 5 6 7 8 9 10
1 2 3 4 5 6 7 8 9 10	54. Do employees have training and career development opportunities that enable them to support the change?	1 2 3 4 5 6 7 8 9 10
1 2 3 4 5 6 7 8 9 10	55. Are employee goals and objectives aligned with the change strategy?	1 2 3 4 5 6 7 8 9 10
1 2 3 4 5 6 7 8 9 10	56. Do change teams or other change infrastructures exist in the organization?	1 2 3 4 5 6 7 8 9 10
1 2 3 4 5 6 7 8 9 10	57. Are change mechanisms in place in the organization to facilitate networking among change agents?	1 2 3 4 5 6 7 8 9 10
1 2 3 4 5 6 7 8 9 10	58. Are information technologies available to facilitate decentralized networks?	1 2 3 4 5 6 7 8 9 10
1 2 3 4 5 6 7 8 9 10	59. Are continuous improvement programs in place?	1 2 3 4 5 6 7 8 9 10
1 2 3 4 5 6 7 8 9 10	60. Are individuals and teams encouraged to learn from their past actions, through after-action reports and other methods of learning?	1 2 3 4 5 6 7 8 9 10

Performance Measurement: ensuring that employee and organizational performance relevant to the change process is measured

PERTINENCE How pertinent is the identified aspect of performance measurement to the change effort? Scale 1–10 1 = Not at All Pertinent 10 = Extremely Pertinent	PERFORMANCE MEASUREMENT		PREPAREDNESS To what extent does the identified aspect of performance measurement exist in the organization? Scale 1–10 1 = Not at All 10 = Throughout
		To what extent:	
1 2 3 4 5 6 7 8 9 10	61. Are programmatic performance measures available to managers in the organization?		1 2 3 4 5 6 7 8 9 10
1 2 3 4 5 6 7 8 9 10	62. Are managers confident that the available performance measures are valid and reliable?		1 2 3 4 5 6 7 8 9 10
1 2 3 4 5 6 7 8 9 10	63. Do leaders in the organization support and reward the use of performance measures in managerial decision-making?		1 2 3 4 5 6 7 8 9 10
1 2 3 4 5 6 7 8 9 10	64. Do performance metrics capture the programmatic outcomes that will be affected by the change?		1 2 3 4 5 6 7 8 9 10
1 2 3 4 5 6 7 8 9 10	65. Are current performance measurement systems satisfactory (i.e., will they need to be modified, or new systems designed, to collect useful performance measures)?		1 2 3 4 5 6 7 8 9 10
1 2 3 4 5 6 7 8 9 10	66. Are resources available to modify current measurement systems or build new systems?		1 2 3 4 5 6 7 8 9 10
1 2 3 4 5 6 7 8 9 10	67. Have all appropriate stakeholders been involved in deliberations about performance measurement related to the change?		1 2 3 4 5 6 7 8 9 10
1 2 3 4 5 6 7 8 9 10	68. Are agreement and buy-in sufficient among critical internal and external stakeholders about how change-related performance should be measured?		1 2 3 4 5 6 7 8 9 10
1 2 3 4 5 6 7 8 9 10	69. Are programmatic performance measures typically used in addressing the performance of managers in the organization?		1 2 3 4 5 6 7 8 9 10
1 2 3 4 5 6 7 8 9 10	70. Is it feasible to tie change-related progress to performance measures for the appraisal of senior leaders in the organization?		1 2 3 4 5 6 7 8 9 10

Example of Scoring Change Complexity

Pertinence Score	Question	Performance Score	Ratio	Percentage
6	1) Number impacted	4	4/6	66%
8	2) Widely dispersed	4	4/8	50%
1	3) Partnering necessary	2	2/1	200%
5	4) Policies and procedures	5	5/5	100%
4	5) New skills	6	6/4	150%
10	6) Change routines	4	4/10	40%
9	7) New technology	6	6/9	66%
10	8) New mission	6	6/10	60%
8	9) Rigid change	4	4/8	50%
8	10) Changing environment	6	6/8	75%
TOTAL: 69		TOTAL: 47	47/69	68%

Analysis

Any score below 100 percent indicates that the organization is not well prepared for this aspect of complexity, and thus has a higher change risk. In this case, the overall score of 68 percent indicates a weakness in organizational readiness regarding the complexity of the change. The organization has done a good job of adjusting policies and procedures for the change and preparing employees with new skills, but is less prepared for the change of routines and the dispersed nature of the change, the use of technology during the change, and the new mission and rapidity of the change—these are the weakest areas for the organization. This assessment provides the organization with a good starting point for developing and implementing corrective actions.

APPENDIX B

Transformational Stewardship 360-degree Assessment

This Transformational Stewardship 360-degree Assessment is designed to enable individual leaders/managers (or those aspiring to become leaders) to determine the extent to which they are practicing the leadership skills of a transformational steward. The assessment consists of 48 questions covering the three broad areas and 16 attributes that define the characteristics of transformational stewards (see Table 3.2 and discussions in Chapter 3).

The leader/manager should have a cross-section of the organization complete the assessment. Ideally, this will include individuals who work for the leader/manager, peers of the leader/manager, and individuals to whom the leader/manager reports. Even if a person has not yet achieved a leadership role in an organization, an assessment by peers and

This instrument incorporates aspects of the U.S. Office of Personnel Management's Management Competency Assessment Tool. The authors would like to acknowledge the suggestions of George Washington University MPA student Audra Clark in formulating this assessment instrument.
© 2008, James Edwin Kee and Kathryn E. Newcomer.

colleagues will provide valuable information on the skills and abilities that the individual displays. The assessment can be anonymous or not, depending on the purpose for using it and the culture of the organization. (The instrument can be returned to a third party, such as the human resources department, for tabulation and to ensure anonymity.)

An individual's absolute score is not as important as the opportunity to see how others view his or her strengths and weaknesses. Comments should be encouraged. In analyzing the scoring, both the answers to specific questions and the totals in the three broad areas should be considered. Weaknesses can be addressed by examining the knowledge, skills, abilities, and experiential ideas discussed in Chapter 10 and summarized in Tables 10.1–10.4.

The questions relate to the three categories of leadership attributes as follows:
Inner-Personal Values: 1, 4, 5, 9, 13, 15, 17, 25, 29, 33, 34, 40, 41, 42, 43, 48.
Operational Mindset: 2, 6, 8, 10, 12, 14, 16, 21, 22, 24, 26, 28, 30, 32, 38, 39.
Interpersonal Abilities: 3, 7, 11, 18, 19, 20, 23, 27, 31, 35, 36, 37, 44, 45, 46, 47.

TRANSFORMATIONAL STEWARDSHIP 360-DEGREE ASSESSMENT

My Name: _____

Position: _____

Thank you for agreeing to participate in my 360-degree evaluation. Below you will find 48 statements designed to provide me with an evaluation of my leadership strengths and weaknesses. Each statement includes an optional area for comments. While comments will be extremely helpful in enabling me to analyze my strengths and weakness, please do not feel you must provide comments for every statement. You may either fill this out electronically or give me a hard copy. **Above all, please be as candid as possible to provide me with the greatest assistance with my personal growth.**

Please complete and return the assessment to _____
by _____. I really appreciate your help!

In scoring, use the following 0–10 scale:

0. **Not applicable or not observed.**
1. Ability, skill, value, and knowledge **rarely or seldom** exhibited.
10. Ability, skill, value, and knowledge exhibited **frequently or always.**

How often do I exhibit the following ability, skill, value, or knowledge?

1	When making a decision, considers various ethical principles before acting.	0 1 2 3 4 5 6 7 8 9 10
	Comments:	
2	When using the organization's resources, acts as a trustee for the organization and the public at large.	0 1 2 3 4 5 6 7 8 9 10
	Comments:	
3	Engages co-workers in trying to see how their own interests fit with the common interests and goals of the organization.	0 1 2 3 4 5 6 7 8 9 10
	Comments:	
4	Encourages initiative and change at all levels of the organization.	0 1 2 3 4 5 6 7 8 9 10
	Comments:	
5	Likes to step back from a situation and consider alternative perspectives before making a decision.	0 1 2 3 4 5 6 7 8 9 10
	Comments:	

6	Thinks it is important to share information about the organization's mission and performance throughout the organization.	0 1 2 3 4 5 6 7 8 9 10
	Comments:	
7	Actively collaborates with colleagues and stakeholders in the organization.	0 1 2 3 4 5 6 7 8 9 10
	Comments:	
8	Thinks strategically about the organization's strengths and weaknesses as part of decision-making.	0 1 2 3 4 5 6 7 8 9 10
	Comments:	
9	Seeks new ideas from and is inspired by others.	0 1 2 3 4 5 6 7 8 9 10
	Comments:	
10	Works to limit any unintended consequences of the organization's actions on the wider community.	0 1 2 3 4 5 6 7 8 9 10
	Comments:	
11	Actively listens to diverse points of view from colleagues.	0 1 2 3 4 5 6 7 8 9 10
	Comments:	
12	Thinks it is important to support fundamental processes and systems even in the midst of major change efforts.	0 1 2 3 4 5 6 7 8 9 10
	Comments:	
13	Is tolerant of colleagues, even when they disagree with her/his point of view.	0 1 2 3 4 5 6 7 8 9 10
	Comments:	
14	Keeps current on events and issues that may affect the organization.	0 1 2 3 4 5 6 7 8 9 10
	Comments:	
15	Treats others, both inside and outside the organization, with dignity and respect.	0 1 2 3 4 5 6 7 8 9 10
	Comments:	
16	Develops risk-mitigation strategies before undertaking any major new initiative.	0 1 2 3 4 5 6 7 8 9 10
	Comments:	

17	Is able to look beyond specific situations and consider the organization's mission in a broader context.	0 1 2 3 4 5 6 7 8 9 10
	Comments:	
18	Recognizes that her/his particular worldview (values, culture) is not the only valid approach to organizational issues.	0 1 2 3 4 5 6 7 8 9 10
	Comments:	
19	Is comfortable sharing power and giving credit to others in the organization.	0 1 2 3 4 5 6 7 8 9 10
	Comments:	
20	Focuses primarily on the changes needed in the organization rather than on who leads the change.	0 1 2 3 4 5 6 7 8 9 10
	Comments:	
21	Feels comfortable with defining specific goals and objectives for her/his unit to meet the organization's overall mission and vision.	0 1 2 3 4 5 6 7 8 9 10
	Comments:	
22	Measures success in multiple ways, not just in terms of profit or loss or number of persons served.	0 1 2 3 4 5 6 7 8 9 10
	Comments:	
23	Recognizes those who resist change and entrepreneurialism in the organization and develops strategies to mitigate their concerns.	0 1 2 3 4 5 6 7 8 9 10
	Comments:	
24	Is good at grasping the total situation (both the whole and the parts) and creating a vision for improvement and change in the organization that integrates various points of view.	0 1 2 3 4 5 6 7 8 9 10
	Comments:	
25	Upon finishing a project, whether a success or a failure, focuses on "What can I learn from the results?"	0 1 2 3 4 5 6 7 8 9 10
	Comments:	
26	Tries to align organizational capabilities and resources to support change initiatives.	0 1 2 3 4 5 6 7 8 9 10
	Comments:	

27	Highest value is maintaining trust with colleagues and with those who interact with the organization.	0 1 2 3 4 5 6 7 8 9 10
	Comments:	
28	Often recognizes the ambiguity involved in decisions and is comfortable making tradeoffs that involve the organization's values and goals.	0 1 2 3 4 5 6 7 8 9 10
	Comments:	
29	Challenges self to continually become more knowledgeable and skilled in dealing with organizational problems and issues.	0 1 2 3 4 5 6 7 8 9 10
	Comments:	
30	Makes sure to set goals and specific objectives for the projects that she/he personally and her/his department collectively undertake.	0 1 2 3 4 5 6 7 8 9 10
	Comments:	
31	Finds ways to give others freedom and choice in determining how to accomplish their goals.	0 1 2 3 4 5 6 7 8 9 10
	Comments:	
32	Finds ways for the organization to incorporate learning opportunities in its day-to-day activities.	0 1 2 3 4 5 6 7 8 9 10
	Comments:	
33	When considering goals and objectives, envisions the organization as a moral and ethical exemplar.	0 1 2 3 4 5 6 7 8 9 10
	Comments:	
34	Routinely takes initiative in experimenting with new approaches to problems or organizational operations.	0 1 2 3 4 5 6 7 8 9 10
	Comments:	
35	Works to build coalitions with others outside the immediate organization (i.e., with other public and nonprofit organizations, individuals, foundations, and corporations).	0 1 2 3 4 5 6 7 8 9 10
	Comments:	
36	Supports the decisions that others make, even when disagreeing with those decisions.	0 1 2 3 4 5 6 7 8 9 10
	Comments:	

37	Celebrates the accomplishments of colleagues.	0 1 2 3 4 5 6 7 8 9 10
	Comments:	
38	Follows through on commitments to co-workers and to the organization.	0 1 2 3 4 5 6 7 8 9 10
	Comments:	
39	Shares information about departmental performance widely to create a sense of collective ownership.	0 1 2 3 4 5 6 7 8 9 10
	Comments:	
40	Looks for ways that she/he and co-workers can do things better to improve the organization.	0 1 2 3 4 5 6 7 8 9 10
	Comments:	
41	Assesses and recognizes own strengths and weaknesses and pursues self-development.	0 1 2 3 4 5 6 7 8 9 10
	Comments:	
42	Behaves in an honest, fair, and ethical manner and shows consistency in words and action; models high standards of ethics.	0 1 2 3 4 5 6 7 8 9 10
	Comments:	
43	Considers and responds appropriately to the needs and feelings of various people in various situations.	0 1 2 3 4 5 6 7 8 9 10
	Comments:	
44	Makes clear and convincing written and oral presentations, listens effectively, and clarifies information as needed to enhance trust in the organization.	0 1 2 3 4 5 6 7 8 9 10
	Comments:	
45	Shows a commitment to serve the public through the organization; ensures that her/his actions meet the public interest.	0 1 2 3 4 5 6 7 8 9 10
	Comments:	
46	Is not overly concerned with own power and authority and relies more on persuasion and group power to achieve the organization's goals.	0 1 2 3 4 5 6 7 8 9 10
	Comments:	

47	Actively consults with others in the organization and key stakeholder groups before making a decision.	0 1 2 3 4 5 6 7 8 9 10
	Comments:	
48	Is able to look beyond the current situation and see future directions for the organization.	0 1 2 3 4 5 6 7 8 9 10
	Comments:	

Your name (optional): _____

Your position (optional): _____

Check one: _____ Peer or colleague

_____ Boss or a person I report to

_____ Person who reports to me

References and Further Reading

Ackoff, Russell L. 1999. *Ackoff's Best.* New York: Wiley.

Acquisition Solutions, Inc. 2001. Independent Assessment of the United States Coast Guard "Integrated Deepwater System." Acquisition Issue Brief, July 14.

Addington, Thomas, and Stephen Graves. 2002. The Forgotten Role. *Life@Work* 1(6):25–33.

Agranoff, Robert. 2003. Leveraging Networks: A Guide for Public Managers Working Across Organizations. IBM Endowment for the Business of Government.

Agranoff, Robert, and Michael McGuire. 2001. Big Questions in Public Network Management Research. *Journal of Public Administration Research and Theory* 11(3): 295–326.

Agranoff, Robert, and Michael McGuire. 2003. *Collaborative Public Management: New Strategies for Local Government.* Washington, DC: Georgetown University Press.

Albright, Kendra S. 2004. Environmental Scanning: Radar for Success. *Information Management Journal* 38(3):38.

Allen, Thad. 2006. Keynote Address. Excellence in Government Conference. Washington, DC.

Alter, Catherine, and Jerald Hage. 1993. *Organizations Working Together.* Newbury Park, CA: Sage Publications.

Altshuler, Allan A., and Robert D. Behn (eds.). 2007. *Innovation in American Government: Challenges, Opportunities, and Dilemmas.* Washington, DC: The Brookings Institution.

Anheier, Helmut K., and Nuno Themudo. 2005. The Internationalization of the Nonprofit Sector. In Robert D. Herman and Associates (ed.), *The Jossey-Bass Handbook of Nonprofit Leadership and Management.* San Francisco: Jossey-Bass.

Asch, Steven M., Elizabeth A. McGlynn, Mary M. Hogan, Rodney A. Hayward, Paul Shekelle, Lisa Rubenstein, Joan Keesey, John Adams, and Eve A. Kerr. 2004. Comparison of Quality of Care for Patients in the Veterans Health Administration and Patients in a National Sample. *Annals of Internal Medicine* 141(12): 938–45.

Atwood, Margaret, Mike Pedler, Sue Pritchard, and David Wilkinson. 2003. *Leading Change: A Guide to Whole Systems Working.* Bristol, UK: The Policy Press.

Autry, James. 2001. *The Servant Leader.* New York: Three Rivers Press.

Autry, James, and Stephen Mitchell. 1998. *Real Power: Business Lessons from the Tao Te Ching.* New York: Riverhead Books.

Axelrod, Richard H. 2000. *Terms of Engagement: Changing the Way We Change Organizations.* New York: Crown Business.

Axelrod, Robert. 1984. *The Evolution of Cooperation.* New York: Basic Books.

Axelrod, Robert. 2006. *The Evolution of Cooperation,* revised ed. New York: Perseus Books.

Badaracco, Joseph L., Jr. 1997. *Defining Moments: When Managers Must Choose between Right and Right.* Boston: Harvard Business School Press.

Banford, Robert, J. Peter Duncan, and Brian Tracy. 1999. *Simplified Strategic Planning: No-Nonsense Guide for Busy People Who Want Results Fast!* Worcester, MA: Chandler House.

Barge, J. Kevin. 2004. Antenarrative and Managerial Practice. *Communication Studies,* 55(1).

Barger, Deborah G. 2005. *Toward a Revolution in Intelligence Affairs.* Santa Monica, CA: Rand.

Barker, Joel Arthur. 1992. *Paradigms: The Business of Discovering the Future.* New York: HarperBusiness.

Barr, Stephen. 2005. Coast Guard's Response to Katrina a Silver Lining in the Storm. *The Washington Post,* September 6, Federal Diary, B2.

Bass, Bernard, and Bruce Avolio. 1994. *Improving Organizational Effectiveness Through Transformational Leadership.* Thousand Oaks, CA: Sage Publications.

BBC Editorial Guide. Available at http://www.bbc.co.uk/guidelines/editorialguidelines/edguide/privacy/publicinterest.shtml (accessed September 5, 2007).

Behn, Robert. 1998. What Right Do Public Managers Have to Lead? *Public Administration Review* 58 (3): 209–224.

Behn, Robert. 2001. *Rethinking Democratic Accountability.* Washington, DC: The Brookings Institution.

Bellinger, Gene. 2004. The Way of Systems. Available at http://www.systems-thinking.org (accessed September 5, 2007).

Bennis, Warren. 1989. *On Becoming a Leader.* New York: Perseus Books.

Bennis, Warren. 2000. Leadership of Change. In M. Beer and N. Nohria (eds.), *Breaking the Code of Change.* Boston: Harvard Business School Press, 113–121.

Bennis, Warren, and Joan Goldsmith. 2003. *Learning to Lead: A Workbook on Becoming a Leader.* New York: Perseus Books.

Bennis, Warren, and Burt Nanus. 1985. *Leaders: The Strategies for Taking Charge.* New York: Harper & Row.

Bennis, Warren, and Burt Nanus. 2007. *Leaders: The Strategies for Taking Charge,* 2nd ed. New York: Collins Business Essentials.

Bishop, Charles H., Jr. 2001. *Making Change Happen One Person at a Time.* New York: American Management Association.

Black, J. Steward, and Hal B. Gregersen. 2002. *Leading Strategic Change: Breaking Through the Brain Barrier.* Upper Saddle River, NJ: Financial Times Prentice Hall.

Blake, Robert, and Jane Mouton. 1964. *The Managerial Grid.* Houston, TX: Gulf.

Blake, Robert, and Jane Mouton. 1985. *The Managerial Grid III.* Houston, TX: Gulf.

Block, Peter. 1993. *Stewardship: Choosing Service Over Self-Interest.* San Francisco: Berrett-Koehler Publishers.

Blunt, Peter. 1997. Prisoners of the Paradigm: Process Consultants and "Clinical" Development Practitioners. *Public Administration and Development* 17: 341–349.

Board Source and Independent Sector. 2006. *The Sarbanes-Oxley Act and Implications for Nonprofit Organizations.* Washington, DC: Board Source and Independent Sector. Available at http://www.independentsector.org/issues/sarbanesoxley.html (accessed August 20, 2007).

Bridges, William. 1991. *Transitions: Making the Most of Change.* Reading, MA: Addison-Wesley.

Brinkerhoff, Derick W. 1991a. Looking Out, Looking In, Looking Ahead: Guidelines for Managing Development Programs. *Working Paper No. 1. Implementing Policy Change Project.* Washington, DC: U.S. Agency for International Development.

Brinkerhoff, Derick W. 1991b. The Program Environment and the Policy Setting: Appreciating, Adapting and Influencing. In Derick W. Brinkerhoff (ed.), *Improving Development Program Performance: Guidelines for Managers.* Boulder, CO: Lynne Rienner Publishers, Inc.: 27–61.

Brinkerhoff, Derick W. 1997. Democratic Governance and Sectoral Policy Reform: Linkages, Complementarities, and Synergies. Paper presented at the American Society for Public Administration. 58th National Conference. Philadelphia, PA.

Brinkerhoff, Derick W., and Benjamin L. Crosby. 2002. *Managing Policy Reform: Concepts and Tools for Decision-Makers in Developing and Transitioning Countries.* Bloomfield, CT: Kumarian Press, Inc.

Brinkerhoff, Jennifer M. 2002. *Partnership for International Development: Rhetoric or Results?* Boulder, CO: Lynne Rienner Publishers, Inc.

Bryson, John M. 2004. *Strategic Planning for Public and Nonprofit Organizations: A Guide to Strengthening and Sustaining Organizational Achievement,* 3rd ed. San Francisco: Jossey-Bass.

Bryson, John M., and Farnun K. Alston. 1996. *Creating and Implementing Your Strategic Plan, A Workbook for Public and Nonprofit Organizations.* San Francisco: Jossey-Bass.

Bryson, John M., Barbara C. Crosby, and Melissa Middleton Stone. 2006. The Design and Implementation of Cross-Sector Collaborations: Propositions from the Literature. *Public Administration Review* 66 (Special Issue): 44–55.

Burns, James MacGregor. 1978. *Leadership.* New York: Harper & Row.

Burns, James MacGregor. 2003. *Transforming Leadership.* New York: Atlantic Monthly Press.

Cavanagh, Roland, Robert Neuman, and Peter Pande. 2002. *The Six Sigma Way: How GE, Motorola, and Other Top Companies Are Honing Their Performance.* New York: McGraw Hill.

Chisholm, Donald. 1989. *Coordination without Hierarchy: Informal Structures in Multiorganizational Systems.* Berkeley: University of California Press.

Ciulla, Joanne B. 2004. *Ethics, the Heart of Leadership.* Westport, CT: Praeger.

Coles, Robert. 2000. *Lives of Moral Leadership.* New York: Random House.

Conger, J.A. 2000. Effective Change Begins at the Top. In M. Beer and N. Nohria (eds.), *Breaking the Code of Change.* Boston: Harvard Business School Press, 99–112.

Darling, Marilyn, Charles Parry, and Joseph Moore. 2005. Learning in the Thick of It. *Harvard Business Review Online,* July–August. Available at http://harvardbusinessonline.hbsp.harvard.edu/hbrsa (accessed August 12, 2005).

Davis, Mike, and James Edwin Kee. 2007. Forward Together: Transformational Stewardship as a Path Toward Collaborative Public Sector Change. Paper presented at American Society for Public Administration's Annual Meeting, Washington, DC.

Deal, Terrence, and Allan Kennedy. 1982. *Corporate Cultures: The Rites and Rituals of Corporate Life.* Reading, MA: Addison-Wesley.

De Geus, Arie. 1988. Planning as Learning. *Harvard Business Review,* March/April: 70–74.

Deming, W. Edward. 1986. *Out of Crisis.* Cambridge: MIT Center for Advanced Engineering Study.

Denhardt, Janet V., and Robert B. Denhardt. 2003. *The New Public Service: Serving, not Steering.* Armonk, NY: M.E. Sharpe.

Department of Systems Management for Human Services (DSMHS), Fairfax County, VA. Website 2007. Vision and mission statements. Available at http://www.fairfaxcounty.gov/dsm (accessed July 16, 2007).

Depree, Max. 1989. *Leadership Is an Art.* New York: Doubleday.

Diver, Colin. 1982. Engineers and Entrepreneurs: The Dilemmas of Public Management. *Journal of Policy Analysis and Management* 1(3): 402–406.

Downs, Anthony. 1962. The Public Interest: Its Meaning in a Democracy. *Social Research* (Spring): 1–36.

Doyle, M.E., and M.K. Smith. 2001. Shared Leadership. The Encyclopedia of Informal Education (infed). Available at http://www.infed.org/leadership/shared_leadership.htm(accessed July 17, 2007).

Dunphy, Dexter. 2000. Embracing Paradox: Top-down versus Participative Management of Organizational Change; A Commentary on Conger and Bennis. In M. Beer and N. Nohria (eds.), *Breaking the Code of Change.* Boston: Harvard Business School Press.

Editorial. 2004. Creating a Culture of Quality: The Remarkable Transformation of the Department of Veterans Affairs Healthcare System. *Annals of Internal Medicine,* 141(4): 316–318.

Editorial. 2005. A Path to Safer Hospitals. *USA Today,* March 29.

Eggers, Robert, with Howard Yoon. 2002. *Begging for Change.* New York: Harper Collins Publishers.

Eggers, William, and Stephen Goldsmith. 2004. *Government by Network: The New Public Management Imperative.* MA: Harvard University. Deloitte Research & Ash Institute for Democratic Governance and Innovation.

Elias, Arun A., and Robert Y. Cavana. 2000. Stakeholder Analysis for Systems Thinking and Modeling. Victoria University of Wellington, New Zealand, School of Business and Public Management. Available at http://www.esc.auckland.ac.nz/organisations/orsnz/conf35/papers/BobCavana.ps (accessed October 16, 2006).

Fairfax County Human Services Council. 1999. 1998–1998: *A Decade of Change in Fairfax County Human Services.* Fairfax, VA.

Fairholm, Gilbert. 1994. *Leadership and the Culture of Trust,* Westport, CT: Praeger.

Fairholm, Gilbert. 1997. *Capturing the Heart of Leadership: Spirituality and Community in the New American Workplace.* Westport, CT: Praeger.

Fairholm, Gilbert. 2000. *Perspectives on Leadership.* Westport, CT: Quorum Books.

Fielder, F.E. 1967. *A Theory of Leadership and Effectiveness.* New York: McGraw-Hill.

Fielder, F.E., and M.M. Chemers. 1974. *Leadership and Effective Management,* Glenview, IL: Scott, Foresman.

Findlay, S. 1992. Military Medicine: The Image and the Reality of Veterans' Hospitals. *U.S. News & World Report,* June.

Fisher, E.S., and H.G. Welch. 1995. The Future of the Department of Veterans Affairs Healthcare System. *Journal of the American Medical Association* 273(8): 651–67.

Fisher, Roger, William L. Ury, and Bruce Patton. 1991. G*etting to Yes: Negotiating Agreement without Giving In,* 2nd ed. New York: Penguin.

Follett, Mary-Parker. In Pauline Graham (ed.) 2003. *Mary Parker Follett: Prophet of Management.* Washington, DC: Beard.

Forsythe, Dall. 2001. *Quicker, Better, Cheaper? Managing Performance in American Government.* Albany, NY: Rockefeller Institute Press.

Fox, Elliot M., and Lyndall F. Urwick (eds.). 1973. *Dynamic Administration—The Collected Papers of Mary Parker Follett.* New York: Pitman.

Frederickson, David G., and H. George Frederickson. 2006. *Measuring the Performance of the Hollow State.* Washington, DC: Georgetown University Press.

Frederickson, H. George. 1999. The John Gaus Lecture: The Repositioning of American Public Administration. PSOnline: *Political Science and Politics* 32(4): 701–711. Available at http://www.apsanet.org (accessed fall 2006).

Freedom of Information (Scotland) Act 2002: Annual Report 2002. Office of the Information Commissioner–Ireland. Available at http://www.oic.gov.ie/en/Publications/AnnualReports/2002/AnnualReport2002TextVersion/Name,2852,en.htm (accessed November 21, 2007).

Freeman, R. Edward. 1984. *Strategic Management: A Stakeholder Approach.* Boston: Pitman.

French, W.L., and C.H. Bell. 1984. *Organization Development: Behavioral Science Interventions for Organization Improvement.* Englewood Cliffs, NJ: Prentice Hall.

Friedman, Thomas L. 2000. *The Lexus and the Olive Tree: Understanding Globalization.* New York: Anchor Books.

Friedman, Thomas L. 2006. *The World Is Flat: A Brief History of the Twenty-first Century,* updated ed. New York: Picador.

Galpin, Timothy L. 1996. *The Human Side of Change: A Practical Guide to Organization Redesign.* San Francisco: Jossey-Bass.

Gaul, Gilbert M. 2005. Revamped Veterans' Healthcare Now a Model. *Washington Post,* August 22.

Gearon, Christopher J. 2005. Military Might: Today's VA Hospitals Are Models of Top-Notch Care. *U.S. News & World Report,* July 18.

Godard, Andrew. 2005. Reform as Regulation—Accounting, Governance and Accountability in UK Local Government. *Journal of Accounting and Organizational Change* 1:1, 27–44.

Goldsmith, Arthur A. 1995. *Making Managers More Effective: Applications of Strategic Management.* Working Paper No. 9. Implementing Policy Change Project. Washington, DC: U.S. Agency for International Development.

Goldsmith, Stephen, and William D. Eggers. 2004. *Governing by Network: The New Shape of the Public Sector.* Washington, DC: Brookings Institution Press.

Goleman, Daniel. 1998. *Working with Emotional Intelligence.* New York: Bantam.

Goleman, Daniel, Annie McKee, and Richard Boyatzis. 2002. *Primal Leadership: Realizing the Power of Emotional Intelligence.* Boston: Harvard Business School Press.

Goodsell, Charles T. 1990. Public Administration and the Public Interest. In G.L. Wamsley et al. (eds.), *Refounding Public Administration.* Newbury Park, CA: Sage Publications.

Gordon, Hal. 2006. *The Speechwriters Slant.* Available at http://blog.ragan.com/ archives/speechblog/2006/08/building_a_cath.html (accessed July 2007).

Greenleaf, Robert K. 1970. *The Servant as Leader.* Newton Centre, MA: Robert K. Greenleaf Center.

Greenleaf, Robert K. 1977 (25th anniversary edition 2002). *Servant Leadership: A Journey into the Nature of Legitimate Power and Greatness.* New York: Paulist Press.

Hale, Sandra J., and Mary M. Williams (eds.). 1989. *Managing Change: A Guide to Producing Innovations from Within.* Washington, DC: The Urban Institute.

Hall, Peter Dobkin. 2005. Historical Perspectives on Nonprofit Organizations in the United States. In Robert D. Herman and Associates (eds.), *The Jossey-Bass Handbook of Nonprofit Leadership and Management.* San Francisco: Jossey-Bass.

Hardin, Garrett. 1968. The Tragedy of the Commons. *Science* 162: 1243–1248.

Hardin, Russell. 2002. *Trust and Trustworthiness.* New York: Russell Sage Foundation.

Harmon, Michael M. 1990. The Responsible Actor as 'Tortured Soul': The Case of Horatio Hornblower. In Henry D. Kass and Bayard L. Catron (eds.), *Images and Identities in Public Administration.* Newbury Park, CA: Sage Publications.

Harmon, Michael M. 1995. *Responsibility as Paradox: A Critique of Rational Discourse on Government.* Thousand Oaks, CA: Sage Publications.

Harmon, Michael M. 2007. *Public Administration's Final Exam: A Pragmatist Restructuring of the Profession and the Discipline.* Tuscaloosa: University of Alabama Press.

Harvard Business Online. 2005. The Three Myths of Collaboration. *Harvard Business Review Online,* July–August. Available at http://harvardbusinessonline.hbsp.harvard.edu/hbrsa (accessed August 12, 2005).

Harvey, Jerry. 1974. The Abilene Paradox: The Management of Agreement. *Organizational Dynamics.* Summer. Reprinted in Walter E. Natemeyer and J. Timothy McMahon. 2001. *Classics of Organizational Behavior.* Prospect Heights, IL: Waveland Press.

Hatry, Harry. 1999. *Performance Measurement: Getting Results.* Washington, DC: The Urban Institute.

Hatry, Harry. 2007. *Performance Measurement: Getting Results,* 2nd ed. Washington, DC: The Urban Institute.

Hatry, Harry, Elaine Morley, Shelli Rossman, and Joseph S. Wholey. 2003. *How Federal Programs Use Outcome Information: Opportunities for Federal Managers.* Washington, DC: IBM Endowment for the Business of Government.

Heath, Vicki. 2006. Resistance to Change and How to Deal With It. Available at http://www.leader-values.com/content/detail.asp?ContentDetailID=1111 (accessed February 5, 2007).

Hendricks, Michael. 2002. Outcome Measurement in the Nonprofit Sector: Recent Developments, Incentives, and Challenges. In K.E. Newcomer, E. Jennings, C. Broom, and A. Lomax (eds.), *Meeting the Challenges of Performance-oriented Government.* Washington, DC: The American Society for Public Administration.

Herman, Robert D., and Associates. 2005. *The Jossey-Bass Handbook of Nonprofit Leadership and Management.* San Francisco: Jossey-Bass.

Hersey, Paul, and Kenneth H. Blanchard. 1993. *Management of Organizational Behavior: Utilizing Human Resources.* Englewood Cliffs, NJ: Prentice Hall.

Hill, Linda A. 1994. Exercising Influence. Note 9-494-080. Cambridge: Harvard Business School.

Hillel: The Foundation for Jewish Campus Life. 2006. *Enriching Lives, Inspiring Commitment, Delivering the Jewish Future: Hillel's Five-Year Strategic Plan for the USA.* Washington, DC: Hillel.

Hillel website. Available at http://www.hillel.org (accessed July 15, 2007).

Horowitz, Sari, and Michael Ruane. 2003. *Sniper: The Hunt for the Killers Who Terrorized the Nation.* New York: Random House.

Hsu, Spencer C. 2007. "Job Vacancies at DHS Said to Hurt U.S. Preparedness." *Washington Post,* July 9, 2007, A1.

Hughes, Charlotte (team leader). Analysis and Planning for Redesign—Region I Team. Submitted to Fairfax County, Virginia Human Services Redesign Steering Committee, December 1993–July 1994.

Hughes, Charlotte (program manager). Customer Services Planning—Region I Prototype, Phase I: July 1994–February 1995. Submitted to Human Services Redesign Steering Committee, March 1, 1995.

Human Services Intake Redesign, Fairfax County, Virginia. Excerpt from *A Foundation for the Future—FY 1993 Strategic Direction,* February 25, 1992: 25–45.

Inglehart, John K. 1996. Reform of the Veterans Health Care System. *New England Journal of Medicine* 335(18): 1407–11.

Ingraham, P.W., P.G. Joyce, and A.K. Donahue. 2003. *Government Performance: Why Management Matters.* Baltimore: The Johns Hopkins University Press.

Jacobs, Robert W. 1994. *Real-Time Strategic Change: How to Involve Entire Organizations in Fast and Far-Reaching Change.* San Francisco: Barrett-Koehler.

Jaworski, Joseph. 1996. *Synchronicity: The Inner Path of Leadership.* San Francisco: Berrett-Koehler.

Jha, Ashish K., Jonathan B. Perlin, Kenneth W. Kizernneth, and R.A. Dudley. 2003. Effects of the Transformation of the Veterans Affairs System on the Quality of Care. *New England Journal of Medicine* 348(22): 2218–27.

Johnson, Craig. 2005. *Meeting the Ethical Challenges of Leadership: Casting Light or Shadow,* 2nd ed. Thousand Oaks, CA: Sage Publications.

Kantor, Rosabeth Moss. 1983. *The Change Masters.* New York: Simon and Schuster.

Kaplan, Robert S., and David P. Norton. 2005. Organizational Capital I, Supporting the Change Agenda That Supports Strategy Execution. In *Managing Change to Reduce Resistance.* Boston: Harvard Business School Press, 58–72.

Kass, Henry D. 1990. Stewardship as a Fundamental Image of Public Administration. In Henry D. Kass and Bayard L. Catron (eds.), *Images and Identities in Public Administration.* Newbury Park, CA: Sage Publications.

Kee, James Edwin. 2003. *Leadership as Stewardship.* Unpublished manuscript. Washington, DC: George Washington University.

Kee, Jed, and Roger Black. 1985. Is Excellence Possible in the Public Sector? *Public Productivity Review* 9(1): 25–34.

Kee, James Edwin, and Mike Davis. 2006. The Leadership Challenge of Managing Change Related Risk. *The Federal Manager.* Alexandria, VA: Federal Managers Association.

Kee, James Edwin, John Forrer, and Seth Gabriel. 2007. Not Your Father's Public Administration. *Journal of Public Affairs Education* 13(2): 253–280.

Kee, James Edwin, and Kathryn Newcomer. 2007. *Leading Change, Managing Risk: The Leadership Role in Public Sector Transformations.* Washington, DC: Center for Innovation in Public Service.

Kee, James Edwin, Kathryn Newcomer, and Mike Davis. 2007. Transformational Stewardship: Leading Public Sector Change. In Ricardo Morse, Terry Buss, and C. Morgan Kinghorn (eds.), *Transforming Public Leadership for the 21st Century.* Armonk, NY: M.E. Sharpe.

Kee, James Edwin, Kathryn Newcomer, and Mike Davis. 2008. A New Vision for Public Leaders: The Case for Developing Transformational Stewards. In Ricardo Morse and Terry Buss (eds.), *Innovations in Public Leadership Development.* Armonk, New York: M.E. Sharpe.

Kee, James Edwin, and Whitney Setzer. 2006. *Change-Centric Leadership.* Working paper. Washington, DC: Center for Innovation in the Public Service, George Washington University.

Keifer, John J., and Robert S. Montjoy. 2006. Incrementalism Before the Storm: Network Performance for the Evacuation of New Orleans. *Public Administration Review* 66: 122–130.

Kelman, Steve. 2005. *Unleashing Change: A Study of Organizational Renewal in Government.* Washington, DC: Brookings Institution Press.

Kerr, Eve A., Robert B. Gerzoff, et al. 2004. Diabetes Care Quality in the Veterans Affairs Healthcare System and Commercial Managed Care: The TRIAD Study. *Annals of Internal Medicine* 141(4): 272–81.

Kettl, Don. 1998. *Reinventing Government: A Fifth-Year Report Card.* Washington, DC: Brookings.

Kettl, Donald F. 2005. The Next Government of the United States: Challenges for Performance in the 21st Century. *Transformation of Organizations Series.* Washington, DC: IBM Center for the Business of Government. Available at http://www.businessofgovernment.org/pdfs/KettlReport.pdf (accessed March 16, 2007).

Kettl, Donald F. 2007. *System under Stress: Homeland Security and American Politics,* 2nd ed. Washington, DC: CQ Press.

Kettl, Don, and R. Jones. 2003. Assessing Public Management Reform in an International Context. *International Public Management Review* 4(1): 1–19.

Kirkpatrick, S.A. and E.A. Locke 1991. Leadership: Do Traits Matter? *The Executive* 5(2): 48–60.

Kizer, Kenneth W. 1995. The "New VA": A National Laboratory for Healthcare Quality Management. *American Journal of Medical Quality* 14(1): 3–19.

Kizer, Kenneth. 1997. *Journey of Change.* Washington, DC: U.S. Veterans Health Administration.

Klein, Susan J. 1999. Intergovernmental Collaboration in the Emergency Response to HIV Transmission in Chautauqua County. *Journal of Public Health Management Practice* 5(5): 12–18.

Kline, Peter, and Bernard Saunders. 1997. *Ten Steps to a Learning Organization,* 2nd ed. Salt Lake City: Great River Books.

Knopman, D. 2003. *Innovation and Change Management in Public and Private Organizations: Case Studies and Options for EPA.* Washington, DC: Rand.

Kotter, John. 1996. *Leading Change.* Boston: Harvard Business School Press.

Kotter, John P., and Leonard A. Schlesinger. 1979. Choosing Strategies for Change. *Harvard Business Review,* March–April: 4-11 (reprint number 79202).

Kouzes, James M., and Barry Z. Posner. 1995. *The Leadership Challenge: How to Keep Getting Extraordinary Things Done in Organizations.* San Francisco: Jossey-Bass.

Kouzes, James M., and Barry Z. Posner. 2003. *Encouraging the Heart: A Leader's Guide to Rewarding and Recognizing Others.* San Francisco: Jossey-Bass.

Kraus, Allen, Jolie Bain Pillsbury, Ajay Chaudry, and Carol Finney. 1993. *Streamlining Intake and Eligibility Systems: A Review of the Practice and the Possible, a Technical Assistance Paper for The Children's Initiative: Making Systems Work*. Funded by the Center for Assessment and Policy Development.

Lazes, Peter, and Jane Savage. 2000. Embracing the Future: Union Strategies for the 21st Century. *Journal for Quality and Participation* Fall: 18–23.

Leape, Lucian L., and Donald M. Berwick. 2005. Five Years After To Err Is Human: What Have We Learned? *Journal of the American Medical Association* 293(19): 2384–90.

Leary, Brent. 2006. Inherit the Web. *Network Journal* 14 (2, November): 34.

Light, Paul C. 1998. *Sustaining Innovation: Creating Nonprofit and Government Organizations That Innovate Naturally*. San Francisco: Jossey-Bass.

Light, Paul C. 1999. *The True Size of Government*. Washington, DC: Brookings Institution Press.

Light, Paul C. 2006. Fact Sheet on the True Size of Government. New York: Wagner School, New York University. Available at http://www.brookings.edu/gs/cps/light20030905.pdf (accessed October 3, 2007).

Linden, Russell M. 1994. *Seamless Government, A Practical Guide to Re-Engineering in the Public Sector*. San Francisco: Jossey-Bass.

Lipnack, Jessica, and Jeffrey Stamps. 1994. *The Age of the Network: Organizing Principles for the 21st Century*. New London, NH: Oliver Wight Publications.

Lipnack, Jessica, and Jeffrey Stamps. 1996. *The Age of the Network: Organizing Principles for the 21st Century* (paperback ed.). Hoboken, NJ: John Wiley & Sons.

Lipton, Eric. 2006. Security Cuts for New York and Washington. *New York Times,* June 1.

Lomas, Jonathan. 2003. Health Services Research: More Lessons from Kaiser Permanente and Veterans' Affairs Healthcare System. *British Medical Journal* 327: 1301–2.

Longman, Phillip. 2005. The Best Care Anywhere. *Washington Monthly* 37(1/2): 38–48.

Lord, R.G., C.L. DeVader, and G.M. Allinger. 1986. A Meta-analysis of the Relation between Personality Traits and Leadership Perceptions: An Application of the Validity Generalization Procedures. *Journal of Applied Psychology* 71: 402–410.

MacNeil, D. James. 1998. The AIC Process: Generating Shared Visions for Community Development in Southeast Asia. Washington, DC: Organizing for Development: An International Institute. Available at http://www.odii.com/ (accessed February 21, 2007).

Majone, Giandomenico. 1989. *Evidence, Argument, and Persuasion in the Policy Process.* New Haven: Yale University Press.

Mandell, Myrna P. 1994. Managing Interdependencies through Program Structures: A Revised Paradigm. *American Review of Public Administration* 24(1): 99–121.

Mandell, Myrna P. 1999. Community Collaborations: Working Through Network Structures. *Policy Studies Review* 16(1, spring): 42–64.

Mann, R.D. 1959. A Review of the Relationship between Personality and Performance in Small Groups. *Psychological Bulletin* 56: 241–270.

Matheson, Scott M., with James Edwin Kee. 1986. *Out of Balance.* Salt Lake City: Peregrine Smith Books.

McKinsey and Company. 2007. Capacity Assessment Grid. Appendix of a report on Venture Philanthropy Partners. Available at http://www.vppartners.org/learning/reports/capacity/assessment.pdf (accessed June 10, 2007).

McLaughlin, J.A., and G.B. Jordan. 2004. Using Logic Models. In J. Wholey, H.P. Hatry, and K.E. Newcomer (eds.), *Handbook of Practical Program Evaluation* (2nd ed.). San Francisco: Jossey-Bass.

McNamara, Carter. 2007. Strategic Planning (in Nonprofit or For-Profit Organizations). Free Management Library. Available at http://www.managementhelp.org/plan_dec/ str_plan/str_plan.htm (accessed January 9, 2008).

McSwite, O.C. 2001. Theory Competency for MPA-educated Practitioners. *Public Administration Review* 61:111–114.

Metzenbaum, Shelley H. 2006. Performance Accountability: The Five Building Blocks and Six Essential Practices. *Managing for Performance and Results Series.* Washington, DC: IBM Center for the Business of Government. Available at http://www.businessofgovernment.org/pdfs/MetzenbaumReport2.pdf (accessed March 16, 2007).

Mihm, Christopher. 2002. Beyond Plans, Promised and Good Intentions: Instilling Results-oriented Management in Federal Agencies. In K.E. Newcomer, E. Jennings, C. Broom and A. Lomax (eds.), *Meeting the Challenges of Performance-oriented Government.* Washington, DC: The American Society for Public Administration: 37–48.

Milward, H. Brinton, and Keith G. Provan. 2006. A Manager's Guide to Choosing and Using Collaborative Networks. *Networks and Partnerships Series.* Washington, DC: IBM Center for the Business of Government.

Mitchell, Terrence R., and William G. Scott. 1987. Leadership Failures, the Distrusting Public, and Prospects of the Administrative State. *Public Administration Review* 47 (6): 445–452.

Moe, Kari J. 2006. *The Challenges of Local Homeland Security Preparedness: A Case Study of the National Capital Region.* Dissertation. Washington, DC: George Washington University.

Moe, Ronald. 1994. The "Reinventing Government" Exercise: Misinterpreting the Problem, Misjudging the Consequences, *Public Administration Review* 54 (2): 446–462.

Moe, Ronald. 2001. The Emerging Federal Quasi Government: Issues of Management and Accountability. *Public Administration Review* 61 (3): 290–312.

Morgan, Gareth. 1988. *Riding the Wave of Change: Developing Managerial Competencies for a Turbulent World.* San Francisco: Jossey-Bass.

N Street Village. 2005. *Annual Report.* Available at http://www.nstreetvillage.org/news/annual-reports.cfm(accessed January 2, 2008).

N Street Village, mission statement. Available at http://www.nstreetvillage.org (accessed July 15, 2007).

National Academy of Public Administration. 2002. *The 21st Century Federal Manager: A Study of Changing Roles & Competencies.* Vienna, VA: Management Concepts.

National Academy of Public Administration. 2003. *Leadership for Leaders.* Vienna, VA: Management Concepts.

National Academy of Public Administration. 2005. *Academy Initiative: Managing Federal Missions with a Multisector Workforce: Leadership for the 21st Century.* Washington, DC: November 16.

National Commission on Terrorist Attacks on the United States. 2004. *The 9/11 Commission Report.* New York: W.W. Norton & Company.

Newcomer, Kathryn (ed.). 1997. *Using Performance Measurement to Improve Public and Nonprofit Programs.* San Francisco: Jossey-Bass.

Newcomer, Kathryn E. 2006. How Does Program Performance Assessment Affect Program Management in the Federal Government? *Public Performance and Management Review* 30 (3 March): 350–371.

Newcomer, Kathryn E. 2008. Assessing Performance in Nonprofit Service Agencies. In P. Lancer Julnes, F. Stokes Berry, M. Aristigueta and K. Yang (eds.), *International Handbook of Practice-Based Performance Management, Public Performance and Management Review.* Thousand Oaks, CA: Sage Publications.

Newcomer, Kathryn, Edward Jennings, Cheryle Broom, and Allen Lomax. 2002. *Meeting the Challenges of Performance-Oriented Government.* Washington, DC: The American Society for Public Administration.

Newcomer, Kathryn, Deborah Trent, Brent Bushey, Charlene Johnson, Mike Davis, and Allen Cermak. 2006. *A Strategic Framework for Implementation of Human Capital Management in the Federal Government.* Washington, DC: Center for Innovation in Public Service.

Northouse, P.G. 2004. *Leadership Theory and Practice.* Thousand Oaks, CA: Sage Publications.

O'Leary, Rosemary et al. (eds.). 2006. *Public Administration Review, Special Issue on Collaborative Public Management* 66(s1).

O'Reilly, Charles, Jennifer Chatman, and David Caldwell. 1991. People and Organizational Culture: A Profile Approach to Assessing Person-Organization Fit. *Academy of Management Journal* 34: 487–516.

O'Rourke, Ronald. 2005. *Coast Guard Deepwater Program: Background and Issues for Congress.* Washington, DC: Congressional Research Service. Available at http://www.house.gov/transportation/cgmt/03-03-05/03-03-05memo.html (accessed January 2006).

Osborne, David, and Ted Gaebler. 1992. *Reinventing Government: How the Entrepreneurial Spirit Is Transforming the Public Sector.* Reading, MA: Addison-Wesley.

Osborne, David, and Peter Plastrik. 1997. *Banishing Bureaucracy.* New York: Penguin Putnam.

Osborne, David, and Peter Plastrik. 2000. *The Reinventor's Fieldbook: Tools for Transforming Your Government.* San Francisco: Jossey-Bass.

Oster, Sharon M. 1995. *Strategic Management for Nonprofit Organizations: Theory and Cases.* Oxford: Oxford University Press.

O'Toole, Larry J., Jr., and K.I. Hanf. 2002. American Public Administration and Impacts of International Governance, *Public Administration Review* 62: 158–169.

Owen, Harrison. 2000. *The Power of Spirit: How Organizations Transform.* San Francisco: Barrett-Koehler.

Pascale, Richard, Mark Millemann, and Linda Gioja. 2000. *Surfing the Edge of Chaos: The Laws of Nature and the New Laws of Business.* New York: Crown Business.

Peters, Thomas J., and Robert H. Waterman. 1982. *In Search of Excellence: Lessons from America's Best-Run Companies.* New York: Harper and Row.

Phillips, J.T., and J.M Loy. 2003. *Character in Action: The U.S. Coast Guard on Leadership.* Annapolis, MD: The Naval Institute Press.

Poister, Theodore H. 2003. *Measuring Performance in Public and Nonprofit Organizations:* San Francisco: Jossey-Bass.

Provan, Keith G., and Patrick Kenis. 2007. Modes of Network Governance: Structure, Management, and Effectiveness. *Journal of Public Administration Research and Theory Advance Access* (August 2).

Putnam, Robert D. 2000. *Bowling Alone: The Collapse and Revival of American Community.* New York: Simon and Schuster.

Raelin, J.A. 2003. *Creating Leaderful Organizations: How to Bring Out Leadership in Everyone.* San Francisco: Berrett-Koehler Publishers.

Random House Dictionary of the English Language, College Edition. 1968. New York: Random House.

Richmond, B. 2001. *An Introduction to Systems Thinking.* Hanover, NH: High Performance Systems.

Romzek, Barbara S., and Melvin J. Dubnick. 1987. Accountability in the Public Sector: Lessons from the Challenger Tragedy. *Public Administration Review* 47 (3): 227–38.

Rosen, Mark I., with analysis by Amy L. Sales. 2006. *The Remaking of Hillel: A Case Study on Leadership and Organizational Transformation.* New York: Fisher-Bernstein Institute for Jewish Philanthropy and Leadership, January.

Rubin, Claire (ed.). 2007. *Emergency Management: The American Experience, 1900–2005.* Fairfax, VA: Public Entity Risk Institute.

Rutzick, Karen. 2006. Coast Guard Chief Stresses Importance of Focusing on Employees. *Government Executive,* December 13. Available at http://www.govexec.com/dailyfed/1206/121306r1.htm (accessed December 14, 2006).

Savas, E.S. 2000. *Privatization and Public-Private Partnerships.* New York: Chatham House.

Schein, Edgar H. 2004. *Organizational Culture and Leadership.* San Francisco: Jossey-Bass.

Schubert, Glendon A. 1960. *The Public Interest.* New York: Free Press.

Selden, Sally C., Jessica E. Sowa, and Jodi Sandfort. 2006. The Impact of Nonprofit Collaboration in Early Child Care and Education on Management and Program Outcomes. *Public Administration Review* 66(3): 412–425.

Senge, Peter. 1990. *The Fifth Discipline: The Art and Practice of the Learning Organization.* New York: Doubleday.

Senge, Peter, Charlotte Robert, Richard B. Ross, Bryan J. Smith, and Art Kleiner. 1994. *The Fifth Discipline Fieldbook: Strategies and Tools for Building a Learning Organization.* New York: Doubleday.

Senge, Peter, Charlotte Robert, Richard B. Ross, Bryan J. Smith, and Art Kleiner. 1999. *The Dance of Change: The Challenge of Sustaining Momentum in Learning Organizations.* New York: Doubleday.

Sentell, Gerald D. 1998. *Creating Change-Capable Cultures.* Provo, UT: Executive Excellence Publishing.

Simmons, John. 2003. Reconciling Effectiveness and Equity in Performance Management: A Stakeholder Synthesis Approach to Organizational Systems Design. *Systemic Practice and Action Research* 16(5): 355–365.

Simone, Maria. 2006. *Processes, Principles and Policies: The Public Interest Standard in U.S. Media.* Policy Paper presented at the annual meeting of the International Communication Association, Sheraton New York, NY. Available at http://www.allacademic.com/meta/p14310_index.html (accessed October 1, 2007).

Slater, R. 1999. *Jack Welch and the GE Way: Management Insights and Leadership Secrets of the Legendary CEO.* New York: McGraw-Hill.

Smith, William E. 1991. *The AIC Model: Concepts and Practice.* Washington, DC: Organizing for Development.

Sorauf, Frank J. 1957. The Public Interest Reconsidered. *Journal of Politics* 19(4): 616–639.

Spears, Lawrence (ed.). 1997. *Insights on Leadership.* New York: John Wiley.

Spears, Lawrence (ed.). 2002. *Focus on Leadership.* New York: John Wiley.

Stillman, Patrick, Admiral. 2005. Remarks December 9. Expert Panel on Transformation and Change, Center for Innovation in the Public Sector, Washington, DC: George Washington University.

Stogdill, R.M. 1948. Personal Factors Associated with Leadership: A Survey of the Literature. *Journal of Psychology* 25: 35–71.

Stogdill, R.M. 1974. *Handbook of Leadership: A Survey of Theory and Research.* New York: Free Press.

Stoker, Robert P. 1991. *Reluctant Partners: Implementing Federal Policy.* Pittsburgh: University of Pittsburgh Press.

Stone, Deborah. 1997. *Policy Paradox: The Art of Political Decision Making.* New York: W.W. Norton.

Strebel, Paul. 1996. Why Do Employees Resist Change? *Harvard Business Review* 74(3): 86–93.

Terry, Larry D. 1995. *Leadership of Public Bureaucracies: The Administrator as Conservator.* Thousand Oaks, CA: Sage Publications.

Terry, Larry D. 1998. Administrative Leadership, Neo-Managerialism, and the New Public Management Movement. *Public Administration Review* 58(3): 194–200.

Thompson, C. Michael. 2000. *The Congruent Life.* San Francisco: Jossey-Bass.

Thomson, Ann Marie, and James L. Perry. 2006. Collaboration Processes: Inside the Black Box. *Public Administration Review* 66 (Special Issue): 20–32.

U.S. Census Bureau. 2002. Federal, State, and Local Governments: 2002 Census of Governments. Available at http://www.census.gov/govs/www/cog2002.html (accessed January 3, 2008).

U.S. Department of Homeland Security. December 2004. *National Response Plan.* Washington, DC: DHS. Available at http://www.dhs.gov/xlibrary/assets/ NRP_FullText.pdf (accessed August 25, 2007).

U.S. Department of Homeland Security. June 2006. *Nationwide Plan Review Phase 2 Report.* Washington, DC: DHS.

U.S. Department of Veterans Affairs. 1995. *Vision for Change.* Washington, DC.

U.S. Department of Veterans Affairs. 1996. *Prescription for Change: The Strategic Principles and Objectives for Transforming the Veterans Healthcare System.* Washington, DC.

U.S. Government Accountability Office (GAO). 1992. *AID Management: Strategic Management Can Help AID Face Current and Future Challenges.* Washington, DC: U.S. Government Printing Office.

U.S. GAO. 1998. *VA Community Clinics: Networks' Efforts to Improve Veterans' Access to Primary Care Vary.* Washington, DC: U.S. Government Printing Office.

U.S. GAO. 1999. *Major Management Challenges and Program Risks: Department of Veterans Affairs.* Washington, DC: U.S. Government Printing Office. Report GAO/OCG-99-15.

U.S. GAO. 2004a. *Results Oriented Government: GPRA Has Established a Solid Foundation for Achieving Greater Results.* GAO Report 04-38. Washington, DC: U.S. Government Printing Office.

U.S. GAO. 2004b. *Contract Management: Coast Guard's Deepwater Program Needs Increased Attention to Management and Contractor Oversight.* Washington, DC: U.S. Government Printing Office.

U.S. GAO. 2004c. *Coast Guard: Deepwater Program Acquisition Schedule Update Needed.* Washington, DC: U.S. Government Printing Office.

U.S. GAO. 2005a. *National Airspace System: Experts' Views on Improving the U.S. Air Traffic Control Modernization Program.* GAO Panel 05-333SP. Available at http://www.gao.gov/new.items/d05333sp.pdf (accessed February 7, 2007).

U.S. GAO. 2005b. *Results Oriented Government: Practices That Can Help Enhance and Sustain Collaboration among Federal Agencies.* GAO Report 06-15. Available at http://www.gao.gov/highlights/d0615high.pdf (accessed October 13, 2005).

U.S. GAO. 2005c. *Framework for Assessing the Acquisition Function at Federal Agencies.* GAO Report 05-218G. Washington, DC: U.S. Government Printing Office.

U.S. GAO. 2007. *Urban Area Security Initiative.* GAO Report 07-381R. Washington, DC: U.S. Government Printing Office.

U.S. Office of Management and Budget (OMB). 2007a. The President's Management Agenda. Available at http://www.whitehouse.gov/omb/budintegration/pma_index.html (accessed January 3, 2008).

U.S. OMB. 2007b. Competitive Sourcing Update. Available at http://www.whitehouse.gov/omb/procurement/comp_src/cs_update_050207.pdf (accessed January 3, 2008).

Urban Institute. 2006. *The Nonprofit Sector in Brief: Facts and Figures from the Nonprofit Almanac 2007.* Washington, DC: The Urban Institute.

Vaill, Peter B. 1989a. *Managing as a Performing Art.* San Francisco: Jossey-Bass.

Vaill, Peter B. 1989b. *Spirituality in the Age of the Leveraged Buyout.* Keynote address to a conference on Spirituality in Life and Work, Georgetown University, Washington, D.C., July 21. Reprinted in Vaill, Peter B. 1998. *Spirited Leading and Learning.* San Francisco: Jossey-Bass.

Vaill, Peter B. 1996. *Learning as a Way of Being: Strategies for Survival in a World of Permanent White Water.* San Francisco: Jossey-Bass.

Van Wart, Montgomery. 2005. *Dynamics of Leadership in Public Service.* Armonk, NY: M.E. Sharpe.

Veterans Health Administration, programs and organization website. 2007. Available at http://www1.va.gov/health/gateway.html (accessed July 16, 2007).

Virginia Tech Review Panel. 2007. *Mass Shootings at Virginia Tech: Report of the Virginia Tech Review Committee.*

Wamsley, Gary L. et al. 1990. *Refounding Public Administration.* Newbury Park, CA: Sage Publications.

Waugh, William L., Jr. 2006–07. Mechanisms for Collaboration: EMAC and Katrina. *The Public Manager* 35(4, winter): 12–15.

Weisbord, Marvin R., and Sandra Janoff. 2000. *Future Search: An Action Guide to Finding Common Ground in Organizations and Communities,* 2nd ed. San Francisco: Berrett-Koehler. See also http://www.futuresearch.net.

Wheatley, Margaret J. 1984. *Leadership and the New Science: Learning about Organizations from an Orderly Process.* Birmingham, AL: University of Alabama Press.

Wheatley, Margaret J. 2005. *Finding our Way: Leadership for an Uncertain Time.* San Francisco: Berrett-Koehler.

White, Barry, and Kathryn E. Newcomer. 2005. *Getting Results: A Guide for Federal Leaders and Managers.* Vienna, VA: Management Concepts, Inc.

Whitehead, Joel. 2005. Remarks at George Washington University, October 22, to PAD 203 Class. Washington, DC.

Wholey, J.S. 2002. Making Results Count in Public and Nonprofit Organizations: Balancing Performance with Other Values. In K.E. Newcomer, E. Jennings, C. Broom and A. Lomax (eds.), *Meeting the Challenges of Performance-oriented Government.* Washington, DC: The American Society for Public Administration: 13–35.

Williams, Sandra J., and Mary M. Hale. 1989. *Managing Change: A Guide to Producing Innovation from Within.* Lanham, MD: University Press of America.

The World Bank Group. 1996. *The World Bank Participation Sourcebook, Appendix I: Methods and Tools, Appreciation-Influence-Control, Collaborative Decisionmaking: Workshop-Based Method.* Washington, DC: The World Bank Group. Available at http://www.worldbank.org/wbi/sourcebook/sba101.htm#B (accessed March 15, 2007).

Young, Dennis R. 2006. Complementary, Supplementary, or Adverserial? Nonprofit-Government Relations. In Elizabeth R. Boris and C. Eugene Steuerle (eds.). *Nonprofits and Government: Collaboration and Conflict.* Washington, DC: Urban Institute Press, pp. 37–81.

Young, Gary. 2000. Transforming Government: *The Revitalization of the Veterans Health Administration.* Washington, DC: PricewaterhouseCooper Endowment for the Business of Government.

Yukl, Gary. 2005. *Leadership in Organizations,* 6th edition. New York: Prentice Hall.

Zeleznik A. 1977. Managers and Leaders: Are They Different? Reprinted in *Harvard Business Review on Leadership.* 1998. Boston: HBS Publishing.

Index